READINGS ON

TWELFTH NIGHT

OTHER TITLES IN THE GREENHAVEN PRESS LITERARY COMPANION SERIES:

BRITISH AUTHORS

Jane Austen
Joseph Conrad
Charles Dickens
J.R.R. Tolkien

BRITISH LITERATURE

Animal Farm
Beowulf
Brave New World
The Canterbury Tales
A Christmas Carol
Frankenstein
Great Expectations
Gulliver's Travels
Hamlet
Heart of Darkness
The Importance of Being
  Earnest
Jane Eyre
Julius Caesar

Lord of the Flies
Macbeth
The Merchant of Venice
A Midsummer Night's
  Dream
Oliver Twist
Othello
A Portrait of the Artist as a
  Young Man
Pride and Prejudice
Romeo and Juliet
Shakespeare: The Comedies
Shakespeare: The Histories
Shakespeare: The Sonnets
Shakespeare: The Tragedies
Silas Marner
A Tale of Two Cities
The Taming of the Shrew
Tess of the d'Urbervilles
Wuthering Heights

THE GREENHAVEN PRESS

Literary Companion

TO BRITISH LITERATURE

READINGS ON

TWELFTH NIGHT

Tanja Notkoff, *Book Editor*

Bonnie Szumski, *Series Editor*

Greenhaven Press, Inc., San Diego, CA

Every effort has been made to trace the owners of copyrighted material. The articles in this volume may have been edited for content, length, and/or reading level. The titles have been changed to enhance the editorial purpose. Those interested in locating the original source will find the complete citation on the first page of each article.

Library of Congress Cataloging-in-Publication Data

Readings on Twelfth night /Tanja Notkoff.
    p. cm. — (The Greenhaven Press literary
companion to British literature)
   Includes bibliographical references and index.
   ISBN 0-7377-0616-3 (pbk. : alk. paper) —
ISBN 0-7377-0617-1 (lib. : alk. paper)
   1. Shakespeare, William, 1564–1616. Twelfth night.
2. Comedy. I. Notkoff, Tanja. II. Series

PR2837 .R43 2001
822.3'3—dc21
                                 00-059321
                                     CIP

Cover photo: © Burstein Collection/Corbis
Library of Congress, 20

Copyright © 2001 by Greenhaven Press, Inc.
PO Box 289009
San Diego, CA 92198-9009
Printed in the U.S.A.

"To see this age! A sentence
is but a chev'ril glove to a
good wit—how quickly
the wrong side may be turned
outward!**"**

—Act III, scene 1, 11–13.

CONTENTS

Chapter 1: The Art of the Play

Shakespeare's writing process is revealed in the very structure of the play which combines popular plots from a variety of sources and demonstrates the use of revision, whether occurring during pre-production, production, or post-production. Shakespeare also revises his own earlier interpretations of the popular plots and it is this heavy borrowing which supports the argument that the play may have been hastily composed.

In the play, the characters' language reflects their state of mind. Shakespeare expertly employs rhetorical devices which intentionally reveal these nuances of character, giving the audience an impression of life-like characters.

The characters of Sir Andrew and Malvolio exhibit Shakespeare's dexterous handling of satire. But it is his innovative and controversial treatment of Malvolio that has stirred up debate concerning the intent of his lampooning.

The close to *Twelfth Night* has always attracted much criticism and commentary in regard to Malvolio's treatment and the quick matches made between couples. In this essay, however, Shakespeare's plotting throughout the play is examined and found to result in an apt and satisfying ending.

Chapter 2: Characters

Chapter 3: Themes and Concepts

theme of self-deception in *Twelfth Night* as only one of many moral themes at work in the play. Other themes such as pride and folly are also apparent yet all these human failings are balanced by the characters' strengths, giving the play a clever moral balance.

FOREWORD

"'Tis the good reader that
makes the good book."

Ralph Waldo Emerson

The story's bare facts are simple: The captain, an old and scarred seafarer, walks with a peg leg made of whale ivory. He relentlessly drives his crew to hunt the world's oceans for the great white whale that crippled him. After a long search, the ship encounters the whale and a fierce battle ensues. Finally the captain drives his harpoon into the whale, but the harpoon line catches the captain about the neck and drags him to his death.

A simple story, a straightforward plot—yet, since the 1851 publication of Herman Melville's *Moby-Dick*, readers and critics have found many meanings in the struggle between Captain Ahab and the whale. To some, the novel is a cautionary tale that depicts how Ahab's obsession with revenge leads to his insanity and death. Others believe that the whale represents the unknowable secrets of the universe and that Ahab is a tragic hero who dares to challenge fate by attempting to discover this knowledge. Perhaps Melville intended Ahab as a criticism of Americans' tendency to become involved in well-intentioned but irrational causes. Or did Melville model Ahab after himself, letting his fictional character express his anger at what he perceived as a cruel and distant god?

Although literary critics disagree over the meaning of *Moby-Dick*, readers do not need to choose one particular interpretation in order to gain an understanding of Melville's novel. Instead, by examining various analyses, they can gain numerous insights into the issues that lie under the surface of the basic plot. Studying the writings of literary critics can also aid readers in making their own assessments of *Moby-Dick* and other literary works and in developing analytical thinking skills.

The Greenhaven Literary Companion Series was created with these goals in mind. Designed for young adults, this unique anthology series provides an engaging and comprehensive introduction to literary analysis and criticism. The essays included in the Literary Companion Series are chosen for their accessibility to a young adult audience and are expertly edited in consideration of both the reading and comprehension levels of this audience. In addition, each essay is introduced by a concise summation that presents the contributing writer's main themes and insights. Every anthology in the Literary Companion Series contains a varied selection of critical essays that cover a wide time span and express diverse views. Wherever possible, primary sources are represented through excerpts from authors' notebooks, letters, and journals and through contemporary criticism.

Each title in the Literary Companion Series pays careful consideration to the historical context of the particular author or literary work. In-depth biographies and detailed chronologies reveal important aspects of authors' lives and emphasize the historical events and social milieu that influenced their writings. To facilitate further research, every anthology includes primary and secondary source bibliographies of articles and/or books selected for their suitability for young adults. These engaging features make the Greenhaven Literary Companion series ideal for introducing students to literary analysis in the classroom or as a library resource for young adults researching the world's great authors and literature.

Exceptional in its focus on young adults, the Greenhaven Literary Companion Series strives to present literary criticism in a compelling and accessible format. Every title in the series is intended to spark readers' interest in leading American and world authors, to help them broaden their understanding of literature, and to encourage them to formulate their own analyses of the literary works that they read. It is the editors' hope that young adult readers will find these anthologies to be true companions in their study of literature.

INTRODUCTION

Nearly four hundred years have passed since William Shakespeare graced humanity with his presence, and fortunately that presence left beauty and thought-provoking entertainment behind in the forms of poetry and plays. Although most of his contemporaries had little to say about him, it was less than a decade before Shakespeare's friends John Heminge and Henry Condell published a collection of his works known as the First Folio. Shakespeare's colleague and friend Ben Jonson contributed his praise to the folio edition, recognizing Shakespeare's worth as "not of an age, but for all time."[1] Jonson's remark is equally appropriate regarding the pivotal work that marks Shakespeare's metamorphosis: *Twelfth Night; or, What You Will* is a work "for all time."

A STRANGE, SYMBOLIC LOCALE

Entering the world of Illyria feels like chasing Alice's white rabbit down the rabbit hole to Wonderland. It is somewhere between a "never never land," as the great Shakespearean director Sir Peter Hall describes it, and the domain of modern-day Yugoslavia. It is also the place where in Greek mythology Cadmus and his wife Harmonia (Hermione) fled to after terrible tragedies befell them and their offspring. Cadmus was the founder of Thebes, and as such the founder of the House of Thebes from which Oedipus was a descendant (great-great-grandson). Actaeon was Cadmus's grandson who was changed into a deer by the goddess Artemis (Diana), whom he saw bathing at a pond in the forest where he was hunting. He was then mauled by his own pack of dogs. It is this story Orsino refers to in the opening scene of the play when Curio asks him if he will go hunting and Orsino replies that Olivia has changed him into a hart upon which his desires attack him like "cruel hounds."

Orsino is overly melodramatic, and in his own pun on "hart" and "heart" he sets the tone of the play, which is a finely tuned orchestration that balances precariously between harmony and discord. The play not only embodies the ideas of harmony and discord, an Elizabethan interest for certain, but is permeated by music from beginning to end. Orsino's discord lies in his exaggerated state of being in which his "humors" are off balance: He is dominated by the melancholic humor. His imbalance requires a harmonizing influence, which appears in the form of the soothing Viola, an instrument-named woman disguised as a page.

The ideas of identity and disguise as well as metamorphosis and change are found throughout the play, and it does seem likely that Shakespeare had Cadmus's Illyria in mind since Cadmus's story appears first in Book 3 of Ovid's *Metamorphoses* (a popular book during Shakespeare's time), followed by the story of Actaeon. *Twelfth Night* is all about changes and changing identities, the meaning of metamorphosis. It is also symbolic of the protean Elizabethan England as the characters in the play search for their identities and positions in the world.

COMEDY AND MISRULE

Leslie Hotson proposes another reason for Shakespeare's choice of locale. What Illyria brings to his mind are "thoughts of wild riot and drunkenness, and the lawless profession of piracy."[2] It is, after all, the time of Twelfth Night, a night of revels and drunken behavior, a night when the world is turned on its head—just like Alice in Wonderland—and the fools rule the kingdom while the kings entertain the fools. Twelfth Night, which comes at the end of the Christmas season on January 6, is the celebration of the Feast of the Epiphany, marking the arrival of the Magi—the three wise men or the three kings—in Jerusalem to see the newborn Jesus. The Feast of the Epiphany is also the Feast of Fools, which was traditionally ruled over by a Lord of Misrule, a Festus. The idea of misrule seems to run throughout Shakespeare's play, and there even appear to be two Lords of Misrule, although it is Sir Toby who embodies the spirit while Feste possesses the name. However, it is Feste's night and it is fool's logic that guides the plot. Feste is not the most festive character, but the festive nature of the comedy full of ruses easily spreads to the audience, so by the time Malvolio shows up cross-gartered and in yellow stockings, the audience can hardly refrain from hysterical laughter.

Shakespeare's comedy couldn't miss. He not only used a tried and true story of the disguised heroine who must court another woman on behalf of the man she loves, but he used the most rambunctious holiday celebration for his setting. *Twelfth Night* is a fantastic combination of all of the best elements: borrowing from Shakespeare's earlier work, Elizabethan ideas of order and balance, and the Renaissance love for the classics. Throw in three independent women, who also represent a tradition of Twelfth Night by taking charge of the men, and Shakespeare cannot go wrong, not as long as he trusts his own abilities to successfully synthesize the parts. Even his scenes seem sporadically placed, but ultimately his careful plotting comes through and all the elements balance as all the humors should balance, and the one ill-willed character, Malvolio, is expunged. Actually, much of the play's appeal becomes evident in its flexibility with interpretation. Not all audiences have felt the same about Malvolio, and different reactions from different audiences suggest a type of participation, a clever method for keeping the audience's attention, especially a Twelfth Night audience full of high spirits. Even the Elizabethan diarist Samuel Pepys who found the play "silly" managed to see it no less than three times over the course of about eight years.

AN ADAPTABLE PLAY

From the moment Shakespeare opted to adapt this story, his own adaptation was taking off in other directions. Perhaps the appeal really is in the delicate balance that can shift according to the mood of the audience. The appeal might also be based, and it is likely so, on the intertextual quality of the play, which lends itself to an endless potential for adaptation. Not only does it stem from numerous derived and translated sources, it continues to expand into other areas. The play itself has been adapted as an opera and as a rock and roll extravaganza. Toby and Andrew have entered on rollerskates and have been considered the original sources for the inspiration of the comic duo Laurel and Hardy. Scenes have been rearranged and the play has been shortened to two and three acts. Sometimes all that remains is fewer than fifty lines. In this day and age of Web surfing when an Internet user may easily jump from one Web page to another, from one country to another, from one piece of virtual reality to another, a play such as *Twelfth Night* easily finds an audience.

NOTES

1. Quoted in Anthony Burgess, *Shakespeare.* Chicago: Elephant-Ivan R. Dee, 1994, p. 237.
2. Leslie Hotson, *The First Night of* Twelfth Night. London: Rupert Hart-Davis, 1954, p. 151.

WILLIAM SHAKESPEARE: A BIOGRAPHY

Four centuries of minimal information about William Shakespeare have produced critics who claim that Shakespeare did not write the plays and poems credited to him. Some believe the famed body of work was penned by Edward de Vere, the seventh earl of Oxford; others attribute the work to English philosopher and statesman Sir Francis Bacon. Still other detractors believe the plays to be the achievement of a great playwright but assume that it was Christopher Marlowe, not William Shakespeare, who authored the immortal works. One of the main reasons for doubting Shakespeare's authorship, as noted by biographer Peter Hyland in *An Introduction to Shakespeare,*

> seems to be . . . a matter of social snobbery, an unwillingness to believe that the works that have become the cornerstone of English culture could have been written by the son of a glove-maker from a tiny country town. Doubters have sought amongst noble literati for the real author: the Earl of Essex, the Earl of Derby, Sir Walter Raleigh, even Queen Elizabeth herself . . . but none of them wrote anything that would convince most people that they were capable of writing Shakespeare's plays, and arguments in their favour have to depend on ingenuity rather than evidence.[1]

Another reason for doubting Shakespeare's authorship could simply be the result of a lack of information about the man.

MINIMAL DOCUMENTATION LEADS TO MYTHMAKING

There are more tall tales and stories about Shakespeare than actual documented facts, making up what can easily be called the Shakespeare mythos: stories about Shakespeare that might mix fact with fiction. There are no biographies from Shakespeare's time that might offer insight, and often legal documents can be misleading, as in the case of a marriage certificate in the Bishop's Register of Worcester, documenting a William Shakespeare engaged to an Anne Whateley of Temple Grafton, dated November 27, 1582, just one day before the playwright Shakespeare married Anne Hathaway. Shakespeare was a common name and spelled in a variety of ways; this most likely was another Will Shakespeare who wooed Miss Whateley. In light of the poor record-keeping of Shakespeare's time and the commonality of the Shakespeare name, it is best to regard Feste's caution of language in *Twelfth Night*: "Words are grown so false, I am loath to prove reason with them" (III. i. 24–25).

Extrapolation also contributes to the Shakespeare mythos. There are numerous stories based on or deriving from Shakespeare's own life and work, ranging from English writer Virginia Woolf's consideration of Shakespeare's fictional sister—what if he had an equally talented sister?—in her 1929 feminist essay *A Room of One's Own* to the 1999 Academy Award–winning film *Shakespeare in Love* in which the young Shakespeare is relieved of writer's block by falling in love with Viola, an actress who must disguise herself as a boy to participate in Elizabethan theater. Shakespeare stories are in endless supply. The legal documents that remain from Shakespeare's time are minimal and frequently confusing, which further prompts storytellers to fill in the gaps. Discerning biographical information about the real man is an arduous task.

A SON OF STRATFORD

William's grandfather Richard Shakespeare was a farmer (a yeoman) in Snitterfield, England, located three and a half miles northeast of Stratford. According to Shakespeare biographer Samuel Schoenbaum, Richard settled there sometime before 1529, renting property from the prosperous Robert Arden of Wilmcote. Richard's son, John Shakespeare, and Robert Arden's daughter, Mary Arden, were to become the future parents of the mysterious William Shakespeare. By the time Shakespeare was born, John and Mary were well established in the thriving town of Stratford.

The first documented fact about William Shakespeare is not his birth certificate (there were no birth certificates then) but, rather, an item in the Parish Register of his baptism on April 26, 1564. He was christened *Gulielmus filius Johannes Shakspere* (William, son of John Shakespeare) in the town of Stratford, now called Stratford-upon-Avon, in the county of Warwickshire, England. Newborns were generally baptized just a couple of days after their birth. Although religious holidays might alter this, for convenience's sake and the great appeal of myth and legend, William Shakespeare is given the birthdate of April 23, the same date of his documented death fifty-two years later in 1616. April 23 is also St. George's Day, the patron saint of England—an appropriate date for the birth and death of William Shakespeare, the "National Poet."

EDUCATING SHAKESPEARE

There is no record of Shakespeare's attendance at the Stratford school, but for that matter there are no records for anyone else (not until the 1700s). It is assumed that he did attend the free local grammar school—the King's New School—and there is no reason to doubt this, especially since his parents were prospering and could afford to have their son educated. John Shakespeare was a successful tradesman working as a glover and had become a town official. Mary (Arden) Shakespeare was an heiress. Therefore, it is more than likely that Shakespeare attended school. With the knowledge that, as researcher Dave Kathman writes, "all the headmasters while Shakespeare was growing up were university graduates with good reputations,"[2] it can be surmised that Shakespeare received a decent education, further evidenced by Shakespeare's own work. However, some scholars believe that William Shakespeare was a self-educated man, a jack-of-all-trades.

Without any academic records, information regarding the curriculum Shakespeare might have followed is at best secondary. Queen Elizabeth I nationalized education in 1553, and the curriculum was probably standard for most or all of the schools. The multitalented writer, critic, and Shakespearean expert Anthony Burgess in his Shakespeare biography explains that students studied Latin grammar in grammar school and nothing more. Scholar Rebecca Brown, on the other hand, suggests in her on-line biography, *Shakespeare at School,* that once the students had mastered the basic grammar using W. Lily's *Short Introduction of Grammar* (first published in 1540), they would have expanded their studies to include advanced grammar, logic, and rhetoric, and possibly arithmetic, geometry, music, and astronomy. Eventually, having mastered Latin, they would have read the works of the great Greek and Roman thinkers, with the Greek texts translated into Latin.

The approach to education was based on imitation, so, in addition to the Greek philosopher Aristotle's works, the works of Roman philosophers Cicero, Quintilian, and Seneca would also have been studied. Toward the end of their schooling, the young men might have studied histories such as those of Livy, Julius Caesar, and Plutarch; poetry was likely studied and would have included the *Metamorphoses* by the Roman poet Ovid; and plays such as the comedies by Terence and Plautus were also examined, probably to study and imitate the style as Shakespeare eventually did in his plays. In addition to the "imitation" method of education, rote memorization was also a preferred approach. Worst of all, as Burgess notes, was the idea "generally acknowledged among Elizabethan educationists that children had to have knowledge crammed, and sometimes beaten, into them."[3]

MARRIAGE AND PATERNITY

Shakespeare was probably fifteen when he left school, and it is fairly certain that he had no college education, yet his writing displays a tremendous knowledge of myth and history, ancient times, and faraway places. He also had a keen comprehension of his contemporary society as well as country wisdom. The only real bit of evidence that Shakespeare studied the grammar school curriculum is what is found in the body of his works; *Twelfth Night*, for example, contains numerous references to Ovid's *Metamorphoses*, and Shakespeare includes a recycled version of the mistaken twin plot in *The Comedy of Errors*, which was based on Plautus's *Menaechmi*. There is always the possibility that Shakespeare educated himself on the topics of which he was writing. He certainly applied his life knowledge. At about age fifteen or sixteen, he probably worked with his dad as a glover. It is hard to miss Shakespeare's abundant metaphoric use of cheveril (kid-skin) gloves throughout his plays. As Feste reports, "A sentence is but a chev'ril glove to a good wit—how quickly the wrong side may be turned outward!" (III. i. 11–13).

Burgess suggests that Shakespeare did not initially start out with an interest in drama since "actors were a kind of masterless men who evaded the charge of vagabondage and sturdy beggardom only by sheltering under the nominal patronage of some noble lord."[4] Rather, Shakespeare might have been a poet, trying to win the queen's praise and make a name for himself while working in his father's shop. Employment would have been important to the young Shakespeare since he was soon to have other responsibilities.

It is documented that

On November 28, 1582, two Warwickshire farmers stood surety for the legality of a marriage between a certain William Shagspere . . . and a certain Anne Hathwey. It is all there in the Bishop of Worcester's register. In the register of Stratford Parish Church we read that, on May 26, 1583, a girl child, daughter to William Shakespeare, was christened Susanna.[5]

William Shakespeare, at age eighteen, married Anne Hathaway, around age twenty-six, who was already (approximately) three months' pregnant with Susanna at the time of the marriage. Shakespeare's twins, Hamnet and Judith, were christened less than two years later on Candlemas, February 2, 1585. According to Schoenbaum, the twins were named after the Shakespeares' lifelong friends and neighbors the Sadlers, who returned the honor in 1598 by naming their son William. Unfortunately, Hamnet Shakespeare, William's only son, was to die at the age of eleven and the Shakespeares would have no more children.

THE LOST YEARS AND THE LURE OF THE LONDON THEATERS

Shakespeare's early employment is only surmised. In addition to perhaps working as a glove maker, other possible occupations for the young Shakespeare include butcher, schoolmaster, tutor, lawyer, and officer in the army—all of which might be demonstrated by the worldliness and proficiency of his tales. It seems unlikely that he was a schoolmaster because all the schoolmasters of his time held degrees from either Oxford or Cambridge. He might have been a tutor in a private house, however, or taught in the petty schools set up under Queen Elizabeth that prepared students for primary education. Although noted for much misinformation, John Aubrey's so-called biographical work titled *Brief Lives,* written during the Restoration Period (mid– to late seventeenth century), refers to Shakespeare as "a Schoolmaster in the Countrey."[6]

There is even a specific period known as the "Lost Years," which Schoenbaum explains lasted "from 1585, when the twins were born, until 1592." Shakespeare's documented history during this time was "a virtual blank."[7] Many of the tales that filled in the Lost Years have made their way into biographies, and some of the tales are fantastic and amusing.

Some biographies note Shakespeare's appearance in the London theater, but even a few of these report that he was actually tending horses outside the theater instead of acting or writing plays.

Obviously, an interest in the theater had to have developed despite his family obligations. Players (entertainers) had been performing at Stratford's Guildhall from at least as early as 1569, so it seems reasonable to believe that Shakespeare would have been exposed to these groups at some time during his youth. Burgess notes that the Queen's Men played in 1587 and Lord Strange's Men played in 1579. Other groups also performed over the years. As a young man, Shakespeare would have had opportunities to come in contact with these groups, and Burgess even suggests that the great actor-comedian Will Kemp, who was with the Queen's Men in 1587, took Shakespeare under his wing as a playwright precisely because Shakespeare was trying to escape his marriage and family life. Another possibility,

William Shakespeare

presented by Schoenbaum in his Shakespeare biography, is that William Shakespeare became an actor when he replaced a member of a touring group who was killed in a duel while performing near Stratford. Even twentieth-century biographers such as Burgess and Schoenbaum admittedly indulge in hypothesizing, which of course contributes to the Shakespeare mythos.

The brilliant actor and director Orson Welles has noted in his introduction to *The Mercury Shakespeare* that the acting companies Shakespeare would have seen in Stratford would have performed religious-themed morality and miracle plays, "but down in London real shows were being put on in place of masques and roustabouts and these plays were about real people," not just the vices and virtues. The University Wits—the group of university-educated playwrights and pamphleteers, including Robert Greene, Thomas Lodge, and Thomas Nashe—were quite successful at this time, and

the theater was growing and developing, in the process of
being refined. The English stage had come "out of the
church when the actors got too entertaining. It lingered for
a couple of hundred years in front of it in the marketplace
and then moved into the inn yard where it stayed until it got
over being a holiday treat and became an institution,"[8]
writes Welles.

SHAKESPEARE BECOMES A PLAYER

In a 1592 pamphlet supposedly written by University Wit
Robert Greene but published posthumously (and possibly
written by someone else), there are derogatory remarks
about another playwright whom Greene refers to as a *"Johannes fac totum"* (jack-of-all-trades) and "the onely Shake-
scene in a countrey."[9] It is likely that these comments refer
to Shakespeare, although it is not known for certain, and
they are often considered the first indication of Shakespeare's presence in the London theaters. During that year,
however, the playhouses in London had closed due to a severe outbreak of the bubonic plague and there are no other
references to Shakespeare's involvement in theater at that
time.

The earliest documents verifying Shakespeare's presence
in London are from 1594 players' records for the Lord
Chamberlain's Men. Queen Elizabeth I had made Henry
Carey, her cousin, Lord Chamberlain in 1585. In 1594, Lord
Chamberlain had taken over sponsorship of a group of play-
ers who had previously worked under another lord's pa-
tronage—known as Lord Strange—and included Will Kemp,
Thomas Pope, John Heminge, Augustine Phillips, and
George Bryan.

Closed since 1592 because of the plague, the playhouses reopened in 1594, and it is at this time that Shakespeare's name
began appearing along with the great actor (and Shakespeare's good friend) Richard Burbage and the rest of the
Lord Chamberlain's Men. In light of Greene's comment, it is
generally believed that Shakespeare had arrived in London
before 1594, at which time he joined Lord Strange's Men.
However, there is no hard evidence of his involvement in theater until the 1594 emergence of the Lord Chamberlain's
Men. And while acting with the company, Shakespeare was
also probably contributing plays; some of his most famous
were penned during these early days in the theater.

DATING SHAKESPEARE'S PLAYS

Determining the dates of Shakespeare's plays is no easy task. As Shakespearean scholar Peter Alexander notes, "There was no copyright in the modern sense in the reign of Elizabeth, or for many years after. A printer or publisher, however, could b[u]y an entry in the Day Book of the Stationers' Company ... [and] secure the sole right of issuing a work in his possession." [10] This type of document registration, known as the Stationers' Register, has been useful in assessing dates of what would constitute publication for some of Shakespeare's plays. However, registers frequently contain only partial information, as seen in the Stratford Parish Register that contains Shakespeare's baptism date but not his birth date. The dates of Shakespeare's plays are ultimately educated guesses.

In addition to using the Stationers' Register, the dates for Shakespeare's plays are taken from other sources as well (basically, any available information helps to approximate dates). Records that contain performance dates for licensing of the plays and contracts drawn up for production preparation provide useful information. The unauthorized (bootlegged) versions of Shakespeare's plays that were printed and circulated during his lifetime and, due to their paper size, are known as the Quartos are also informative. Some of the Quartos date the various plays, but their counterfeit nature leaves many critics suspicious of their accuracy, and not all of the plays appeared in the Quarto editions.

The First Folio, the first authorized collection of Shakespeare's works, was published in 1623, seven years after Shakespeare's death, by Shakespeare's fellow actors and friends John Heminge and Henry Condell. The First Folio is also used to date Shakespeare's plays. Yet overall, the dates of the plays are constantly shifting, changing as research and study reveal patterns and development in Shakespeare's writing, as documents such as personal journals and letters belonging to spectators are discovered, and as historical references within Shakespeare's plays are identified.

PROSPERITY DURING THE 1590s

By 1594 (and no earlier than 1589), it is believed that Shakespeare had already written and published the poems "Venus and Adonis" and "The Rape of Lucrece," which were dedicated to the third earl of Southampton, Henry Wriothesley, who had become Shakespeare's patron. The *Sonnets* were also written at this time but would not be published until 1609. About a quarter of the plays had been composed by 1594: *Henry VI,* Parts 1, 2, and 3; *Richard III; The Two Gentlemen of Verona; The Comedy of Errors; Titus Andronicus; The Taming of the Shrew;* and *Love's Labour's Lost.*

Romeo and Juliet, Richard II, A Midsummer Night's Dream, King John, The Merchant of Venice, and *Henry IV,* Parts 1 and 2 appeared sometime between 1594 and 1598. The untimely death of Hamnet Shakespeare in 1596 would have certainly seemed to take its toll on the playwright, although all that is evident is Shakespeare's prosperity, indicative, perhaps of a saddened father who buried himself in his work. The same year Hamnet died, the Shakespeares were finally granted the family coat of arms, which William's father had tried and failed to obtain in the 1570s. By 1597 it is known that Shakespeare was well established and financially secure; he purchased New Place, the second largest house in Stratford, and owned other property as well.

The work that Shakespeare produced between 1598 and 1601 consists of the poem "The Phoenix and the Turtle" and the plays *The Merry Wives of Windsor, Much Ado About Nothing, Henry V, Julius Caesar, As You Like It, Hamlet,* and *Twelfth Night; or, What You Will.* In this group of plays, it is quite difficult to determine the chronological order, and *Twelfth Night* seems to fall somewhere in between it all, a testimony to what might be seen as a transitional time for Shakespeare.

TURNING POINTS AND *TWELFTH NIGHT*

At the turn of the century, Shakespeare, along with the rest of his country, seems to have been going through major changes. The queen was aging (and only a few years from death), and Shakespeare himself was quickly approaching his forties. He was a successful playwright, poet, and actor, and as of 1599 a theater owner too—he owned about one-tenth of the Globe theater. Supposedly, the Globe had been built from the wood originally used to construct the Theatre, which had been built in 1576 as the first public playhouse in London, just outside the city limits. It is believed that the wood was recycled into the Globe when an agreement could not be met between the landowner and the theater owners, so, in 1597, the Theatre was disassembled and moved across the Thames River where it was rebuilt as the Globe, opening in 1599.

That same year, 1599, Will Kemp left the Lord Chamberlain's Men. Kemp, who had always played the role of the fool in the performances by the Lord Chamberlain's Men (which included Shakespeare's plays), was replaced by Robert Armin, an entirely different type of fool. Armin's wit destined him to be Feste in *Twelfth Night*, a part that might have been created or revised for him when he replaced Kemp.

Until the discovery of the diary kept by law student John Manningham in which he reports the performance of "Twelue night or what you will"[11] on Candlemas (February 2) 1602, it had been believed that the play was composed sometime in 1614 and was Shakespeare's last play. Now, *Twelfth Night* is usually considered the last of Shakespeare's festive and romantic comedies, but critics frequently find themselves at odds with this comedy, which lays the foundation for the later problem plays and the tragedies. Its chronological placement in relation to *As You Like It, Troilus and Cressida,* and *Hamlet* is questionable. In his recent masterpiece *Shakespeare: The Invention of the Human,* the great literary scholar Harold Bloom places the play as "bridging the interval between the final *Hamlet* and *Troilus and Cressida*. There are elements of self-parody in *Twelfth Night,* not on the scale of *Cymbeline*'s self-mockery, but holding a middle ground between Hamlet's ferocious ironies and the rancidity of *Troilus and Cressida*."[12] Robert Ornstein in his book *Shakespeare's Comedies* points out that "there is no convincing evidence that *Twelfth Night* was written after *As You Like It,* we usually say that it was because *As You Like It* is not somber enough to be 'the last of the romantic comedies.'"[13] Meanwhile, J.M. Gregson notes in his study of *Twelfth Night* that

> the construction of *Hamlet* may even have overlapped that of *Twelfth Night*. In many ways the play is the climax of the pure comedies, in others it foreshadows the mighty achievements at hand. The miraculous fusion of these disparate materials into a work which is almost perfectly balanced dramatically and aesthetically constitutes one of the major interests of the play.[14]

THE TWILIGHT YEARS: FROM "PROBLEM PLAYS" TO PLAYS OF RECONCILIATION

There are numerous dark aspects to be found in *Twelfth Night* such as the pending return to the real world, fleeting youth, and the treatment Malvolio receives. For a comedy, these dark tones are unusual in their quantity and as such would seem like natural precursors to Shakespeare's "problem comedies" although the problem plays could just as easily come before *Twelfth Night.* "Around the year 1600," Hyland explains that Shakespeare "took on a new direction with a series of puzzling plays," composing *Troilus and Cressida* (ca. 1601–1602), *All's Well That Ends Well* (1602–1603), and *Measure for Measure* (ca. 1604). They "may be called comedies but are much harsher in tone than anything he had written before."[15]

Shakespeare's next artistic move was to master the tragedy. He penned the majority of his great tragedies over the next several years, including *Othello* (ca. 1603–1604), *King Lear* (ca. 1605–1606), and *Macbeth* (ca. 1605–1606). Perhaps the death of his father, John Shakespeare, who was buried on September 8, 1601, and the death of Queen Elizabeth I in 1603 affected the direction of Shakespeare's writing. It is, after all, his artistry at representing life that has proven popular for more than four hundred years. Changing times and loss of youth could easily have influenced his work, as it so often does with people in general.

Change is inevitable and the results that first might appear disheartening can just as easily lead to new opportunities. When in 1603 James I became the king of England, the Lord Chamberlain's Men, to which Shakespeare still belonged, received the honor of becoming the King's Men. This meant that they were the favored performers in London. By 1608, the King's Men, who already owned the Globe theater, also acquired the Blackfriars theater. All this prosperity and notoriety might have boosted Shakespeare's ego and propelled him in yet another creative direction, for, as Hyland points out, it was "around 1608 he changed direction again, ending his career with the group of plays of forgiveness and reconciliation known as romances."[16] Burgess, however, attributes this final stage of Shakespeare's writing to his return to Stratford and family life, noting that "Shakespeare certainly, if the last plays are any evidence, took pleasure in the company of his daughters. The charm and beauty of *Perdita* [*The Winter's Tale*], *Miranda* [*The Tempest*], and *Marina* [*Pericles*] may be taken as a reflection of fatherly pride and love."[17]

SHAKESPEARE'S LEGACY

On June 5, 1607, Shakespeare's oldest daughter, Susanna, married Dr. John Hall of Stratford, and by 1608 she had given birth to Elizabeth; that same year, 1608, Shakespeare's mother, Mary, was buried on September 9. It was in 1608 also that Shakespeare would permanently retreat to New Place. The last of his plays were written at this time, between 1606 and 1612, and include *Antony and Cleopatra* (ca. 1606–1607), *Timon of Athens* (ca. 1607–1608), *Coriolanus* (ca. 1607–1608), *Pericles* (ca. 1607–1608), *Cymbeline* (ca. 1609–1610), *The Winter's Tale* (ca. 1610–1611), and *The Tempest* (ca. 1611), after which he is considered to have retired from solo playwrighting.

Shakespeare's life was winding down. The last works attributed to him, *Henry VIII* (ca. 1612–1613) and possibly *The Two Noble Kinsmen* (ca. 1612–1613), are now considered collaborative endeavors with John Fletcher. *Henry VIII* is generally considered Shakespeare's last play, which suggests that, even if he did collaborate with Fletcher, Shakespeare wrote the majority of the play. On June 29, 1613, a fire broke out during the premier performance of *Henry VIII* and completely destroyed the Globe theater.

The last couple of years of Shakespeare's life seem uneventful at least until a few months before his death at which time Shakespeare made the first draft of his will. He altered it just a month later when Judith, his youngest daughter and the surviving twin, finally married at the age of thirty-one on February 10, 1616. Burgess, in his biography, proposes that Shakespeare was unhappy with Judith's choice of a husband, Thomas Quiney. In fact, Burgess reports that it was discovered just a month after the marriage that Quiney had impregnated another woman not less than a year before—both mistress and child had died. Consequently, according to Shakespeare's last will and testament of March 25, 1616, "Shakespeare willed all his personal property, New Place, two houses on Henley Street, a house in Blackfriars, London, and 'all my other landes and tenementes and hereditamentes whatsoever'"[18] to his eldest daughter, Susanna. To his wife, Shakespeare left nothing more than "the second-best bed," which of course has kept the scholars wondering about what he meant by such an odd statement. He also left money to his friends John Heminge and Henry Condell for the purchase of mourning rings, as was customary. Heminge and Condell in turn would edit the First Folio of Shakespeare's collected works and get them posthumously published.

William Shakespeare died on April 23, 1616, and was buried two days later at Holy Trinity Church in Stratford. Even his death remains a mystery, for nothing is known of its cause. As for the epitaph on his gravestone, which is attributed to Shakespeare, scholars do not generally accept that Shakespeare wrote it, but, regardless of its authorship, it certainly belongs to the Shakespeare mythos:

> Good friend, for Jesus' sake forbear
> To dig the dust enclosed here.
> Blessed be the man that spares these stones
> And cursed be he that moves my bones.[19]

NOTES

1. Peter Hyland, *An Introduction to Shakespeare: The Dramatist in His Context.* New York: St. Martin's Press, 1996, p. 16.
2. Dave Kathman, "The Stratford Grammar School," *Critically Examining Oxfordian Claims,* Part 11. April 2000. www.clark.net/pub/tross/ws/school.html.
3. Anthony Burgess, *Shakespeare.* Chicago: Elephant-Ivan R. Dee, 1994, p. 30.
4. Burgess, *Shakespeare,* pp. 43–44.
5. Quoted in Burgess, *Shakespeare,* p. 51.
6. Quoted in Burgess, *Shakespeare,* p. 44.
7. S.[amuel] Schoenbaum, *William Shakespeare: A Compact Documentary Life.* Abr. ed. New York: Oxford University Press, 1977, p. 95.
8. Orson Welles, "On Staging Shakespeare and on Shakespeare's Stage," *The Mercury Shakespeare:* The Merchant of Venice, Twelfth Night, Julius Caesar. Eds. Orson Welles and Roger Hill. New York: Harper & Brothers, 1939, pp. 22–23.
9. Quoted in Bruce R. Smith, *Roasting the Swan of Avon: Shakespeare's Redoubtable Enemies and Dubious Friends.* Washington, DC: Folger Shakespeare Library, 1994, p. 4.
10. Peter Alexander, *Shakespeare's Life and Art.* Amer. ed. New York: New York University Press, 1967, p. 32.
11. Quoted in J.M. Lothian and T.W. Craik, eds., "Introduc-

tion," *The Arden Edition of the Works of William Shake-speare:* Twelfth Night. London: Routledge, 1995, p. xxvi.
12. Harold Bloom, *Shakespeare: The Invention of the Human.* New York: Riverhead Books, 1998, p. 226.
13. Robert Ornstein, *Shakespeare's Comedies: From Roman Farce to Romantic Mystery.* Newark: University of Delaware Press, 1986, p. 153.
14. J.M. Gregson, *Shakespeare:* Twelfth Night. London: Edward Arnold Ltd., 1980, p. 9.
15. Hyland, *An Introduction to Shakespeare,* p. 13.
16. Hyland, *An Introduction to Shakespeare,* p. 13.
17. Burgess, *Shakespeare,* p. 214.
18. Quoted in Burgess, *Shakespeare,* p. 233.
19. Quoted in Hyland, *An Introduction to Shakespeare,* p. 14.

CHARACTERS AND PLOT

CHARACTERS

Sir Andrew Aguecheek: Like his friend Sir Toby Belch, Sir Andrew is a knight, and although he is educated, he is not very bright. Rather, he is quite a fool, and he is especially fooled by Sir Toby, who uses him for money and laughs. Sir Andrew, gutless and pathetic in character, ultimately ends up in a duel with Viola/Cesario that is orchestrated for laughs by Sir Toby.

Antonio: A sea captain (possibly the same one from the beginning of the play) who saves Sebastian, Viola's twin brother thought to have drowned. Antonio is a wanted criminal in Illyria but risks capture in order to help Sebastian. He also mistakes Viola/Cesario for Sebastian and aids her just in time during the duel. In the end, as with Sir Andrew, he is not one of the lucky characters to be paired off in a relationship and is therefore excluded from the final happiness shared by the reconciled characters.

Sir Toby Belch: Olivia's kinsman, most likely her uncle according to Sir Toby's reference to Olivia as his niece. He is probably a good bit older than Olivia and Viola. Sir Toby is a knight and represents a bygone era when the knights protected the estates in exchange for room and board. Sir Toby has too much time on his hands and is consequently always soused and mischievous. He partakes in revelry and ruses and holds a great interest in making Malvolio mad, although eventually he fears the future of his livelihood because of the mischief he has done. Furthermore, he uses Sir Andrew not only to pay for his amusement but to supply it as well, such as when he gulls Sir Andrew by setting a duel between Sir Andrew and Viola/Cesario. In the end, Sir Toby marries Maria as a reward for her crafty plot against Malvolio.

Captain: A kind man, although he doesn't appear so on the outside, who aids Viola in her disguise. The captain ends up in jail at Malvolio's request, but it is never revealed for what reason.

Curio: A gentleman attending on Orsino.

Fabian: A member of Olivia's household and possibly a fool in training since he is often linked to Feste. Fabian also does not like Malvolio, who has betrayed him to Olivia regarding his penchant for bearbaiting. Fabian primarily serves to aid in the great ruses played on Sir Andrew, Viola, and Malvolio. He moves the plot along by witnessing Malvolio's discovery of the falsified letter, summing up the "gulling" and the perpetrators to Olivia, and then reading Malvolio's letter to Olivia.

Feste: Once Olivia's father's fool, Feste now belongs to Olivia. He is insightful into the folly of humans and as a result appears less than a happy fool. He is witty and wise, and he possesses a beautiful singing voice. He moves between Orsino's and Olivia's households, constantly begging for money in exchange for his talents. In the guise of the priest Sir Topas, Feste takes part in the humiliation of Malvolio; however, Feste does eventually aid Malvolio's attempt to prove his sanity to Olivia. The ambiguity of Feste's loyalty shows that he does not want to take sides, preferring to point out the folly of all the players.

Malvolio: Characterized as a puritan and therefore disdainful of play and idleness, Malvolio is the source of ill will in Illyria. He is a social climber with delusions of grandeur, and his rudeness makes him disliked by most of the other characters. He harbors feelings for Olivia and is tricked into believing she desires him by an elaborate ruse carried on by Maria and Sir Toby. So deceived, his behavior makes Olivia and others believe he is mad, and he is even temporarily locked up for his "insanity." The sympathy engendered by his mistreatment, however, is forfeited since he refuses to forgive the conspirators when he is released. He flees the last scene while threatening revenge on everyone.

Maria: Olivia's lady-in-waiting is possibly around Sir Toby's age, undoubtedly older than Olivia. She is antagonistic toward Malvolio, choosing to reprimand and mock his puritanical stance in life ("no more cakes and ale") since he is of such an ill will. Maria gulls Malvolio by writing a love letter that appears to come from Olivia. The letter suggests how Malvolio should dress and act around his mistress, and by following the ludicrous advice of the letter, Malvolio makes a fool of himself when in the presence of Olivia. For orchestrating this ruse, Maria is rewarded by her marriage to Sir Toby, a fellow conspirator who appreciates Maria's wit and cleverness.

Olivia: A young and beautiful noblewoman who is desired by Orsino but does not return his affection. With both her father and brother dead, the latter of whom she mourns as an excuse to keep Orsino away, Olivia is in control of her household. She is independent and willful, pursues Viola/Cesario, and finally marries Sebastian, whom she mistakes for Viola/Cesario. Olivia is patient, as evidenced by her tolerance of her uncle Sir Toby and his friend Sir Andrew. She is even sympathetic toward Malvolio, who, unbeknownst to her, acts the fool to win her love. Once she is aware of the ruse against him, she is concerned about the treatment Malvolio has received at the hands of the jesting conspirators.

Orsino, Duke of Illyria: A handsome and melodramatic man who obsesses about what he cannot have. He seems to love the idea of being in love more than he loves Olivia. He is moody and melancholic but Viola loves him steadfastly, eventually winning his love in return.

Priest: He performs the marriage between Olivia and Sebastian (thought to be Cesario) and confirms the marriage when required.

Sebastian: Sebastian is the handsome and strong twin brother to Viola. At the outset of the play, he is thought to have drowned in the shipwreck that tossed Viola to shore. However, unbeknownst to his sister, Sebastian was rescued by Antonio and brought to Illyria. Sebastian desires to see Illyria and in the process of his explorations encounters the beautiful Olivia, whom he instantly weds. He also runs into Sir Toby and Sir Andrew as they await the duel with Viola/Cesario. He finally encounters Viola in the final act, providing some resolution to the play.

Valentine: A gentleman attending on Orsino who, prior to Viola's arrival, delivers Orsino's messages to Olivia.

Viola (later disguised as Cesario): A young woman who is shipwrecked in Illyria. Although she survives the tragedy, she believes that her twin brother, Sebastian, has drowned in the wreck. Unsure of her future but recognizing the "noble duke" Orsino's name as someone her father used to speak of, Viola dons a male disguise to serve the duke. She falls in love with the duke but ends up courting the Lady Olivia at his request. She eventually wins Orsino over at the same time she is reunited with her brother. Viola is witty and wise and especially charming to the Lady Olivia, who is taken by Viola/Cesario's effeminate beauty and charm.

PLOT

Act 1, Scene 1: Orsino's house. The melodramatic Duke Orsino compares music to love, asks for more music in order to deaden his appetite (for love), then changes his mind and asks for the music to stop. His attendant Curio asks if he wants to hunt, which leads Orsino to speak of Olivia, his obsession. Valentine, Orsino's other attendant, enters and delivers a message to Orsino: The Lady Olivia refused to see him and she has sworn to hide herself from the world for seven years to mourn her dead brother. This information excites the duke, who thinks that Olivia, once his, will worship him even more than she does her dead brother's memory.

Act 1, Scene 2: The beach. The shipwrecked Viola arrives in Illyria with the sea captain and some sailors. She fears that her brother, Sebastian, drowned in the wreck. The captain tells Viola that she is lucky to not have been drowned herself and that when he last saw her brother, he was swimming. This pleases Viola, so she gives the captain money and asks him who rules this land. The captain tells her Orsino's name (which he says is as noble as the man). Viola remembers hearing her father speak of Orsino. She also recalls that he was then a bachelor. The captain tells Viola that Orsino is still a bachelor, but the last information he has heard is of Orsino's pursuit of Olivia, a fine, noble lady. Viola asks about Olivia and the captain informs her that Olivia's father died just a year ago, and her brother a short time after that, and now Olivia has cloistered herself. Viola considers going to serve the noble lady, but is advised that even she will not be admitted to Olivia's house. Viola praises the captain for his kind nature and requests his help in disguising her as a eunuch so that she can instead serve the duke.

Act 1, Scene 3: Olivia's grounds. Sir Toby, a boisterous and surly knight, questions why Olivia has cloistered herself. Olivia's handmaiden Maria comes to rebuke Sir Toby for keeping late hours that disturb Olivia and make him fall out of favor with her. Sir Toby is not concerned with Maria's admonishment. Maria tells Sir Toby that her mistress believes Toby's drinking will be the end of him. She also relates that Olivia thinks that Sir Andrew Aguecheek, another knight that Sir Toby has brought to woo Olivia, is a fool. Sir Toby defends his friend but when Maria questions his purpose in uniting the two, Sir Toby admits it is for the money. Sir Toby tries to save face with Maria and praises Sir Andrew's abilities, but

Maria is not convinced. Sir Andrew enters and immediately makes a fool of himself. He is introduced to Maria but misunderstands a remark of Sir Toby's and thinks Maria's last name is Accost. Sir Andrew continues to make a fool of himself. Only after Maria departs does Sir Andrew recognize his foolishness, yet he rationalizes it away. Sir Andrew also admits that he is not knowledgeable in the arts, such as language and courtship, only in activities such as fencing, bearbaiting, and dancing. Sir Andrew asserts that his chances to woo Olivia are slim since she will not see any suitors—even the duke—under the pretext of mourning for her brother. Sir Toby assures him that Olivia is not looking for someone as lofty as the duke. Sir Andrew resigns himself to stay another month, and the scene ends with Sir Toby encouraging Sir Andrew to show off his talents by cutting a caper.

Act 1, Scene 4: Back at Orsino's. Valentine and Viola (now disguised as Cesario for the remainder of the play) are speaking about Orsino's favoritism toward Viola, namely, that in three days Orsino has taken Viola into his confidence. The duke enters with Curio and his other attendants, looking for Viola. Orsino elaborates on what Valentine has said, admitting that Viola now knows all of his deep secrets. Orsino then asks Viola to visit Olivia. Viola does not think it is possible to get in to see Olivia, but Orsino insists on it and wants Viola to woo Olivia on his behalf. Orsino thinks Olivia will be more receptive to Viola because of Viola's youthful and effeminate appearance. Orsino promises Viola great wealth if she succeeds. Viola says she will do it but once alone confesses her dilemma: She wants to be Orsino's wife.

Act 1, Scene 5: Back at Olivia's. The fool Feste enters with Maria, who is concerned that Feste will be turned out for being away from Olivia's household for so long. She offers to defend his absence if he tells her where he has been, but Feste will not tell her. Feste obviously appreciates Maria's gesture and tells her that if Sir Toby could ever quit drinking, Maria should wed him. Maria hushes Feste and upon Olivia's approach urges him to be on his best behavior with the lady, then exit. Feste attempts to please Olivia with his cleverness, but at first she will have none of it and wants him to leave. He finally convinces her through witty proofs that he is a worthwhile fool. Malvolio, a gentleman who secretly aspires to marry Olivia, is in attendance and rudely criticizes Feste's wit. Olivia defends Feste, lightly reprimanding Malvolio for being self-serving. Feste is grateful. Maria reenters to announce Viola's presence at the gate and her insistence on remaining until Olivia admits her. Sir Toby is currently detaining Viola, and Maria is sent after Sir Toby while Malvolio is sent to deal with Viola. Sir Toby returns and, to Olivia's amazement, he is already near-drunk. After Sir Toby leaves, Olivia sends Feste to look after him. Malvolio then returns to inform Olivia that Viola still refuses to leave. Olivia tells Malvolio to tell Viola that she will not be seen, but, when Olivia asks about Viola's manner and appearance, she seems to be taken by Malvolio's description of the effeminate Viola and grants Viola access. Olivia has Maria get her veil before Viola approaches.

When Viola enters, she does not know if the veiled lady is Olivia, and after the two dialogue back and forth (with Viola alluding to her own disguise), Olivia finally admits that she is the lady. Viola at first begins to carry out Orsino's will, but Olivia quickly dismisses the wooing. Viola then convinces Olivia to lift her veil and is impressed with what she sees, consequently accusing Olivia of keeping her beauty from others. Olivia's facetious response brings Viola to call Olivia vain and again plead Orsino's case. Olivia does admit that Orsino is a noble person but insists that her answer still stands and Orsino should have accepted it a long time ago. Viola defends Orsino's perseverance as being a result of his love and thus leads to her own imaginings of what she would do to woo Olivia. Olivia is completely overwhelmed by Viola's romantic plea and begins to find herself growing attracted to the disguised Viola. Olivia tells Viola to inform Orsino that she still refuses his hand, but she welcomes Viola's return with Orsino's response. After Viola leaves, Olivia reveals that she is taken with Viola. She sends Malvolio after her with a ring, telling Malvolio to return it to Viola—falsely claiming that Viola left it with her—and to invite her again to return for an answer.

Act 2, Scene 1: Between town and the Illyrian countryside. Antonio, a sea captain, implores Viola's brother, Sebastian, to remain with him but Sebastian insists that he must go, although he does not know where, for he fears his bad luck—which he blames for the shipwreck—will rub off on Antonio. Sebastian tells Antonio about Viola, whom he believes is dead, and Antonio is so struck by Sebastian's character that he offers to be Sebastian's servant. Sebastian tells Antonio that he is off to Duke Orsino's court and Antonio admits having many enemies there, but he cares for Sebastian so much that he decides to risk it.

Act 2, Scene 2: Just outside Olivia's property boundaries.

Following Olivia's directions, Malvolio locates Viola and attempts to return the ring Olivia has given him. Viola claims she left no ring and will not take it, so Malvolio throws it down and departs. Viola realizes that Olivia has truly mistaken her as male and that Olivia is attracted to her. Viola curses her disguise that has fooled Olivia.

Act 2, Scene 3: Olivia's kitchen. Sir Toby and Sir Andrew are up late, eating and drinking. Feste joins them and entertains them with a love song, for which they pay him. Sir Toby and Sir Andrew praise Feste, then Sir Toby entreats both Sir Andrew and Feste to sing a round. Maria comes in, concerned that their noise might disturb Olivia, who in turn might send Malvolio to quiet them. Sir Toby continues singing and Malvolio enters, reprimanding the four others for disrespecting Olivia. Malvolio informs Sir Toby that Olivia has made it known that Sir Toby should either behave himself or leave. Sir Toby continues to sing, then Feste joins in until Sir Toby cuts off the singing by accusing Malvolio of trying to force his will on the others. Feste backs up Sir Toby, as does Maria. Malvolio departs and Sir Andrew brings up the notion of challenging Malvolio, which Sir Toby encourages, but Maria says she has a plan to embarrass Malvolio. With prompting from Sir Toby, Maria explains that she will forge a love letter in Olivia's handwriting and will drop it in Malvolio's path. Malvolio, reading the letter, will think that the letter is from Olivia and that Olivia harbors the same feelings for him that he holds for her. The conspirators can then laugh when Malvolio humiliates himself while acting under the delusion that Olivia loves him. All agree the plan is ingenious and the men sing Maria's praises. When she leaves, Sir Toby admits that Maria adores him, to which Sir Andrew says rather cryptically and forlornly that he, too, was once adored.

Act 2, Scene 4: Orsino's house. Orsino again requests music, and he asks Viola to sing an accompanying song. But Curio corrects Orsino, telling him that it was Feste who previously sang for the duke and that Feste is still in Orsino's court. Curio is asked to get Feste. Orsino asks Viola what she thinks of the music that is playing. She finds that it matches what the heart feels. She and Orsino begin a conversation about love, and Orsino asks Viola if she has ever loved. She replies by describing her beloved as resembling Orsino's complexion and age, which causes Orsino alarm, and he cautions Viola (as Cesario) to not pursue an older woman. Orsino then refers to men's love as fickle and to women's beauty as fleeting. By now, Curio has returned with Feste, who sings and is paid. Feste blesses Orsino and acknowledges Orsino's fickle mind. All but Orsino and Viola depart. Orsino again entreats Viola to call on Olivia, and Viola is told not to take no for an answer if Olivia will not accept Orsino's will. Viola asks what Orsino would do if the roles were reversed and it was he who kept refusing some lady's undying love. Orsino doesn't find Viola's scenario plausible since no lady's love could compare to his love for Olivia. Viola corrects him by sharing her own story about her "sister's" untold love, which is really a description of her love for the duke. Orsino does not know that Viola is talking about herself even though she makes allusions to loving the duke. Viola concludes that women are truer to their love, but when Orsino asks about the outcome of the "sister's" love, Viola is elusive, unsure herself. She quickly changes the subject back to Olivia, and Orsino gives Viola a jewel to take to Olivia.

Act 2, Scene 5: Olivia's garden path. While awaiting Maria's next direction in her plan, Sir Toby, Sir Andrew, and Fabian, a servant, are expressing their disgust for Malvolio and how good it will be to see him gulled. Maria, having just seen Malvolio putting on airs to his shadow, comes to tell the three to hide as Malvolio is coming down the walkway. They hide behind a boxtree while Maria drops the letter and exits. Malvolio comes on the scene speaking of fortune and the possibility of wedding and bedding Olivia. Meanwhile the others eavesdrop, growing increasingly furious with Malvolio, who continues to fantasize about being Count Malvolio. Malvolio even pretends to call for Sir Toby, whom he envisions as curtsying in front of "the count," the notion of which infuriates the real Sir Toby. Malvolio then imagines having enough power to tell Sir Toby to give up drinking, which angers Sir Toby to the point of threatening murder, but Fabian keeps Sir Toby quiet enough to witness Maria's scheme. Malvolio, finding the letter and reading it, falls right into Maria's trap, which specifically lays out the behavior Malvolio is to follow to make his love known to Olivia. Maria returns after Malvolio's exit and is highly commended for her ruse. Sir Toby thinks it just might make Malvolio mad. Maria finds it humorous that Malvolio, following the letter's advice, will soon show up in Olivia's presence wearing yellow stockings, a color Olivia hates. The conspirators depart to watch the ruse unfold.

Act 3, Scene 1: Somewhere on the edge of Olivia's property.

Viola encounters Feste on her way to see Olivia. He demonstrates the fickleness of words and makes a reference to Orsino, Olivia, and Viola being fools. Viola pays Feste a coin, but he asks for another, which she pays once Feste tells her whether Olivia is in the house. Feste leaves to let Olivia's party know that Viola is present. Viola reflects on Feste's wit and occupation as a fool, which has impressed her. Sir Toby and Sir Andrew come out to meet Viola and lead her in to Olivia, but Olivia joins them outside, along with Maria. Viola praises Olivia and Olivia asks her people to leave. She takes Viola's hand and asks her name. Viola calls herself Cesario. Viola again asserts that she is there to see Olivia on behalf of Orsino, but Olivia is not interested and switches the conversation back to Viola and herself. Olivia wants to know what Viola thinks of her, but her question makes them both feel awkward and Viola responds cryptically, telling Olivia that Olivia is not what she thinks she is. Olivia quickly tells Viola that Viola is also not what she appears, to which the disguised Viola concurs. Olivia says she wishes Viola were in love with her, but Viola affirms that there will never be a mistress of her own heart, save herself. Upon Viola's departure, Olivia asks Viola to return, saying she might begin considering Orsino's pledged love.

Act 3, Scene 2: Olivia's household. Sir Andrew is ready to depart, having seen Olivia treat Viola, a mere page, better than she treats him. Sir Toby and Fabian entreat him to stay. Fabian convinces Sir Andrew that Olivia was only trying to make him jealous and that he missed his opportunity to challenge Viola on behalf of Olivia. In order to regain favor, Fabian and Sir Toby encourage Sir Andrew to challenge Viola to a duel. Sir Toby promises to deliver the fearsome letter of challenge that Sir Andrew is to write. After Sir Andrew departs, Fabian reveals that he knows Sir Toby will not deliver the letter. Sir Toby says that there is no way Sir Andrew and Viola will ever duel since Sir Andrew is too terrified and, as Fabian acknowledges, Viola appears equally timid. Maria enters to inform them that Malvolio is cross-gartered and in yellow stockings as she predicted.

Act 3, Scene 3: Illyrian countryside, close to Orsino's. Antonio tells Sebastian that he couldn't help but follow his friend for fear of Sebastian's safety and well-being. Sebastian thanks Antonio and desires to tour the town, which Antonio cannot do. Antonio informs Sebastian that he is in danger walking the streets of Illyria since he has fallen out of sorts with the duke for pirating. Antonio gives Sebastian his purse in case he wants to buy something and tells Sebastian that he will be at the Elephant Inn, where they shall board. They go their separate ways.

Act 3, Scene 4: Olivia's household. Olivia is pleased that Viola has accepted her dinner invitation and wonders what to serve. She calls for Malvolio but is warned by Maria that he is behaving oddly. Olivia asks Maria to get him and Maria enters with Malvolio, who is cross-gartered and in yellow stockings. Malvolio's incessant smiling leads Olivia to question his state of mind and through their conversation she concludes that he is stricken with midsummer madness. She is unaware that he is merely enacting the directions included in the letter. Olivia's servant enters to inform her that Viola has returned. Before Olivia leaves, she asks Maria to send for Sir Toby to look to Malvolio's care. Malvolio, still not realizing he has been set up, thinks Olivia is acting out some of the promises in the letter, and this leads him to be curt with Sir Toby, Fabian, and Maria, as directed by the letter. They in turn treat Malvolio as if he were possessed and, in order not to let the trick run out, pursue Malvolio with the intent of locking him up in a dark room, a punishment that Fabian suggests might actually make Malvolio mad.

Sir Andrew enters the scene with the challenge he has written to Viola. The others read it and make fun of it, but to Sir Andrew they are encouraging. Sir Toby volunteers to deliver the letter, and Maria informs him that Viola is currently with Olivia but that he will have the opportunity to deliver it shortly. In the meantime, Sir Toby tells Sir Andrew to go stand in the orchard and when he sees Sir Toby with Viola to wave his sword and swear in order to intimidate Viola. When Sir Andrew leaves, Sir Toby announces that he will not deliver the letter since it is obvious that Viola is of good breeding and will not be intimidated by Sir Andrew's puny threat. Rather, Sir Toby promises to paint a frightful picture of Sir Andrew's abilities so that by the mere exchange of glances between Viola and Sir Andrew, both will be terrified and run off. Fabian spots Viola with Olivia and tells Sir Toby that it will soon be a good time to approach Viola. Viola is still trying to convince Olivia to love Orsino and Olivia is still trying to gain Viola's favors. Olivia wonders how she can be expected to love Orsino when she already loves Viola; she gives Viola a jewel with her picture and asks her to return. Olivia departs and Sir Toby and Fabian enter.

Sir Toby tells Viola that he does not know what offense Viola committed against Sir Andrew, but Sir Andrew is waiting in the orchard to fight Viola. Viola insists that she has no quarrel with any man. Sir Toby builds up Sir Andrew's reputation to the point where Viola wishes to retreat into Olivia's house, but Sir Toby won't allow it since Sir Andrew's injury is (supposedly) justified. Viola entreats Sir Toby to discover what her offense has been and Sir Toby obliges. Viola asks Fabian about Sir Andrew, but Fabian, like Sir Toby, exaggerates Sir Andrew's combative abilities. Fabian offers to try to dissuade Sir Andrew from dueling. Meanwhile, Sir Toby is exaggerating Viola's skills to Sir Andrew. Sir Andrew no longer wishes to follow through and is willing to offer his horse in order to stop the duel, but Sir Toby insists that Viola will not back down. Sir Toby returns to Viola claiming he still does not know Viola's offense, stating that for Sir Andrew the duel is now on principle alone. Viola is fearful and nearly ready to reveal her disguise. Fortunately, Antonio arrives on the scene and is ready to duel on behalf of Viola, whom he mistakes for Sebastian. Sir Toby is also ready to join in but the officers arrive and arrest Antonio, who asks Viola for some of his money. Viola does not know what Antonio is talking about but offers him some of her own money for his assistance. Before being taken off, Antonio tells the officers that earlier he had rescued Sebastian from drowning, but the officers don't care and take him away. Viola is excited and hopeful on hearing this and being mistaken for Sebastian. She departs but Sir Toby calls her a coward, especially for not helping her friend Antonio. As an excuse to flee, Sir Andrew says he'll go after Viola to exact justice.

Act 4, Scene 1: Olivia's property. Feste is sent to find Viola but instead encounters Sebastian, whom he mistakes for Viola. Sebastian is annoyed at Feste's persistence and after paying him threatens worse if he is not left alone. Sir Andrew, Sir Toby, and Fabian then come upon Sebastian and also mistake him for Viola. Sir Andrew takes advantage of the moment and strikes Sebastian, but Sebastian is not afraid and strikes him back, three for one. Sebastian wonders if all the Illyrians are mad. Feste goes to tell Olivia while Sir Toby keeps hold of Sebastian. Olivia arrives just as Sir Toby and Sebastian have drawn swords. Reprimanding Sir Toby for his ill treatment of Sebastian, whom she mistakes for Viola, she orders Sir Toby, Sir Andrew, and Fabian to leave. Olivia offers to take Sebastian back with her in order to make light of the situation. Sebastian now thinks he must be dreaming or mad, but either way he is pleased. Olivia asks Sebastian to marry her and he says yes.

Act 4, Scene 2: Olivia's property. Feste joins the ruse against Malvolio by impersonating Sir Topas the curate as a means of revenge against Malvolio for his earlier rudeness towards Feste. Maria gives Feste a gown to wear while she retrieves Sir Toby, who, upon seeing Feste, is impressed with his masquerade. As the priest, Feste calls to Malvolio, who is still locked up nearby in a dark room. Feste treats Malvolio as if he were insane and even tries to convince him that the room is not dark. Malvolio insists that he is not insane and that the room is dark. Feste asks Malvolio's opinion regarding Pythagoras's idea of the soul, which after death might inhabit the body of a bird. Malvolio agrees that the soul is noble but does not believe the rest. Feste uses this excuse to leave Malvolio confined in his dark cell. Sir Toby is very pleased with the scene, although Maria does not know why Feste bothered to wear the attire of Sir Topas since Malvolio could not see him. Sir Toby asks Feste to return to Malvolio, but this time as himself. Feste begins singing, which Malvolio hears. Malvolio calls to Feste and asks him for pen and ink, paper, and a candle. Malvolio insists that he is sane and that he is notoriously abused. He asks Feste to deliver the letter he will write, promising him great rewards for his assistance. Feste says he will help and leaves to get writing materials.

Act 4, Scene 3: Olivia's property. Sebastian wonders where Antonio is since he wasn't at the Elephant and he wants Antonio's advice regarding Olivia. Sebastian concludes that Olivia is not crazy since she can control her house. Olivia shows up with the priest and asks Sebastian to assuage her jealous soul by going to the church and marrying her right then.

Act 5, Scene 1: Olivia's household. Fabian asks Feste to show him Malvolio's letter but Feste will not. Orsino, Viola, Curio, and the lords approach. The duke recognizes Feste and inquires into Feste's well-being. Feste explains how he is worse for his friends and Orsino pays him for his wit. Feste convinces Orsino to pay him another coin. He asks for a third coin but Orsino refuses, although he does tell Feste to retrieve Olivia and in doing so he will perhaps be paid again. When Viola sees Antonio approaching with the officers, she tells Orsino that he has helped her; she also claims that he oddly addressed her. Orsino recognizes Antonio as a pirate and asks him what could possibly lead him to risk capture by returning to Illyria. Antonio explains that he has been bewitched by Sebastian, (whom he thinks Viola to be) whose life he saved just a short while ago, and he has even given him his purse. Orsino asks when Antonio arrived in Illyria, and Antonio tells him it was just the present day and that Sebastian had been with him for the three previous months. Orsino, who sees Olivia approaching, calls Antonio mad since Viola has been in Orsino's company for three months.

Meanwhile, Olivia, who is now present among the others, reprimands Viola for not keeping Sebastian's promise to return to her rather than to her prior duty to the duke. Orsino, still pursuing Olivia, calls her cruel, to which she defends herself as constant. Realizing that Olivia loves Viola, Orsino threatens to kill Viola, although he loves his servant well. Viola is willing to follow Orsino and be killed; Olivia asks where she is going. Viola says she loves Orsino, and Olivia—addressing Viola as her husband—claims Viola must be beguiled, thus calling for the priest. Orsino asks Viola if she is indeed Olivia's husband, but Viola denies it. The priest arrives and confirms that he has in fact performed a wedding between Viola (actually Sebastian) and Olivia; Orsino tells Viola to take the lady but to never cross his path again. Viola protests. Sir Andrew now arrives, wounded, and tells Olivia to send a surgeon to Sir Toby, who is also wounded, both by Viola's hand, which she denies. Sir Toby, drunk, arrives, accompanied by Feste and makes the same claim as Sir Andrew. Olivia sends Sir Toby and Sir Andrew to be looked to, but Sir Toby belittles Sir Andrew, for he does not think he can help him since he is so pathetic. They leave with Feste and Fabian while Olivia questions who has done this.

Sebastian arrives on the scene, apologizing to Olivia for what he has done to her kinsman. Sebastian notices that Olivia is regarding him in a strange manner. He also notes Antonio's presence and Antonio's perplexed manner. When Sebastian finally sees Viola disguised as Cesario, their recognition slowly progresses from questioning family ties to acknowledgment and finally glee. Viola reveals her true identity to all, admitting that she is not the page Cesario but is in fact Viola of Messaline. Sebastian gladly accepts Olivia's confusion as truly fortunate, and Orsino says that he too will participate in these happy circumstances by sharing the occasion with Viola, although he still addresses her as "boy."

When Orsino asks to see her in her woman's clothes, Viola says that she has left them with the captain, who is now imprisoned at Malvolio's unknown request. This brings to mind Malvolio's condition and Olivia asks for Malvolio to be retrieved and brought forth, but just then Feste and Fabian arrive with Malvolio's letter, which Fabian reads aloud.

Orsino comments that Malvolio's letter does not seem to belong to a madman, and Fabian goes to retrieve Malvolio. When Malvolio arrives, Olivia asks how he is. He tells her that she has wronged him and shows her the love letter, which Olivia immediately recognizes as being written by Maria. Olivia assures Malvolio that they will get to the bottom of this ruse, but Fabian steps in, hoping to alleviate the situation and not place blame on Maria by exposing all the perpetrators. Fabian tells Olivia that Maria wrote the letter at Sir Toby's request, for which Sir Toby has married her. Feste also announces his role in the scheme, which sets Malvolio off, threatening revenge on them all as he departs. Orsino sends someone after Malvolio and tells Viola that once she has changed into her woman's attire she will be his mistress. They all depart except for Feste, who sings his song about the ages of man and finally informs the audience that the play is done.

CHAPTER 1

The Art of
the Play

Revising and Recycling: Composing *Twelfth Night*

Molly Maureen Mahood

Some disjointed aspects of *Twelfth Night* suggest that
the play may have been revised or in the process of
revision. Professor Molly Maureen Mahood explores
these inconsistencies in her introduction to the 1968
Penguin edition of *Twelfth Night*. The author of several books on Shakespeare, Mahood offers insight
into Shakespeare's writing process. Besides possibly
reworking the play after various performances,
Shakespeare incorporated revised plots and characters from some of his previous plays into *Twelfth
Night*. He also borrowed from other playwrights who
dealt with themes that Shakespeare wanted to explore. Mahood concludes that all of Shakespeare's
revisions and borrowing reveal his writing technique, but the overall tone of the finished play exem-
plify his unique style.

The mood of *Twelfth Night* is so subtle and at the same time
so unified that it comes as a surprise to the producer or to
the careful reader to discover how many minor confusions
and inconsistencies there are in the play's construction. The
second scene, for example, raises expectations which are
never satisfied. Viola's remarks about the Captain's reliable
appearance are so pointed that we expect him to have a
fairly influential part in the plot. But he fades out of the play
at once. Shakespeare himself seems uneasy about his disap-
pearance, because he suddenly informs us in the last scene
that the Captain is detained on a charge brought against him
by Malvolio. But this fresh evidence of Malvolio's ill will towards men is used only to bring him back himself on to the
stage, and when he finally stalks off we are still—as Olivia

Excerpted from the Introduction by Molly Maureen Mahood to *Twelfth Night*, by
William Shakespeare. Copyright © to the Introduction 1968 by M.M. Mahood. Reprinted with permission from Penguin, UK.

exclaims—in the dark about the Captain. A further puzzle created by the second scene is that it leads us to expect Viola will sing to the Duke, but she never does so. Other mysterious features of the action are the unexplained substitution of Fabian for Feste in the trick played on Malvolio, and the sudden entrance in Act V of Sir Toby and Sir Andrew bleeding from a second encounter with Sebastian of which we have been told nothing. In the same scene, events which seem to have happened in a couple of days are said to have occupied three months. This kind of double time is so common in Shakespeare's plays that it is of no significance in itself, but here it does contribute to the general effect that *Twelfth Night*, for all its harmony of mood, is far from being a conventionally well-made play.

INCONSISTENCIES SUGGEST THE PLAY WAS REVISED

There are two ways of explaining these inconsistencies. One explanation is that the text of the play as we now have it represents a revision made some years after the first performance. Another is that the play was written at speed without having been thought out and planned in consistent detail. A test case for deciding, however tentatively, between these two views is offered by the scene that seems to bear the most obvious signs of revision, that between Viola and the Duke Orsino in the second Act. This starts with Orsino calling, in verse, for "That old and antique song we heard last night." He is told, in prose, that the singer is not present but can be found, and while Feste is fetched the tune is played and Orsino explains to Viola that the song is "old and plain." The song that Feste sings, however, is not a ballad or folk-song, but an up-to-date "air."

The explanation usually offered for all this is that, when the play was revived, perhaps about 1606, Feste had to be substituted for Viola as the singer because the voice of the boy who played Viola in the revival was breaking; and that Feste chose to sing a different song from the one Viola had sung in the original production. . . . But there are no awkwardnesses that suggest revision in Act II, scene 4 of *Twelfth Night*. The scene is a dramatic climax, perfectly conceived and perfectly executed. Viola, in her disguise as Cesario, is no longer the Duke Orsino's singer, but has been "much advanced" to someone who summons others to sing for him— a sort of Master of the Duke's Music. Feste's entrance is delayed in order that background music may be used to stress the stagy melancholy of Orsino's love, and in order to draw the audience's attention to Viola's feelings for Orsino. Feste not only furnishes the song but also, by his slight asperity and mockery of Orsino, separates the Duke's more shallow feelings from the scene's final statement of Viola's double sorrow: her unspoken, hopeless love for Orsino and her grief for her missing brother.

Shakespeare in fact speaks "masterly" in this scene, and it is hard to believe that the writing of it was not part of his original inspiration. If we are to call it a revised scene we need perhaps first to revise our own notions of what constitutes a revision. A playwright can revise his intentions while he is actually writing a play, and the practice of [Bertolt] Brecht and other modern dramatists has shown how much further revision can go on in rehearsals, as the author improves on his script, or adapts it to the abilities of his actors. All such revisions will be incorporated into the acting copy, or promptbook, and precede the play's first performance. Other revisions may be carried out later by the playwright to meet the theatrical exigencies of a revival; it is fairly clear that "God" was replaced by "Jove" at several points in the text of *Twelfth Night* which has come down to us, in order to make the play conform with the 1606 statute against profanity in the theatre. Yet other changes in a play may be made years later and without the playwright's knowledge. Shakespeare's fellow actors presumably saw no harm in adding the odd topical joke to his plays from time to time. The mysterious allusion in Act II, scene 5 to the lady of the Strachy who married the yeoman of the wardrobe may well be a piece of Blackfriars gossip current after Shakespeare's death; perhaps it was slipped in for the Court performance of 1623.

THE WRITER'S PROCESS: REASON, RE-SEE, RE-USE

But most of the other so-called revisions of *Twelfth Night* could be of the kind that precede the first performance. Shakespeare at first meant Viola to sing to Orsino, and tells us as much in the second scene; later, when he came to write Act II, scene 4, he realized that he could create an enthralling effect by having Viola sit listening beside her master, as moved as he by the music but able to give only indirect expression to her feelings. Having written this scene as it now stands, Shakespeare perhaps realized that Feste's part was becoming very heavy, and accordingly substituted Fabian for him in the plot against Malvolio. A sound dramatic instinct was also at work in this change of plan. The box-tree episode was Malvolio's big scene, and the Fool's popularity with the audience might have detracted from the effect Shakespeare was aiming at here. So the main encounter between Malvolio and Feste is deferred until the dark house scene in Act IV, in which Malvolio is heard but not seen and in which Feste can therefore be given full scope.

Shakespeare's admirers have often been reluctant to see in the inconsistencies of his texts the result of rapid *ad hoc* decisions by the playwright in the very course of composition. But a degree of improvisation is natural to drama; and the tradition that Shakespeare wrote *The Merry Wives of Windsor* in a fortnight at Queen Elizabeth's request, whether it is true or not, at least suggests that plays could be commissioned at very short notice. As a brilliant improvisation, *Twelfth Night* offers us the pleasure of tracing the artist's hand at work. It is no less an achievement for having been written at speed and perhaps for a special occasion. . . .

A sign of Shakespeare's rapid writing in *Twelfth Night* is the freedom with which he borrows from his own work. When he was pressed for time it was inevitable that his thoughts should fly to incidents and characters which had gone down well with the audiences for his earlier comedies. Indeed there are so many self-borrowings in *Twelfth Night* that the play has been called "a masterpiece of recapitulation." The deeply loyal friend Antonio comes without so much as a change of name from *The Merchant of Venice;* Slender of *The Merry Wives of Windsor* brings his mincing oaths with him when he becomes Sir Andrew Aguecheek, and Shakespeare was counting on his fellow-shareholder in the company, Abraham Cowley, to repeat his success in interpreting this "silly ass" type of role. The comic possibilities of eavesdropping, explored in *Much Ado About Nothing*, and of girl disguised as boy, exploited in *As You Like It,* are stretched yet further in *Twelfth Night,* the one in the box-tree scene and the other in the duel.

Two situations in particular Shakespeare knew from experience to be ready sources of laughter. One was the arrival of a stranger in a town where he was immediately mistaken for his twin brother. . . . Shakespeare had already borrowed this unfailingly funny device from Plautus when writing *The*

Comedy of Errors—a play which had entertained another Inn of Court at their feast eight years previously. Equally attractive was the [Old English tune] Polly Oliver theme: the girl who follows her lover disguised as a page. Shakespeare had tried this out in *The Two Gentlemen of Verona,* a play which appears to have left him discontented since he kept trying to find new uses for its components. The inherent liveliness of the plot of *Twelfth Night* owes a great deal to the skill with which Shakespeare has combined these two comic situations. But he was not the first to combine them. A whole family group of plays and stories merging the twin situation with the Polly Oliver situation already existed by 1602, and Shakespeare certainly knew some of this group. . . . We find among them two Italian plays called *Gl'Inganni*— the Deceptions—but these are less close to *Twelfth Night* than is an earlier play which was a source for both of them, *Gl'Ingannati*— the Deceived—acted at Siena in 1531.

DECEPTIVE ORIGINS FOR *TWELFTH NIGHT*

Discussions of a literary source are often hard or tedious to follow because of the differences in names to be met with in two versions of the same plot. The use of generic names may help us to keep things clear here: the lover, for the character corresponding to Orsino; the brother, for Sebastian's counterpart; the lady, for Olivia's; and the heroine, for the character in Viola's situation. In *Gl'Ingannati,* the heroine assumes her disguise in order to follow and serve a lover who has apparently forgotten all about her during her temporary absence front Modena, the scene of the play, and who in fact now woos a lady to whom he sends the heroine as emissary. The lady promptly falls in love with the disguised heroine. Next the heroine's father and his friend, the ageing father of the lady (himself a suitor to the heroine) hear of her disguise, intercept her—or so they think—and shut her up with the lady. Actually they have seized the heroine's long-lost brother, who has just arrived in the city. On discovering what has occurred, the lover flies into a rage of jealousy and frustration; but he is brought to realize, through the eloquence of the heroine's old nurse, what a treasure he already has in the heroine's devotion.

This bald narration of its plot makes *Gl'Ingannati* sound very much as if it were the direct source of *Twelfth Night.* Actually the two plays are quite different in spirit. . . . In her heartless amusement at the lady's predicament, the heroine of *Gl'Ingannati* is a very long way from Viola. The whole play is in fact a heartless work; a bright, bustling, and often salacious comedy of intrigue. But it must have been very popular: French and Spanish translations soon appeared, and the plot was adapted for short stories by the Italian Bandello, the Frenchman Belleforest, and the Englishman Barnaby Rich. Each of these narrative versions carries us a little farther away from the harsh topicality of *Gl'Ingannati*, towards the Illyrian world represented in the sixteenth century by many translations of late Greek romances. . . .

Several verbal echoes confirm Shakespeare's debt to Rich's story, which had the advantage of being in English and being easily available. . . . What happened may have been something like this. Asked for a comedy, Shakespeare recalled and almost certainly re-read Rich's "Apolonius and Silla" because he liked its blend of two themes that he had already used with success. Then he must have remembered or discovered that there were in fact dramatic versions of this tale already extant. One, a Latin translation of *Gl'Ingannati*, had been acted at Cambridge before the Earl of Essex as recently as 1595, and Shakespeare could have borrowed a manuscript of this from his Stratford acquaintance and future son-in-law John Hall, who had been at Cambridge at the time. Or he could have glanced through a copy of the original Italian play; or come across the close translation of it into French, which had the distinction of being the first prose comedy in that language. He certainly knew *Gl'Ingannati* in the original or translation, since some details in *Twelfth Night* derive from no other source: the brother's sightseeing in the city, the heroine's hopeless passion described as though (II.4.106) it were experienced by someone else—

My father had a daughter loved a man . . .

—and the servant's invitation to the brother, whom he mistakes for the disguised heroine, to come and visit the lady. Moreover, Shakespeare was familiar with the tale in the collections of Bandello and Belleforest. Not only are their retellings echoed verbally several times in *Twelfth Night*, but both writers place the emotional climax of the story in the heroine's attempt to dissuade the lover from his pursuit of the lady; and we have already seen that the episode in *Twelfth Night* which corresponds to this, Act II, scene 4, is a highlight of the play. It has no counterpart in Rich's story.

SHAKESPEARE'S INNOVATIONS

All these recollections did not prevent Shakespeare from handling the tale in his own way. His Viola does not assume her disguise in pursuit of the man she loves; she falls in love with Orsino only after she has found service with him. Olivia is not a widow (her mourning must have misled Manningham) but a young girl who repels the Duke Orsino's suit because she is stricken with grief for her brother's death. Viola too loves a brother she believes to be dead; and the brother himself is not brought in merely to complicate the plot and then disappear, but is a positive and likeable character whose impetuous marriage to Olivia establishes, in a world of fantasies, one irrefutable fact from which the dénouement can be swiftly and gaily reached. All these changes help to normalize and humanize Rich's melodramatic tale. However many versions of the story may have been known to Shakespeare, he succeeded in shaping it afresh with deftness and confidence.

What Rich calls a leash of lovers derives, then, from "Apolonius and Silla" and from some of the tales and plays that preceded it. But there are no hints in these earlier versions of Antonio, nor of Malvolio and his tormentors. Yet for Manningham, the memorable scenes were those in which Malvolio figured, and his response was typical of its time. When the play was acted at Court in 1623, it was called *Malvolio,* and Charles I changed the title to this in his own copy of the second edition of Shakespeare's works.

A suggestion for the baiting of Malvolio could have come from Rich's book. One of his tales is about a man who married a scold. Driven to desperation by her clamour, he shut her up

> *in a dark house that was on his back side; and then, calling his neighbours about her, he would seem with great sorrow to lament his wife's distress; telling them that she was suddenly become lunatic; whereas, by his gesture, he took so great grief as though he would likewise have run mad for company. But his wife (as he had attired her) seemed indeed not to be well in her wits but, seeing her husband's manners, showed herself in her conditions to be a right Bedlam. She used no other words but curses and bannings, crying for the plague and the pestilence, and that the devil would tear her husband in pieces. The company that were about her, they would exhort her, 'Good neighbour, forget these speeches which doth so much distemper you, and call upon God, and he will surely help you.'*

In just the same way, Feste exhorts Malvolio to leave his vain bibble-babble and Maria bids him remember his prayers. But if this passage gave Shakespeare his first idea for the trick played on Malvolio, Malvolio himself quickly grew far beyond the stature of a mere dupe in his creator's mind. In fact he is so sharply particularized that there is a strong likelihood that when he appeared "in the habit of some sir of note" he was recognized as the caricature of some unpopular figure of the time, well known to a Court, or Middle Temple, audience. Malvolio's alleged Puritanism, his dislike of bear-baiting, his "august regard of control," and his interruption of a noisy revel, have all been taken to point to Sir William Knollys, the Controller of the Queen's Household. Even the name Malvolio has been read as a reference to Knollys's notorious infatuation with his ward Mary Fitton ("I-want-Mall"), whose disgrace at Court in the winter of 1600–1601 may be alluded to when Sir Toby speaks of the picture of Mistress Mall which has taken dust.

Whether or not this and other identifications of characters in *Twelfth Night* with real people are correct, they help to remind us of one aspect of the play which stage designers, eager to hoist sail for the Mediterranean, too easily overlook: its Englishness. Shakespeare's Illyria is within hailing distance of the Thames watermen, and the visitor from Messaline puts up in the south suburbs, at the Elephant—as did many other visitors to London. Shakespeare had learned a good deal about the possibilities of realistic social comedy when he had acted in Ben Jonson's *Every Man in His Humour* some three years before *Twelfth Night* was written. The oddities of Jonson's Stephano were still vivid in Shakespeare's memory when he invented the part of Sir Andrew Aguecheek. Both are typical English country "gulls"—the Elizabethan word for anyone easily taken in—both echo the phrases of more inventive characters, both demean themselves by abusing their social inferiors, both waver between bluster and timidity, both are convinced they have a very pretty leg worth clothing in fine hose. Yet to speak of *Every Man in His Humour* as a "source" for *Twelfth Night* is to be reminded once more of Shakespeare's skill in subjugating all the elements that go to make up the play to its dominant mood of festivity. Stephano is an object of real contempt to Jonson; but such is the spirit of *Twelfth Night* that Shakespeare, a bad hater at all times, enjoys his Sir Andrew and endears him to us as somebody who "was adored once, too."

Rhetorical Devices Are Used for Characterization

Karen Newman

Part of what makes characters seem lifelike is their use of language. In *Twelfth Night* the characters reveal their personalities through their various dialogues and monologues. Professor Karen Newman of Brown University analyzes Shakespeare's rhetorical methods for revealing aspects of the characters' identities in the play. For Orsino and Olivia, it is their erratic language which demonstrates an imaginative state of mind for both and the potential for change, and yet their irrational attitudes are counterbalanced with a bent for clever and measured poetry. Other characters reveal their personalities through inner monologues which take the form of soliloquies directed at the audience. Viola, on the one hand, demonstrates great self-insight utilizing what Newman calls a "rhetoric of consciousness" which establishes an audible inner debate of rhetorical questions, signifying growth. Malvolio, however, as demonstrated in his soliloquy in scene V of act II, is neither endowed with poetry nor self-insight. In fact, his soliloquy becomes a dialogue with comments from the eavesdroppers.

In *Twelfth Night* Shakespeare uses mistaken identity not only as a means of complicating the plot, but also as a figure for self-delusion, for the mistakes men make about themselves. Though the central mistakes in identity arise from Viola's disguise as Cesario and the eventual confusion between Cesario and Sebastian, there are also, as many readers have noted, the "identities" created by the imagination: Orsino as melancholy lover to Olivia; Olivia as mourner to her brother; Malvolio as lord to Olivia and her household; and even Sir Toby's fictitious version of Sir Andrew.

LANGUAGE REFLECTS MULTIPLE IDENTITIES OF ORSINO AND OLIVIA AND INSIGHT FOR VIOLA

Both Olivia and Orsino demonstrate the limits of their "identities" by their erratic behavior, which they express primarily through language. In the course of his first six lines, the duke praises music as the food of love and then declares "Enough, no more;/'Tis not so sweet now as it was before." He calls attention to his own irrational behavior, attributing it to the "spirit of love" and equating love with fancy. So in II, iv, in his conversation with Viola, first Orsino affirms that like all true lovers he is "Unstaid and skittish in all motions else,/Save in the constant image of the creature/That is belov'd" (II, iv, 18–20). But following this avowal of constancy, and marked by the emphatic full stop in the middle of the line, is an abrupt change of subject: the question to Viola "How dost thou like this tune?", a tune which we learn, ironically enough, helps to relieve his passion. Within fifteen lines he then contradicts himself when he affirms that instead of being constant, men's "fancies are more giddy and unfirm,/More longing, wavering, sooner lost and worn/Than women's are" (lines 33–5). And finally he tells Viola, "Make no compare/Between that love a woman can bear me/And that I owe Olivia" (lines 102–4). As in so many of Shakespeare's comedies, the clown speaks truth; he affirms the duke's changeableness: "Now the melancholy god protect thee, and the tailor make thy doublet of changeable taffeta, for thy mind is a very opal" (II, iv, 73–5).

Some critics observe only the absurdity of Orsino and Olivia, but Shakespeare endows them with poetry which makes them sympathetic rather than ridiculous. . . . Orsino plays with the clichés and expected behavior of the lover in highly figurative verse, but he is not governed by them. For him, the postures of love provide tropes [figures of speech] which he uses creatively, as in his imaginative reworking of the pun on hart in I, i, 19 ff. He plays self-consciously with the conventions—with the relation between love and music, with the analogy between love and the hunt, with mythological allusions—measuring the distance between himself and ideal romantic behavior. Despite his affectation, the quality of his poetry proves him a worthy lover to Viola.

Olivia also suffers from an unlimited imagination, first in creating her fictive identity as "cloistress" and then, like Orsino, showing her changeable nature and unreadiness for love by loving the epicene [effeminate] Cesario. The clown exposes her "disguise" as mourner in I, v, 50 ff. when he "proves" her a fool, but her relation to Cesario is more complex. Again like the duke she recognizes something in Cesario which attracts her, but her feelings also betray a fear of marriage and adult love. Orsino has already described the ambiguous nature of Cesario's sexuality; Malvolio's description, which precedes their first meeting, emphasizes the page's effeminancy. Olivia's soliloquy at the end of the scene effectively conveys a sense of her inner life by revealing the change wrought in her by love:

> '. . . I am a gentleman.' I'll be sworn thou art:
> Thy tongue, thy face, thy limbs, actions, and spirit
> Do give thee five-fold blazon. Not too fast: soft! soft!
> Unless the master were the man. How now?
> Even so quickly may one catch the plague?
> Methinks I feel this youth's perfections
> With an invisible and subtle stealth
> To creep in at mine eyes. Well, let it be.

> (I, v, 295–302)

Shakespeare makes Olivia seem lifelike by casting her musings about Cesario's enigmatic responses about his parentage in dialogue; she uses rhetorical questions, self-address in the admonition to herself "Not too fast: soft! soft!" and the caesura [a break in the flow of verse] to indicate shifts in thought. . . . Her willingness to accept love's transforming power ("Well, let it be") rather than lament it wins our sympathy and prepares us for her marriage to Sebastian. The final lines continue the courtly metaphor [that love enters through the eyes] used to present Olivia's divided mind: she fears her eye is opposed to her mind. . . . Shakespeare . . . is careful to establish and confirm our comic expectations for Olivia's love. The lady resigns herself to fate rather than human agency, but she is willing enough to help fate along by sending Cesario her ring. More important is the immediately following scene in which we learn Sebastian is alive and well, knowledge which reassures us that the comic confusion of Olivia's love for the disguised Viola will be resolved happily.

Disguise and wooing by proxy are nevertheless dangerous business. Viola's beauty, sincerity, and particularly her

description of how she would woo (I, v, 254 ff.), win Olivia's
love. In her soliloquy which follows Sebastian's first scene
we find many features of the rhetoric of consciousness . . . in
comedy:

> I left no ring with her: what means this lady?
> Fortune forbid my outside have not charm'd her!
> She made good view of me, indeed so much,
> That methought her eyes had lost her tongue,
> For she did speak in starts distractedly.
> She loves me, sure; the cunning of her passion
> Invites me in this churlish messenger.
> None of my lord's ring? Why, he sent her none.
> I am the man: if it be so, as 'tis,
> Poor lady, she were better love a dream.
> Disguise, I see thou art a wickedness,
> Wherein the pregnant enemy does much.
> How easy is it for the proper false
> In women's waxen hearts to set their forms!
> Alas, our frailty is the cause, not we,
> For such as we are made of, such we be.
> How will this fadge? My master loves her dearly,
> And I, poor monster, fond as much of him,
> And she, mistaken, seems to dote on me:
> What will become of this? As I am man,
> My state is desperate for my master's love:
> As I am woman (now alas the day!)
> What thriftless sighs shall poor Olivia breathe?
> O time, thou must untangle this, not I,
> It is too hard a knot for me t'untie.

(II, ii, 16–40)

Rhetorical questions establish the I/you opposition characteristic of inner debate, as do the semantic reversals of an-
tithesis ("As I am man . . . As I am woman"), and the inserted
parenthetical elements which convey the confusion Viola
feels. But because she understands full well how the mistakes have come about, Viola does not fear madness or believe she dreams. It is Sebastian, her other self, who is subjected to those aspects of mistaken identity, who believes he
is mad or dreaming.

Shakespeare divides Viola's speech into three distinct sec-
tions. The first ten lines comment upon the preceding inter-
change with Olivia. They include a mirror passage in which
Viola describes and interprets Olivia's gestures and behavior; their function is essentially reportorial. Viola's apostro-
phe of "Disguise" marks the second section. She shifts from
the first person singular to the plural to extend her audience

much as Angelo does in *Measure for Measure* [II, i, 17–31]. But whereas Angelo's pronoun shift signals his recognition of a shared humanity, Viola's transfers responsibility for her predicament from herself to her sex and its alleged susceptibility to Satan's inventiveness. Though she personifies disguise, Viola attributes Olivia's confusion and her predicament not finally to a supernatural power, but to human nature, or more precisely, women's "frail" natures. And because she captivated Olivia without guile, she does not believe herself responsible for the consequences of her disguise. In the soliloquy's final section, Viola rehearses the complications of the intrigue. Shakespeare emphasizes Viola's comic plight and her sexual ambiguity through the alternating pronouns, the "I" versus "him" (line 33) and "she" versus "me" (line 34), and through the succeeding lines which describe her situation as man and as woman. In a final rhyming couplet, Viola decides to let time untangle the knot her love has tied. . . .

Malvolio's Rhetoric Lacks Self-Consciousness but Gains an Audience

Many readers have seen in Malvolio a satirical portrait of the puritan or melancholic, or a foil whose delusions parody the delicate or rowdy aberrations of the court characters. But . . . some critics have claimed Malvolio as a tragic figure who learns from his error. Certainly Shakespeare endows him with an inner life in his series of revealing monologues, but unlike the other characters for whom the rhetoric of inner debate suggests conflict, struggle and development, Malvolio's soliloquies are diffused in various ways to emphasize Malvolio's unselfconsciousness. He neither questions his own behavior nor is willing to abandon reason to rely on time or fortune to resolve his predicament.

Shakespeare creates for Malvolio an inner life that consists of little more than fantasies of wish-fulfillment in which he imagines himself lording it over Olivia, Sir Toby and his cohorts. In II, v, Malvolio enters in soliloquy:

'Tis but fortune, all is fortune. Maria once told me she did
affect me, and I have heard herself come thus near, that
should she fancy, it should be one of my complexion.
Besides, she uses me with a more exalted respect than any
one else that follows her. What should I think on't?

(lines 23–8)

These lines come at a time in the play that allows us to judge whether or not Malvolio's reflections correspond with his actions and character thus far presented. We have seen Olivia in I, v, chastise him for his "self-love" and "distempered appetite" and our memory of her words discredits his claim that she treats him with "a more exalted respect." We are amused by his fantasy that Olivia's wanting a lover of a melancholy temperament means she fancies him. The rhetorical question which ends the passage would seem to initiate an inner debate, establishing the I/you opposition of dialogue. . . . But, in what follows, the role of interlocutor [to whom the speaker speaks] is taken over by the eavesdroppers, and Malvolio's soliloquy, instead of inner debate, becomes stage dialogue. Malvolio, far from questioning himself, immediately takes off into his social and sexual fantasy of "Count Malvolio." That fantasy is questioned of course, not by a created inner self, conscious of the discrepancy between an imagined reality and the lived world, which in his view ("There is example for't") serves only to confirm his desires, but by the outraged comments of Sir Toby, Andrew, Fabian and Maria. The fantasy becomes a dialogue with Sir Toby, not with conscience or self. Like Berowne in *Love's Labour's Lost*, Malvolio's interlocutor is not the self. But whereas for Berowne, an imaginative created persona and his own rhetorical inventiveness prevent self-analysis, for Malvolio it is prevented by the limits of his egotism and by the dramatic scene itself in which he gets his come-uppance from the eavesdroppers' malicious commentary.

When Malvolio finds the forged letter, his responses parody the parallel speech of Olivia's that we have already considered in which she discovers her love for Cesario. Instead of mental movement back and forth as she struggles with newly discovered feelings, the forged *billet-doux* simply confirms what Malvolio has just been fantasizing. His *softly* (line 122) and *soft* (line 142), parallel Olivia's in I, v, 297, but far from holding him back or suggesting conflict and the need for caution, they are linked to moments of impetuosity. At line 122, *softly* leads to his discovery of the anacrostic on his name, and at line 142 *soft* leads on to the text of the letter itself about which he exclaims after having read it, "Daylight and champaign discovers not more! This is open." To Malvolio, everything, every action, every silence, every gesture, is self-evident, generates no debate, and can only serve to confirm his already firm good estimate of himself. Far from suggesting development or change, Malvolio's monologue here simply emphasizes what we already know of him; he is full of self-love. So also in his next soliloquy at III, iv, 64 ff. in which the dialogue is not with the self, but with the letter. In a moment of unwitting self-revelation he gloats "nothing that can be can come between me and the full prospect of my hopes." Certainly not good sense, self-doubt, a sense of decorum or of social place.

Shakespeare's Use of "Humor" and Satire

Oscar James Campbell

In the following article, the late Oscar James Campbell discusses the humor play subplot and satire in *Twelfth Night*. Campbell, an expert on Shakespeare and satire, believes that it was most likely Shakespeare's firsthand experience acting in Ben Jonson's *Every Man in His Humour* (in September 1598) which led him to incorporate the humor character traits into his own plays. The satiric elements common to Jonson and his contemporaries often took the form of poking fun at self-absorbed or foolish characters. In *Twelfth Night* Shakespeare utilized this strategy in creating the comic subplot that involves Sir Andrew Aguecheek and Malvolio. Campbell notes, however, that while satirists typically redeemed their victims at play's end, Shakespeare added a dark dimension to his comic portrayal of Malvolio by leaving him bitter and outcast. The reason for this is unclear and has fostered entertaining debate. Interestingly, *Twelfth Night* marks the last appearance of humor characters in Shakespeare's plays.

The first agents of Shakespeare's satire were . . . his louts and clowns. The first objects of his systematic ridicule were "humor" figures. In selecting these somewhat mechanically conceived eccentrics for his victims, he followed the lead of certain dramatists who began to write in the last decade of the sixteenth century, notably George Chapman and Ben Jonson. Employing the world-old psychological theory of humors, they developed a very effective comic technique for ridiculing absurd human beings.

The term "humor" seems to have come into common use about the year 1592 as a substitute for "temperament" or "complexion," words which up to that time had been used to denominate the distinguishing characteristic of a man's nature. The theory that the personality of a human being was sanguine, phlegmatic, choleric, or melancholy, as one of the four humors predominated in his bodily composition, was as old as Galen, the celebrated Greek physician of the second century. The system, still universally accepted in Shakespeare's day, was thoroughly expounded in the many handbooks of medicine, one of which was a cherished possession of almost every middle-class Elizabethan household.

In popular parlance the term "humor" . . . came more often to describe a mere eccentricity or foolish mannerism. But the most common meaning of the word was that explained by [the character] Cash in [Ben Jonson's] *Every Man in His Humour.* To Cob's question, "What is this humour?" "It's some rare thing I warrant," Cash replies, "Marry I'll tell thee what it is (as 'tis generally received in these days): it is a monster bred in a man by self-love and affectation, and fed by folly." [III, i, 154–8]

A "humor" figure thus came to be a man impervious to everything in the world except the folly which dominated him. He was a creature ridden by idiosyncrasy. Characters much like these "humorous" figures first appear in some of the morality plays. Abstract vices or virtues, as soon as they became only a little humanized, developed a family likeness to humor types. . . .

Humor characters with this mixed ancestry began to appear frequently in every type of literature written during the 1590's, but the first work properly called a humor play was George Chapman's *An Humorous Day's Mirth* (1597). . . .

About a year after *An Humorous Day's Mirth* had been produced at the Rose Theatre, Jonson's *Every Man in His Humour* was brought out by Shakespeare's company [the Lord Chamberlain's Men]. By adopting practically all the distinctive features of Chapman's play, Jonson, as it were, fixed the conventions of a typical humor comedy. The main purpose of this new form of dramatic satire was the exhibition of the humorous characters. The sole function of the plot was to relate them to each other and to provide effective methods of ridiculing them. Jonson improved on Chapman's structure. . . .

Another feature of Chapman's play that Jonson retains and develops is the relation of the gull to the sham gentleman whom he chooses to imitate. The cream of the jest is that the gull becomes a fool's zany [imitator]. The gull as a type was created by the formal satirists of the 1590's. They made him a simpleton who desired to be a social exquisite, but who, in choosing a model, could not distinguish the true from the fraudulent gentleman. . . . *Every Man in His Humour* thus represents Jonson's perfection of humor comedy. Though based on comic conventions of Roman comedy and orthodox according to the canons of classical theory, it drew its incidents from contemporary life and its spirit from the English satire still free and vigorous in 1597.

A Comedy in the Manner of Jonson

Shakespeare first showed the influence of the "humorous" conception of character after Jonson's comedy had enjoyed a success on the stage. Since Shakespeare had acted one of the principal roles in this drama, he obviously knew just what parts of it Elizabethan audiences had received with most delight. It is not surprising, then, to find that humor characters first play important parts in *Henry V* and *The Merry Wives of Windsor*, plays written shortly after the production of *Every Man in His Humour.*

In both those dramas the eccentrics lurk on the edges of the main plot and so provide the spectators with only incidental satire. In *Twelfth Night*, however, they take charge of the important sub-plot and so make the story of Sir Toby, Sir Andrew, and Malvolio a humor comedy in the manner Jonson had adopted in *Every Man in His Humour* with conspicuous success. . . .

Acute critics have long recognized the similarities between *Twelfth Night* and Jonson's first humor comedy. . . . The characters in the comedy who are most obviously Jonsonian are Sir Andrew Aguecheek and Malvolio. The former is a gull, who imitates Sir Toby Belch. . . .

Sir Andrew, the Gull

Sir Andrew also possesses some of the characteristics of Stephen, Jonson's country gull. The two are alike in being unadulterated fools and in their countrified imitation of what they believe to be the manners of a gentleman. Before Sir Andrew's first appearance Sir Toby and Maria collaborate in sketching a satiric portrait of the gull:

MARIA. . . . He's a very fool and prodigal.

TOBY. Fie that you'll say so! He plays o' the viol-de-gamboys, and speaks three or four languages word for word without book and hath all the good gifts of nature.

MARIA. He hath, indeed, almost natural! for, besides that he's a fool, he's a great quarreller; and but that he hath the gift of a coward to allay the gust he hath in quarrelling, 'tis thought among the prudent he would quickly have the gift of a grave.

(I. iii. 24–35)

Sir Andrew then enters immediately to belie every word of Sir Toby's encomium and to illustrate every detail of Maria's detraction. He understands no foreign language and only the simplest of English words. Sir Toby's suggestion that he "accost" Maria, he mistakes for her surname and calls her "Good Mistress Mary Accost." He asks whether *pourquoi* means "do or not do"; then sighs "I would I had bestowed that time in the tongues that I have in fencing, dancing, and bear-baiting. O, had I but followed the arts" (I. iii. 96–9). This speech gives Sir Toby the idea of prodding him to display his grotesque inability to dance.

But most of the time Sir Andrew needs no urging to exhibit his fatuity [foolishness]. Like Stephen in *Every Man in His Humour* he requires only an ear into which to pour his fat-witted talk. He echoes every remark of his hero. To the Clown's exclamation that Sir Toby is "in admirable fooling," Sir Andrew proudly replies, "Ay, he does well enough if he be disposed and so do I too. He does it with a better grace, but I do it more natural" (II. i. 87–9). Yet when he hears the graceful compliments which Viola pays Olivia, he is greatly impressed and determines to learn by heart all her most glowing words:

VIOLA. Most excellent accomplished lady, the heavens rain odors on you.

ANDREW [*aside*]. That youth's a rare courtier. 'Rain odors'—well!

VIOLA. My matter hath no voice, lady, but to your own most pregnant and vouchsafed ear.

ANDREW [*aside*]. 'Odors,' 'pregnant' and 'vouchsafed'—I'll get 'em all three ready.

(III. i. 95–102)

This perfectly simple dramatic method serves admirably for the display of Sir Andrew's fatuity. . . .

SHAKESPEARE TAKES THE GULLING FURTHER

But Shakespeare clearly felt that the unmasking of his [Sir Andrew's] cowardice demanded more artifice. Accordingly he falls back upon a booby trap which he has Sir Toby and Fabian set. They urge the gull to send an eloquent and insulting challenge to Cesario, his apparent rival for the hand of Olivia.

Be curst and brief . . . Go about it! Let there be gall in thy ink
though thou write with a goose-pen, no matter.

(III. ii. 52–4)

The challenge in which he covers his fear in bluster is even
more absurd than that of Stephen, Jonson's country gull.
Having thus emboldened Sir Andrew, Sir Toby turns to
Fabian and tells him for the enlightenment of the audience:

For Andrew, if he were opened, and you find so much blood
in his liver as will clog the foot of a flea, I'll eat the rest of his
anatomy.

(III. ii. 64–7)

Then Sir Toby takes charge of the plot which is to expose
Sir Andrew's cowardice. He praises the rage, skill, fury, and
impetuosity of each of the duelists to the other, and so fright-
ens them that when they meet they almost "kill one another
by the look, like cockatrices." Andrew is willing to do anything to avoid the combat:

Plague on't, an I thought he had been valiant, and so cunning
in fence, I'd have seen him damned ere I'd have challenged
him. Let him let the matter slip, and I'll give him my horse,
grey Capilet.

(III. iv. 311–15)

But Toby sees to it that the duel takes place. So the two draw
their swords and approach each other with farcical attitudes
of fright, only to be interrupted by Antonio, who is searching
for Sebastian, Viola-Cesarios's twin brother. The next time
that Andrew thinks he has overtaken Viola, he encounters Sebastian, who soundly thrashes both Sir Andrew and Sir Toby.

The last view that we gain of the precious pair is when
they later appear before Olivia and the Duke with their
heads broken. Toby is drunk and Andrew completely crest-
fallen. As they go off to have their wounds dressed, Sir Andrew offers to help Sir Toby out. Then Toby, turning on him
fires a parting shot, a final characterization of the gull: "Will
you help—an ass-head and a cox-comb and a knave—a thin-
faced knave—a gull?" (v. i. 212–4).

Sir Andrew then is a gull—Shakespeare's composite of
Matthew and Stephen, Jonson's city and country gulls. He is
derided, exposed, and ejected from the company of the wise
and the sane, as are all ridiculed figures in satire of any sort.
But Shakespeare's lampooning of Sir Andrew is utterly de-
void of malice. The gull entertains every audience in the
same hilarious fashion in which he entertains Sir Toby. His

folly is inoffensive. No one expects or desires his reform. We
cannot share Sir Toby's final disgust with his dear manikin
[little man]. We hope that he has run away only to return to
amuse us on another day. At no point is the difference between the comic art of Jonson and that of Shakespeare more
obvious than in their conception of their gulls. Jonson's
Matthew and Stephen are personifications of an eccentricity—frank caricatures. Sir Andrew is just as farcically
drawn, but always a human being, even when he is most id-
iotic. His follies may be wild exaggerations of human foibles,
but they never completely obliterate the silly man.

"SICK OF SELF-LOVE," MALVOLIO IS RIPE FOR PURGING

In his characterization of Malvolio, Shakespeare approaches
much closer to Jonson's satiric methods. Malvolio is a humor
figure in being, as Olivia tells us, "sick of self-love," or as
Maria puts it, "The best persuaded of himself, so crammed,
as he thinks, with excellencies, that it is his ground of faith
that all that look on him love him" (II. iii. 155–8). His self-
conceit so puffs him up with false dignity that he thinks simple fun of every sort utterly, exasperatingly trivial. . . .

Malvolio's self-love has filled him with an ambition pre-
sumptuous in one of his lowly social position. "Art thou any
more than a steward?" asks Sir Toby contemptuously, when
Malvolio rebukes him and Sir Andrew for their riotous noise
in the hall. Maurice Evans in his [1940] production of *Twelfth
Night* made Malvolio's social inferiority immediately obvious
to his audiences by the anachronistic [out of place] device of
giving the steward a cockney accent. This established him at
once as a rank social outsider. His aspiring to be Olivia's husband is therefore colossal presumption, gross and palpable
self-conceit.

The plot which Maria devises to drive his humor into exaggerated display is quite properly based on his faith that
Olivia has but to look on him to love him. Maria explains in
detail the nature of the trap in which she is to catch the
booby, and even describes the grotesque struggles in which
he will indulge when securely caught in the toils. She will
drop in his path some obscure epistles of love which he will
imagine come from Olivia. She knows he will then act most
like the "affectioned ass" he is. In no humor play is the conventional device for exhibiting the fool made more obvious
or its mechanism more carefully described. . . .

Maria's device is also of great value to the satire, because it effects an exaggerated display of Malvolio's self-love and social presumption. He enters practicing courtly behavior to his shadow, imagining how he will act when he becomes Count Malvolio. In this mood he picks up Maria's letter and gulps down the bait.

The full revelation of his fatuous self-love comes when he appears before Olivia in yellow stockings, a color she abhors, and cross-gartered, a fashion she detests—both adornments peculiar to serving-men, social underlings. As he smiles with empty-headed insistency, kisses his hands, and acts out with great care every one of Maria's instructions, Olivia becomes more and more certain that his mind is touched. This gives Toby his chance to improve upon Maria's plot. He has Malvolio bound and imprisoned in a dark room in the vaults of Olivia's house. There the rogues, with the help of Feste, torture Malvolio in a way which seems cruel to modern spectators, but to an Elizabethan audience was merely a hilarious form of deserved purgation. For Malvolio is purged; at least for the moment he seems to be washed clean of his ambition to marry Olivia and of the crudest of his social affectations.

MALVOLIO, THE UNREDEEMABLE UPSTART

Twelfth Night, however, does not close, as did *Every Man in His Humour,* with a merry ceremony in which the humor figures take joy in their reformation and are welcomed back into the company of the psychologically balanced and socially competent, by a Dionysiac [wild and drunken] celebration. Malvolio appears in the final scene to learn all about the plot of which he has been the victim. He is neither amused nor purged. Instead he rushes off the stage in a passion of anger and wounded pride, shouting, "I'll be revenged on the whole pack of you!" And he is followed by the scornful laughter of satire.

Malvolio is Shakespeare's representative of the upstart, who was the butt of all the satirists, formal and dramatic, of the 1590's. Like the rest of the writers of the age, Shakespeare takes the conservative side in the struggle of the new classes for social recognition. Malvolio is a "coystril" [a base fellow]. Having no right to bear arms, he is regarded by the gentlemen as a menial and therefore an impossible husband for the lady Olivia. Shakespeare clearly agrees with them that the steward's hope to marry his mistress is consummate impudence.

In another respect Shakespeare seems to take sides against Malvolio. He is the major-domo of the Tudor country house, and, as the official responsible for the economy of Olivia's establishment, he is dead against the extravagances which are relics of life in the medieval castle. He quite properly regards Sir Toby as an anachronism, as a debased representative of the armed retainers who once defended the castle from its foes and in return were given their board and keep. Though when off duty they brawled indoors and out, they were tolerated because of their help in time of trouble. Sir Toby contributes as much uproar to Olivia's household as his forebears used to do, but he performs no other service. Yet he demands all the cakes and ale that he can swallow and the right to introduce his boon companions into the hall to roister when and how they please. To this conduct Malvolio objects. He is an enemy to the time-honored English hospitality and liberality because of the strain it puts upon his lady's purse. He detests Toby's revelry, not because it is wicked, but because it is both indecorous and expensive. Shakespeare is obviously against this upstart of the new social dispensation. . . .

To Shakespeare . . . this change in social custom was something to lament. He believed that the security of gentle folk was endangered by the transition going on in noble households like that of Olivia. Consequently he makes the merchant-minded enemy of the good old days a kill-joy, a conceited ass, an inept social parvenu.

Malvolio is thus elevated above the artificial simplicity of the typical humor figure. In the process he has become an almost pathetically ridiculous human being. In spite of this transformation Shakespeare puts him through the conventional satiric routine of a man caught in the toils of his humor and forced to struggle and grimace there for our amusement. It is Malvolio's routine that forms the center of the robust comic sub-plot of *Twelfth Night.* It provides merry interludes to the sentimental story of Viola, Orsino, and Olivia. It also enables Shakespeare to employ satiric conventions established by Chapman and Jonson in a way to create the most vivid and human of all the humor figures in Elizabethan comedy. No humor characters appear in any of Shakespeare's plays written after *Twelfth Night.*

A Skillfully Constructed Ending

Ejner J. Jensen

The ending to *Twelfth Night* is often considered problematic because it lacks closure. University of Michigan's Ejner J. Jensen, director of the Sweetland Writing Center and professor of English Language and Literature, takes a writer's approach by de-emphasizing plot closure and focusing instead on the comic achievement of the individual scenes and story lines. By considering the *means* rather than the end, Jensen demonstrates Shakespeare's process—his set-up and manipulation of self-contained episodes that fulfill dramatic and comic expectations individually instead of collectively. To Jensen, then, the ending of the play is merely a restatement of the relationships already developed in the individual story lines. Viewed as such, the end is appropriate and satisfying.

Among the comedies, none has had more attention focused on its close than *Twelfth Night*. In part this can be explained with reference to the character of Malvolio . . . but the more general reason for closure's status as a critical issue in understanding *Twelfth Night* lies in the play's position in the canon, where it is seen as bringing to an end the line of romantic comedy even as it bears the seeds of the darker plays to come. . . .

IT'S PLOTTING, NOT PLOT, THAT MATTERS HERE

It should . . . be possible to suggest an approach to *Twelfth Night* that takes pressure off its ending and judges it in terms of its overall function as dramatic comedy. What emerges will not be unfamiliar, but familiar things may, viewed from a different angle, seem new. The notion of plot provides a useful starting point. It is perhaps the most often employed element of analysis for fictions of all kinds; . . . it places helpful emphasis on structure—beginning, middle, end.

What, then, can be said of plot in *Twelfth Night?* The short answer is "not much." Not much, that is, if plot is thought of as the soul of the comedy. Certainly one can chart a plot in the conventional way, with the impetus and shifts of direction reflected in the graph. But Shakespeare in *Twelfth Night* seems far less interested in plot than in plotting. His attention seems directed to short-term effects rather than to the solution of a comprehensive dramatic question. Moreover, it is the emphasis on plotting that allies him with the other great comic dramatists, with [British playwright Ben] Jonson and [French playwright] Molière, for example. . . .

What *Twelfth Night* shares with Jonsonian comedy is an abundance of such comic events subsumed to the requirements of the play's major action but generating an energy that makes them almost independent episodes. Two instances of plotting on this level stand out. The first is . . . a matter of introducing a character, in this case Olivia. . . . In the play's opening scene we learn of Olivia through Orsino, who gives first an unprompted view of her magical powers—"O, when mine eyes did see Olivia first, / . . . . / That instant was I turn'd into a hart"—and then an interpretation of Valentine's report, in which Orsino chooses not to see rejection of his suit but "a heart of . . . fine frame" (1.1.18, 20, 32). The next three scenes of the play continue this line of plotting. Shakespeare never lets us forget Olivia's importance, and through the use of a marvelous dramatic retard he increases our eagerness to see her and the demands on the actress playing the role. She must meet the high expectations the playwright has set for her in scenes 1 through 4. In this respect, Shakespeare exploits the technique of delayed gratification, with the attendant risk of disappointing his audience. . . .

Twelfth Night's fifth scene is the culmination of this plotting line considered as a discrete episode. Shakespeare unveils Olivia at last. But even here the retard continues, for the scene begins with Feste and Maria, who warns the clown, as she had earlier warned Sir Toby, of her lady's displeasure. Olivia's initial verbal jousting with Feste performs two functions: it helps to separate her from the earnest solicitude of Malvolio, and it prepares her for the whimsical act of admitting the messenger. . . . Defeated in her contest with Feste, she chooses to continue the sport with a competitor who promises to be less skillful. What follows, of course, is one of the great comic confrontations in all of Elizabethan drama, and for a brief while I want to reserve comment on its detailed workings. As comic preparation, the whole of act 1, up through 5.26, works magnificently to establish a context for Olivia's appearance. When she does at last enter, she ought to be both as wonderful as Orsino suggests and more real than the creature of his delicate imaginings. She does not disappoint us. At once removed from the world and in it, she jokes with Feste and pronounces her authoritative judgment on Malvolio: "You are sick of self-love." Then she turns, or Shakespeare turns her, to enact yet another miraculous appearance, this time to Orsino's clamorous messenger.

THE PLOTTING THICKENS: VIOLA AND ANDREW ARE SET UP

The care Shakespeare lavishes on plotting of this sort appears in another episode in *Twelfth Night,* one quite different from the introduction of Olivia. This is the duel scene between Viola and Andrew, stage-managed by Sir Toby and Fabian. Again, the knitting of this incident to the main plot is brilliantly successful. . . . Sir Andrew's shortcomings as a wooer and linguist are so prominently set out in his first appearance (1.3) that Maria's comment on his reputation as a fighter is often overlooked. Andrew, she says, is "a great quarreller; and but that he hath the gift of a coward to allay the gust he hath in quarrelling, 'tis thought among the prudent he would quickly have the gift of a grave" (1.3.30–33). This is the first stage in Shakespeare's preparation for the duel. . . .

Shakespeare advances this comic preparation next in the aftermath of Malvolio's interruption of the midnight revels (2.3). He does so, however, in an indirect way. Sir Andrew, casting about as usual in an effort to gain approval (often his method is simply to repeat the words of others), imagines a way to get back at the killjoy steward: "'Twere as good a deed as to drink when a man's a-hungry, to challenge him to the field, and then to break promise with him, and make a fool of him" (2.3.126–28). Sir Toby, quick to scent good fun, offers his full support: "Do't knight. I'll write thee a challenge, or I'll deliver thy indignation to him by word of mouth" (129–30). Maria, of course, has a better idea for Malvolio . . . but Shakespeare wastes neither Sir Andrew's empty gesture nor Sir Toby's offer of support: both function as preparation for the collision that will take place later in the play between Sir Andrew and the terrified Viola.

In 3.2 Sir Andrew petulantly announces that he is leaving, hurt by the sight of Olivia's favors to "the count's serving-man." Fabian then comes to the aid of Sir Toby, who is unwilling to lose his purse, and argues that Olivia's attention to Cesario was a pretense displayed for Sir Andrew's benefit. The countess's act was calculated, Fabian tells the disappointed suitor, "only to exasperate you, to awake your dormouse valor" (19–20). Andrew, he claims, has lost an opportunity: "You should then have accosted her, and with some excellent jests, fire-new from the mint, you should have bang'd the youth into dumbness" (21–23). . . .

While Andrew is thus by indirect and crooked ways led to the point of writing his challenge, Viola has been picking her way through the snares laid by her own disguise. With Orsino, she only narrowly refrains from self-discovery; with Olivia, she is torn between rivalry and loyalty to her master; with both, she gains a measure of relief by telling the truth riddlingly. Now, for the first time, [in 3.4] she confronts a situation for which she has not prepared. . . .

As the reluctant duelists move toward one another and draw, the scene both fizzles and explodes. Antonio's entrance issues in the series of manifestations that will define the play's close and its final atmosphere of revelations, recognitions, and miracle. That is the explosion. Meanwhile, safely apart from the main action on stage, Viola and Andrew come together. . . .

What follows . . . is the unfolding of layer upon layer of misapprehension and masking. But that unfolding should not obscure the immediate pleasure of the duel episode. Artfully designed, that episode furnishes an abundance of rewards both in the theatre and in the study. It takes its place in the total plot of the play, but its value is far greater than that of a link in the chain of plot or one piece (even a large piece) in a puzzle. In this respect, *Twelfth Night* is a less linear construction than most critics would have us believe. Its episodes have their own logic; they are not elements shaped wholly to serve the play's purposes as those are finally revealed at the point of closure.

SHAKESPEARE'S USE OF TONE HELPS THE ORDER OF THINGS

In fact, *Twelfth Night* is of all Shakespeare's comedies least dependent on plot in the ordinary sense of that word. It finesses the whole idea of plot by appealing to another order of things. That order takes its most striking form . . . in the appearances of Antonio and, later, Sebastian, where it provides experiences that are epiphanic [suddenly understood, on a spiritual level] in their nature. Its more pervasive and subtle form lies in an extraordinary reliance on atmosphere and tone [such as] when Viola, in her role as Cesario, finally gains an audience with Olivia. . . . This episode possesses such tonal variety that no criticism can do justice to it; and any single stage version, though it might capture some elements of that variety, would sacrifice others in being forced to make choices.

This much, though, should be clear. At the beginning of the encounter, the women are in different situations. Viola, who in 1.2 was the pattern of self-assurance and decisiveness, now exhibits those characteristics only in her assumed role. At Orsino's court, she is caught by her disguise, used as an emissary to woo on behalf of one she desires to wed. Olivia, secure as mistress of her house, claims strength from both her social position and her adopted role as mourning sister. By the scene's end, Olivia has caught the plague [she thinks she's in love] and Viola has discovered the beauty and wit of her rival. They have been reduced to a shared condition of hopeless yearning. . . .

The end of this encounter, completed for Viola by Malvolio's delivery of the ring, places the women in opposite but emotionally identical situations. Olivia loves a disguised female who cannot accept her overtures; Viola loves a male who believes her to be a boy. They declare a shared powerlessness in calling upon forces greater than those at their disposal, Olivia by an invocation—"Fate, show thy force; ourselves we do not owe"—Viola, more humbly, in an admission of weakness:

> O time, thou must untangle this, not I,
> It is too hard a knot for me t'untie.

(1.5.310, 2.2.40–41)

The effect of this movement through 1.5 is to bring the two women, whose initial situation is so dissimilar, into a shared condition. . . . Our attention, however, is focused not on what will happen to these characters, not on how Fate and Time will contrive to effect a solution to their problems, but simply on the facts of the problems themselves. Because Shakespeare achieves his effects through the deft manipulation of tone, the urgency of Viola and Olivia is only a small part of the spectator's or reader's experience. Instead, our focus is on the comic achievement; and our pleasure, a pleasure akin to satisfaction, comes from perceiving how Shakespeare has brought these two young women to the same pass, bound to wait in hope for the beneficial operation of forces that we know to be guaranteed by the laws of comedy itself.

Shakespeare's manipulation of tone, then, creates local and particular effects that gain for individual scenes and episodes their own importance. They are not merely way stations on the route to the play's end but ends in themselves which fulfill dramatic expectation, excite comic pleasure, and even provide vivid pre-enactments of closure that will make the play's actual ending seem less a surprising or problematic answer than a restatement of relationships and a reordering of matters that have already won our assent. No episode in the whole body of Shakespearean comedy registers these achievements so fully as *Twelfth Night* 2.4. Considered as an element in the play's plot, this scene appears nearly inconsequential. Orsino, attended by Viola, Curio, and others, calls for a song. Feste is summoned, performs the song, and—after some banter—departs. At Orsino's command, "all the rest give place" (79), and he is left alone with Viola, whom he directs to return to Olivia and once more plead his case. Then, after a brief dialogue that recapitulates matters familiar from the play's first scene, Viola recounts the history of her father's daughter, who "never told her love," but breaks off her account rather than respond to Orsino's desire to learn the story's closure: "But died thy sister of her love, my boy?" (110, 119). . . .

In this early scene, then, Shakespeare has his characters pre-enact a closeness that is promised but deferred in the actual closure of the play. There, Orsino tells Viola, "you shall from this time be / Your master's mistress" (5.1.325–26); and yet he calls her Cesario until the end, though with the promise that "when in other habits you are seen" she will take up her true identity as "Orsino's mistress, and his fancy's queen" (5.1.387–88). Critics who find difficulty with the close of the play, especially those who find in it hints of darkness, fasten on this apparent incompleteness. Yet the fulfillment they miss is one of the pleasures *Twelfth Night* affords; it is not to be found at the close of the play, however, but in this scene, where Viola and Orsino come together in a wholly credible and persuasive way. The tonal sureness of this scene is a major source of both its dramatic power and its clarity. It demonstrates early in the play the rightness of the design that finally brings Orsino and Viola together. Theirs may not be a marriage made in heaven, but it is made secure by this episode in Orsino's court. Thus Shakespeare's management of tone in 2.4 of *Twelfth Night* takes interpretive pressure off the play's ending, whose key union has been anticipated and even displayed for the audience's approval. The marriage of Viola and Orsino should not be viewed exclusively as either a festive triumph or a disenchanted comment on the failure of life to achieve the easy victories of comic convention. Its rightness is the rightness of comic drama, an order to which Shakespeare has gained our assent early in the play.

IT'S PROCESS, NOT PRODUCT, IN *TWELFTH NIGHT*

Other matters occur or are anticipated early in *Twelfth Night,* and this prematurity of events affords one last indication that Shakespeare asks less of his comic endings than his critics seem driven to ask. Chief among these is the audience's knowledge (from 2.1) that Sebastian is still alive, and the suggestion, and more than suggestion, to Viola (in 3.4) that her brother has not drowned after all. To a thoroughgoing believer in the strength of dramatic conventions, early disclosure of Sebastian's safety is hardly an issue. Viola herself, in her opening dialogue with the captain, provides hope if not assurance. To her wishful speculation "Perchance he is not drown'd," the captain offers no great comfort: "It is perchance that you yourself were saved" (1.2.5–6). But Viola continues to imagine a fortunate outcome: "so perchance may he be" (7). . . .

But the point, surely, is that in *Twelfth Night* Shakespeare takes all the burden off the question of whether and places it entirely on the question of how. Two aspects of his management of Sebastian's return suggest this emphasis. The first is the playwright's use of Antonio; the second, a preenactment of union for Olivia and Sebastian that repeats in

another key that of Orsino and Viola in 2.4. . . . In terms of
the play's comic needs, Antonio serves . . . [a] role . . . concerned with the work's construction. . . . His entrance, rescue of Viola, and subsequent arrest bring the duel to a close
and provide opportunity for revelations about Sebastian that
excite Viola to hope her brother is alive. Since Viola's cowardice is now apparent to all, Sir Andrew's "dormouse valor"
emerges again in his resolve to "after him again and beat
him" (3.4.391).

Shakespeare might have brought Sebastian in at this point
instead of Antonio, whose place in the play's final scene presents some difficulty because his function is so minimal. But
Sebastian has to be saved for more important matters, first
the great comic moment when Sir Andrew, mistakenly emboldened, strikes him and earns three for one—"Why,
there's for thee, and there, and there!" (4.1.26), then his rescue by Olivia, who dismisses Toby ("Rudesby, be gone!")
and takes Cesario's double under her rule. . . . Before the final act begins, then, Shakespeare joins Olivia and Sebastian
just as he had earlier joined Viola and Orsino in a pre-
enactment of their eventual union. In the latter case, the
method involved a subtle use of tone reinforced by music;
here he employs unrestrained farce and a full measure of
physical action and fooling. The upshot of all this means that
with his final act Shakespeare can attend to other matters: to
the resolution of the Malvolio line of action, and to the delight to be had in allowing the characters' understanding of
matters to grow equal to the audience's knowledge. That
these are Shakespeare's main concerns can be seen in his
handling of the skirmish that gives Sir Andrew, at long last,
an earned wound and Sir Toby a bloody coxcomb. . . .

The bested warriors exit, then, before Sebastian returns
apologetically to the stage—"I am sorry, madam, I have hurt
your kinsman" (209)—and they are thus denied the pleasure
of the recognition scene. . . . Sebastian comes at once to
Olivia, but the first character to voice surprise is Orsino.
Then Sebastian spies Antonio, who, beset by joy and puzzle-
ment, asks, "Which is Sebastian?" (224). Only then does
Olivia speak. Cued perhaps by a gesture implicit in Antonio's
question, she looks at first one twin, then the other; and her
words are as expressive as they are brief: "Most wonderful!"
(225). These are her only words in the entire recognition
episode (209–58), a testimony to Shakespeare's confidence

in his actors, since Olivia (and Antonio, for that matter) must spend most of this episode in mute amazement and delight. Once again, the moment is full. . . .

It would have served this argument well if Shakespeare had stopped here at the point of union, with the matches made and his lovers in full accord. But Malvolio is brought to mind again when Viola, responding to Orsino's comically direct request—"let me see thee in thy woman's weeds"—explains that her garments are with the captain and that he "is now in durance, at Malvolio's suit" (273, 276). Olivia then recalls hearing of the steward's distraction and, distracted herself, gives the command to "fetch Malvolio hither" (278). . . .

No Big Surprise Ending, Just Fulfillment

The need to discuss Shakespeare's handling of Malvolio poses a critical dilemma, however, for a full response to previous critics would necessarily entail still further attention to his last appearance and thus further concentration on the play's close. One way to resolve this impasse may be to ask what dramatic needs remain after the recognition scene, or —better, perhaps—what dramatic needs Shakespeare attends to after that episode. He must, of course, deal with the question of Malvolio. . . .

The Malvolio of Shakespeare's fifth act is no different from the Malvolio we have observed earlier in the play. He remains a rigid and uncompromising figure. Just as, earlier, he condemns others for their late-night license while he himself luxuriates in his imagination, leaving Olivia sleeping on a day-bed as he goes to rebuke Sir Toby, so here he finds himself "notoriously abused" by his treatment in a makeshift cell while the Captain suffers actual imprisonment. Despite this, other characters make an effort to mollify him, not only Olivia and Orsino but Fabian as well, who urges Olivia to

> let no quarrel, nor no brawl to come,
> Taint the condition of this present hour,
> Which I have wond'red at.
>
> (356–58)

Malvolio's exit, then, is of a piece with his behavior throughout the play, and it is therefore not merely accepted but almost predictable. . . .

Now, in the play's last moments, Olivia and Orsino, its ranking figures, assume dominance. She introduces the question of Malvolio and, at his departure, agrees that "he hath been most notoriously abus'd" (379). Orsino makes the final judgment, accepting Olivia's view but imposing on the steward a responsibility as well:

> Pursue him, and entreat him to a peace;
> He hath not told us of the captain yet.
>   (380–81)

In doing so, he fulfills the last necessity in Shakespeare's design. He assumes control, sending Fabian on his errand and conducting the final exit of the lovers. Fate and time having done their admirable work, Illyria's Duke assumes his proper role. . . .

It remains for Feste to negotiate the play's final transaction, a movement away from the world of Illyria into the workaday world where spectators, denied access to the "golden time" anticipated by Orsino, must contend with the wind and the rain. . . . His act of mediation here is but another illustration of Shakespeare's consistency and care in the design of *Twelfth Night.* Like other matters built on a detailed preparation, this bridge between the play world and the world of the audience fulfills or extends its pre-enactment. Throughout the play, Feste has moved between the two houses of Orsino and Olivia and the two plots—the romantic world of love in which Orsino has "unclasp'd / . . . the book even of [his] secret soul" and the heartier, more plainspoken world of Maria and Sir Toby, in which Maria is praised for being "as witty a piece of Eve's flesh as any in Illyria" (1.4.13–14, 1.5.27–28). Now he engages in a similar movement between two worlds, that of the play and that of the world outside the theatre. They are, he assures us, two quite different spheres. . . .

Thus closure in *Twelfth Night,* far from being the key to interpretation and far from being problematic, is a dramatically skillful realization of connections prepared for and pre-enacted in the play's earlier events. It provides satisfaction not because it answers questions but because it presents the promised answers in such dramatically satisfying ways.

CHAPTER 2

Characters

READINGS ON
TWELFTH NIGHT

Viola's Search for Gender Identity

Marilyn French

Feminist writer and critic Marilyn French believes Illyria to be a "feminine" world, one ruled primarily
by emotion. Into this world is thrust Viola, a sensitive
female who lacks gender identity and any sense of
place in this foreign land. Opting to pass herself off
as a man, Viola becomes entangled in a confusing
gender web, becoming the object of Olivia's affections and the frustrated desires of Orsino. As an androgynous character Viola remains emotionally un-
fettered but also ungrounded. Only when she is
involved in an aggressive, "masculine" duel is she
forced to recognize what French calls her natural
identity and acquiesce to the expectations of her gender. In doing so Viola resolves the confusing relations she has had with other characters, restoring
order to the play. The characters are then free to
pursue true male/female relationships and find pleasure in life by play's end. French interprets this as
Shakespeare's commentary that acceptance of socially defined gender roles is necessary to reign in
the "terrifying freedom of emotional life" and pave
the way for true contentment and joy.

On the mythic level of this play, a sensitive person (in comedy: therefore a female) is thrown up by the sea on a land of
emotion to which she is a stranger, and in which she does
not know how to behave. She has no identity because she
has no role; she lacks even gender identity. She is beloved by
Antonio (her social inferior, and composite with the captain
who aids her in the beginning of the play), Olivia (her social
equal and like), and Orsino (her social superior), among
whom she finds it painful to choose. Finding herself in an

impossible emotional bind, she does not herself attempt to act, but rather leaves the situation to time. Events themselves and her own unconscious feelings lead to a choice among Antonio, who loves her in a subordinate way, serving and caring for her; Olivia, who loves her with passion and demands requital; and Orsino, who loves her in a superior way, for her charm, her subordination, and her fidelity.

THE SEARCHING, UNCERTAIN PART OF THE SELF

The world of *Twelfth Night* is often viewed as mad. Its title indicates such a condition, but the madness of Illyria resembles that of Ephesus: it has the frenzy and disconnection attendant to emotional life not structured by role. *Twelfth Night* is, in a sense, a reseeing of the problems first approached in *Comedy of Errors.*

As in *As You Like It,* love is the central fact of emotional experience, but *Twelfth Night* is concerned not only with forms of sexual love (and its denial and repudiation), but with forms of love of life (and its denial and repudiation). Insofar as the play has a norm, it is Viola, but she represents essentially an absence, the searching, uncertain part of the self. All of the sensitive characters suffer some impediment to wholehearted embracing of life. That Orsino and Olivia seem to derive pleasure from feeling pain does not change the fact that they feel that pain. Viola suffers from complete disorientation, a loss of home and sibling that amounts (as in *Comedy of Errors*) to loss of place, and therefore identity. . . .

All of the major characters except Malvolio are connected through love or love of pleasure with the feminine principle. Maria, that opaque figure, is sensitive to other people—she *sees* them. So she understands Olivia's needs and Malvolio's delusions. She seems to suffer from a love that has not been legitimated; nevertheless, she revels in Toby's world.

Orsino and Olivia are "feminine" because they exist totally in feeling. Orsino drowns in his own emotion. Despite his passion for Olivia, he does little to show it: as Viola points out, if *she* loved Olivia, she would build "a willow cabin at your gate, / And call upon my soul within the house" (I, v, 268–269). Olivia drowns in mourning. . . .

SEARCH FOR STRUCTURE

The major characters, then, are all floundering in feeling—the revelers [Toby, Andrew, and Maria] because they choose

to, and are not aware of possible consequences of their behavior; Orsino and Olivia because of their natures; Viola because she has been set adrift and does not know how to
structure her life. In the terms of the play-world, she has no
identity because she has no place, but she is in a way the
psyche or searching mind of all the characters. It is perhaps
impossible to live with anarchy of the soul: something(s)
has to be more important than others, which is to say, structure is probably necessary. But a happy structure—one

FEMININE NATURE

*Similar to how French perceives a prescribed role for Vi-
ola, some critics positively interpret Viola as exemplary
of the feminine character. Anna Brownwell Jameson—* "Mrs.
Jameson"*—was a governess turned scholar who, in her 1832
book* Characteristics of Women *(renamed* Shakespeare's
Heroines*), classified Viola as a character of passion and
imagination.*

If we carry our thoughts back to a romantic and chivalrous
age, there is surely sufficient probability here for all the purposes of poetry. To pursue the thread of Viola's destiny:—she is
engaged in the service of the Duke, whom she finds "fancy-
sick" for the love of Olivia. We are left to infer (for so it is
hinted in the first scene), that this Duke—who, with his accom-
plishments and his personal attractions, his taste for music, his
chivalrous tenderness, and his unrequited love, is really a very
fascinating and poetical personage, though a little passionate
and fantastic—had already made some impression on Viola's
imagination; and when she comes to play the confidant, and to
be loaded with favors and kindness in her assumed character,
that she should be touched by a passion made up of pity, admi-
ration, gratitude, and tenderness, does not, I think, in any way
detract from the genuine sweetness and delicacy of her character, for *"she never told her love."*

Now all this, as the critic wisely observes, may not present a
very just picture of life; and it may also fail to impart any moral
lesson for the especial profit of well-bred young ladies; but is it
not in truth and in nature? Did it ever fail to charm or to interest, to seize on the coldest fancy, to touch the most insensible
heart?

Viola then is the chosen favorite of the enamored Duke, and
becomes his messenger to Olivia, and the interpreter of his suf-

which merges the gender principles—cannot be imposed, it must be discovered. For the revelation of this, Viola trusts to time. And just as she represents a part of all the characters, Viola becomes pivotal in the discoveries they make, as well. Her place, when discovered, determines theirs.

The structure, or design of the comedy, reiterates this movement on another level. The design is intricately interwoven, and demonstrates a gradual and complex integration. The first three scenes present Orsino and his court; Vi-

---

ferings to that inaccessible beauty. In her character of a youthful page she attracts the favor of Olivia, and excites the jealousy of her lord. The situation is critical and delicate; but how exquisitely is the character of Viola fitted to her part, carrying her through the ordeal with all the inward and spiritual grace of modesty! . . . She has not . . . a saucy enjoyment in her own incognito; her disguise does not sit so easily upon her; her heart does not beat freely under it. . . . In Viola a sweet consciousness of her feminine nature is for ever breaking through her masquerade—

> And on her cheek is ready with a blush,
> Modest as morning, when she coldly eyes
> The youthful Phoebus.

She plays her part well, but never forgets, nor allows us to forget, that she is playing a part—

> OLIVIA. Are you a comedian?
> VIOLA. No, my profound heart! and yet, by the very fangs of
> malice I swear, I am not that I play!

And thus she comments on it—

> Disguise, I see thou art a wickedness,
> Wherein the pregnant enemy does much.
> How easy is it for the proper-false
> In women's waxen hearts to set their forms!
> Alas! our frailty is the cause, not we.

The feminine cowardice of Viola, which will not allow her even to affect a courage becoming her attire, her horror at the idea of drawing a sword, is very natural and characteristic, and produces a most humorous effect, even at the very moment it charms and interests us.

Mrs. Jameson, *Shakspeare's Heroines: Characteristics of Women Moral, Poetical, and Historical.* Philadelphia: Henry Altemus Company.

ola and the Captain; and Toby, Maria, and Andrew Aguecheek. In the next scene, Viola is integrated into Orsino's court. Then Olivia, Malvolio, and Feste are brought together with Toby and Maria, and the scene concludes with Viola's introduction into this world. II, i presents Sebastian and Antonio, providing the audience early in the drama with an "if," a device for revocability. Thereafter, there are encounters between Viola and Malvolio, Feste and Orsino, and Viola and Feste. The complex III, iv integrates Viola with Toby, Fabian, and Andrew, and its conclusion places Antonio among them. Sebastian runs swiftly through the course of Olivia's people in IV, 1. The last scene integrates the whole as Orsino finally confronts Olivia, and Sebastian and Viola appear together. In each place she goes, Viola changes the mix, becoming openly important to Olivia, and to Orsino for different reasons, and comically important for Toby's crew.

The moral design of the play is concentric-circular, and exemplifies kinds and degrees of life denial, life acceptance. At its center are Toby and his circle, vital, amoral, irresponsible, joyful—in Freudian terminology (which is appropriate to this play), libido figures. At its outer rim stands Malvolio, the superego, the force that would leash, repress, muzzle, or, if it could, eradicate that vitality. Orsino/Olivia hover listlessly below Malvolio; both are possessed of vitality which neither can use. Between them and Toby's group are Viola/Sebastian, coming up courageously and with mirth from near death into survival and final joy. Outside the whole figure, looking in, are the starving dispossessed, Feste and Antonio. Neither is a restrainer or potential oppressor, but both have been prevented, by the circumstances of their lives and natures, from being part of the general dance.

[Critic] C.L. Barber writes that "the most fundamental distinction the play brings home to us is the difference between men and women." Gender is indeed crucial in a play that assumes one's identity is partly, perhaps mainly, dictated by one's place in society, a society in which gender difference is primary.

ANDROGYNY AND GENDER PROBLEMS

Orsino cannot realize (make real, fulfill) the pleasure he takes in his page because of Cesario's apparent gender; Olivia cannot realize the pleasure she takes in Cesario because of his actual gender. Viola, a still center in this hurricane, cannot act. Viola is *emotionally* androgynous, something Rosalind [*As You Like It*] and Portia [*The Merchant of Venice*], despite their "masculine" qualities, are not. No matter how much she disclaims Olivia, Viola's wooing of her is fervent—far more so than that of the Orsino whose work she is supposed to be doing. Indeed, it is the passion and genuineness of that wooing which are partly responsible for Olivia's passion. Viola woos Olivia assertively—like a Renaissance hero. With Orsino, on the other hand, she is patience on a monument, she is diffident and deferential. She woos him with patient chaste constant adoration so subtle as not to appear to be wooing.

All of this functions workaday well in the plot—close scrutiny of revocable plots does not do, isn't fruitful. On the mythic level, however, it provides an extraordinary glimpse into the predicament of an androgynous gender identity. Olivia is irresistible in her passion; the Duke's sensibility is charming, taking, his treatment of subordinates admirable. Viola herself is utterly *sympathique*.

Yet Shakespeare does to Viola something he does to no other heroine: he humiliates her and makes her the object of group mockery. The seemingly comic threat of having to fight a duel operates in this play as the bruises of the various characters of *Comedy of Errors* operate on them: to force a recognition of *natural* identity. In actuality, most men would be as frightened as most women at having to engage in physical aggression. And some women would be able to handle that as well as some men. But in Shakespeare's division of experience, this is not true: men are aggressive *by nature*, women cowardly and gentle *by nature*. Viola is forced to recognize that she is a woman by nature, and therefore by nature loves men, not women. At bottom, she must depend not on her feelings but on natural distinctions to teach her her identity, her place.

The situation at the beginning of the final scene of *Twelfth Night* is all impasse, and has led to critical questions about logic (plot). Why does Viola not question Antonio when she hears his protest? It must suggest to her that Sebastian is alive, and in actuality (could such a situation occur in actuality), she certainly would. Why does she not speak up immediately when Sebastian appears? He is her lost, beloved brother, and it violates realism that she remains silent. Suppositions, based on Shakespeare's sources, about fictive pasts, the original home of Viola/Sebastian, or her prior knowledge of the Duke, are irrelevant. What is being played out is the myth.

Thus, Viola stands silent in V, i, as both the Duke and Olivia lay claim to her, and Antonio regards her with bitter disappointment. The implications of ambiguity about gender are pushed to the limit—indeed, to the (also unrealistic, given Orsino's character and his previous relationship with "Cesario") threat of death.

AN ENDING OF ORDERED EMOTION

The comic resolution, however, makes the situation revocable by splitting Viola into two genders. She, with her other half, Sebastian, are able to live out two kinds of love, leaving only Antonio the outsider he has been. However, as in *Much Ado About Nothing*, the central problem is so serious that the joyousness of the conclusion is a bit dampened. For the final resolution of all these relationships suggests that love of life, vitality and joyousness, is not fully a personal matter, something people would prefer not to believe because it diminishes the control they prefer to believe they have over their lives. It suggests that hardship and poverty, an unacceptable gender identity, or confusion about one's desires can destroy one's chances of sitting at life's feast.

All of the characters appear in the final scene: in the world of emotion, every tendency is valid, even the denial of Malvolio. But the ending is abrupt, and there is no final ceremony: not everyone can be included in the rites of pure joy. There is room for everyone in the world of the emotions, but the table is stratified: some people get much to eat and some get almost nothing.

The conclusion is "feminine": Toby and Andrew have been forcibly taught that irrevocability exists: they suffer real injuries. But there is no suggestion they will change their ways. Neither will Malvolio: he will endure and threaten with his rules and regulations. Feste and Antonio are doomed to live out their deprived lives. The rest move, it is intimated, into transcendence, happiness ever after. . . .

Twelfth Night presents the opposite situation to that of *As You Like It* in that the latter comedy emphasizes the primacy of individual feeling in determining one's place in a community. *Twelfth Night,* like *Comedy of Errors,* emphasizes the primacy of communal structures and codes in determin-

ing one's place in emotional life. There is a formality, a stiff-
ness at the end of *Twelfth Night* which seems to recognize
possibilities abandoned, renounced, roles accepted that are
constrictions of the full self. *Twelfth Night* is a far more
aware, profound play than *Comedy of Errors,* which suggests
that acceptance of societal role will bring contentment and
joy. *Twelfth Night* suggests that societal role is determining
and necessary to structure the still terrifying freedom of
emotional life, but that the price is high.

Orsino's Narcissism

Joseph Westlund

In a psychoanalytic approach to understanding
Orsino, Professor Joseph Westlund of Northeastern
University in Boston, Massachusetts, considers the
various critical assessments of Orsino that range
from self-indulgent to vaguely mad. Westlund, however, focuses on Orsino's unhealthy narcissism
which is evidenced by his inability to sincerely woo
Olivia, to accurately assess the world, and to let others exist beyond himself. Viola disguised as Cesario
both feeds and tempers Orsino's narcissism. In Cesario's presence, Orsino begins to move away from
his self-absorption. For a time Orsino even comes to
see Cesario as an autonomous individual. In the end,
though, Westlund acknowledges some backsliding in
Orsino as the Duke turns on Cesario for stealing
Olivia and claims, in self-indulgent tones, that he
will have his revenge.

I begin with Orsino, and want to show that he is more life-
like and sympathetic than the usual portrait of him allows.
Some see him as conventionally romantic, or comically self-
indulgent, or rather mad. . . .

Orsino's first speech strikes critics as a romantic apostro-
phe to love, or an amusing instance of self-indulgence. They
are right, as are those who see something vaguely mad
about him. I find the speech disconcerting in ways which
need to be sorted out. His attitude toward love is both self-
indulgent and dissatisfied:

> If music be the food of love, play on,
> Give me excess of it, that, surfeiting,
> The appetite may sicken, and so die.
> (1.1.1–3)

He wants to surfeit on music, to deaden his appetite for love
itself. The terms "surfeit," "appetite," and "die" do not, as we

Excerpted from *Shakespeare's Reparative Comedies: A Psychoanalytic View of the Middle Plays*, by Joseph Westlund. Copyright © 1984 by the University of Chicago Press.
Reprinted with permission from the author and the University of Chicago Press. This
excerpt is a much-reduced version of the original.

expect, refer to sexual activity; this is odd, for it would be an obvious way to sate his hunger. Nor does he refer to a beloved, or even to women. Instead he obsessively concentrates on his dissatisfaction:

> That strain again, it had a dying fall:
> O, it came o'er my ear like the sweet sound
> That breathes upon a bank of violets,
> Stealing and giving odour. Enough, no more;
> 'Tis not so sweet now as it was before.
>
> (1.1.4–8)

He grows sick of music; its action seems vaguely analogous to some loving activity—yet he seems to have no person in mind, nor does it seem to *mean* very much to him:

> O spirit of love, how quick and fresh art thou,
> That notwithstanding thy capacity
> Receiveth as the sea, nought enters there,
> Of what validity and pitch soe'er,
> But falls into abatement and low price,
> Even in a minute! So full of shapes is fancy,
> That it alone is high fantastical.
>
> (1.1.9–15)

Critics refer to Orsino as being in love with love, or with himself; but this does not explain much. He likes to talk about himself and love, yet seems curiously detached from the dismaying situation which he describes: one in which love loses value either through satiety or abatement. . . .

THE AILING ORSINO EXHIBITS NARCISSISTIC TENDENCIES

Orsino has much in common with his fellow contender [Malvolio] for Olivia. The Duke also is sick of self-love, and tastes with a distempered appetite. Either he sates himself on what he takes in: "Enough, no more; / 'Tis not so sweet now as it was before"; or he devalues it: "nought enters there . . . But falls into abatement." Orsino claims that love and music do not satisfy, but the failure really seems to lie within himself. It is due to what [critic Anne] Barton calls an "essentially sterile and self-induced . . . state of mind," but does not depend upon Olivia's absence and lack of response. Indeed, his mood has remarkably little to do with her. We cannot be sure what he really wants, which leads critics to say that he is in love with love; but we can be fairly sure that he does not want Olivia, and the play bears this out. Nor does he seem to desire sexual union, for he never plays with sexual implications of words such as "dies," "dying fall," or of metaphors about appetite and the sea. He longs for something extremely good, yet feels that it will never satisfy him.

The problem seems to be—as for Malvolio—a precarious sense of self-esteem. Healthy narcissism is love of oneself, without which we cannot enter into a loving relation with others. Unhealthy narcissism is fragile, defensive self-absorption; it results in being unable to enter fully into relations with others. . . .

Orsino's self-esteem seems precarious, which is why he concentrates almost all his interest on himself (not others), and why he cannot endure the frustrations of reality. Whatever he idealizes in an effort to confirm his perfection—love, music, Olivia—eludes him. It never confirms his grandeur, because it is never as perfect as he demands that it be: "Enough, no more; /'Tis not so sweet now as it was before." In addition, he idealizes himself in a grandiose way. Orsino's sense of his own excellence rings hollow to us (but not to Viola); he is so self-involved, so much a perfectionist, that he never engages himself in anything (hence the charge that he moons about). He courts an idealized lady at a distance by sending messengers, rather than pursue her more vigorously in person.

Another indication of Orsino's narcissistic imbalance is the wonderfully vitalizing effect which Viola has upon him. In her presence he becomes quite different. . . . She provides (to quote [scholar Harold] Jenkins . . .) a "genuineness of feeling against which the illusory can be measured." Viola does something which Olivia could not do: as Cesario she confirms Orsino's innate sense of vigor, greatness, and perfection. Viola makes him feel rather elated: respected and loved for his own worth. But at the same time, she frustrates and tempers—but never tries to destroy—his illusory sense of omnipotence with regard to Olivia, to love, and to herself as Cesario. Using this perspective, we have a way of seeing the truth to nature which informs Shakespeare's apparently arbitrary treatment of the relationship between characters.

Let us look back at the first scene. Immediately after Orsino's languorous speech, Curio asks if he will go hunt. "What, Curio?" Orsino replies, as if in a love-sick daze—or as if he had not thought of hunting anything or anyone. Olivia would be the likely object, if he is as smitten as he appears to be. Instead, he responds to Curio's suggestion, "the hart," by playing with it as a pun. Instead of hunting the hart—or Olivia—he *becomes* it:

Why so I do, the noblest that I have.
O, when mine eyes did see Olivia first,
Methought she purg'd the air of pestilence;
That instant was I turn'd into a hart,
And my desires, like fell and cruel hounds,
E'er since pursue me.

(1.1.18–23)

He makes himself the center of attention, and in the idealized world of myth: she is Diana, he Acteon. The choice suggests two basic reasons for his ineffectual relation to Olivia.
First, he idealizes her as Diana (who, by definition, will
marry no one); she frustrates him in actuality, and perse-
cutes him in fantasy (as revealed in the myth). Second, he
reveals an ennervated sense of self-worth: Diana/Olivia is so
perfect that Acteon/Orsino can never win her; pursuit can
only be futile. Finally, Orsino, as the hart, becomes the object of his own desires—roughly the situation that Narcissus
found himself in, and a classic instance of the sterile state of
the narcissist.

ORSINO'S PERCEPTIONS ARE WARPED AND SELF-CENTERED

Orsino's major failing is an inability to assess the world
around him with any accuracy. When he learns that Olivia
has vowed to mourn her brother for seven years, he ignores
the excess, unlike Feste and Sir Toby; they see it as unrealistic and life-defeating, but Orsino has no sense of how it ru-
ins his suit. To him, her mourning is solely a sign of her perfection. More important, it allows him to concentrate upon
his own excellence:

O, she that hath a heart of that fine frame
To pay this debt of love but to a brother,
How will she love, when the rich golden shaft
Hath kill'd the flock of all affections else
That live in her; when liver, brain, and heart,
These sovereign thrones, are all supplied, and fill'd
Her sweet perfections with one self king!

(1.1.33–39)

The "rich golden shaft" would in other contexts be a sign of
sexual interest; but given Orsino's decided lack of such a
drive, it serves here as an expression of his narcissistic
grandeur. He will kill "the flock of all affections else / That
live in her." The way he phrases this indicates that he sees
her as having no life of her own, apart from what he be-
stows. If he supplies and fills her thrones of liver, brain, and

heart "with one self king"—his literally aggrandized self—
she will not exist in her own right. Orsino seeks to fuse with
an idealized object—"her sweet perfections"—but in doing
so, he invades and fills her up. He can no longer get what he
wants, for the very good reason that, in his imagined fusion,
it no longer exists. He has taken it over. The process is similar to the one at the start of the play: he longs for music or
love, but spoils it because for him enough is never enough.
Whatever he tries to merge with proves unsatisfying—like
the music—and in reaction he immediately isolates himself
and devalues what he sought. His goal is so unrealistic in itself—and so far beyond anyone's capacities—that he cannot
pursue it. Instead, he relies upon messengers and never
meets Olivia until the last scene. This allows him to preserve
his idealization, and to avoid the frightening, painful acknowledgment that she is someone outside his control—an
individual in her own right, rather than merely a gratifying
extension of himself. . . .

CESARIO STABILIZES ORSINO

As Cesario, Viola becomes an ideal companion for the Duke:
someone loyal, steady, and selfless who respects and understands him in ways which are, apparently, new to him. He
begins to grow progressively less self-absorbed and a better
companion. From his first, restless speech we know that he
longs for something or someone whose worth will satisfy
and endure—will have meaning. We discover from the
opening lines of the first scene between him and Cesario
that he has evidently begun to find it. . . . Several factors allow for the new stability. For one thing, Cesario remains
faithful to the end, and shows no negligence; this quiets
Orsino's fear of inconstancy and loss. Another factor trou-
bles critics more than audiences: Orsino treats Cesario as a
young man, and remains oblivious to his true gender. Perhaps this is why Orsino never feels tempted to fuse, or to iso-
late. Until the very end, he treats Cesario as a reflection of
himself—and what could be better? He treats Cesario as a
reflection of his own excellence. . . .

Viola behaves in the way a friend, or therapist, might in
dealing with someone whose self-esteem is precarious because it fluctuates between the extremes of being too low or
too grandiose. Her passivity allows a mild narcissistic elation
to flourish in Orsino; and thus she bolsters his sense of worth

by confirming his vigor, greatness, and perfection. She serves as a loving, selfless, respectful friend and servant. But also—in the most delicate of maneuvers—she tames his grandiose sense of himself and of his idealized object, Olivia. . . .

In Viola's presence, Orsino begins to modify the view he developed in his very first speech:

> Give me some music. Now good morrow, friends.
> Now, good Cesario, but that piece of song,
> That old and antic song we heard last night;
> Methought it did relieve my passion much.
> (2.4.1–4)

VIOLA IS INSTRUMENTAL IN ORSINO'S RELIEF

We can safety attribute to Viola's influence his new attitude to music. This central metaphor suggests both fusion, and a more harmonious relationship. Now music can comfort him. One reason is Viola's presence. Another is his awareness that music exists outside himself. . . . We find him beginning to experience someone as distinctly other than himself. A first hint is that he says "good morrow, friends" rather than simply ignore others as in his first scene. Cesario exists as a relatively autonomous person of whom he asks a series of questions, and listens to the answers; and with whom he begins to transcend his rapt concentration of interest upon himself. Orsino takes a more serious interest in others, although he is still the center of attention. . . .

He still idealizes women; we know that Olivia has forgotten her brother and giddily begun wooing Cesario. Orsino now says that women love in a better way than men do. He sees some chance for stability, for women can provide constant and devoted love. Since he speaks to a woman without knowing it, we spot the irony. Steadfast Viola says, perhaps eagerly, "I think it well, my lord." She must hope for one, and only one, shift in his fidelity. . . .

HAS ORSINO CHANGED?

Perhaps the greatest puzzle is Viola herself. She gets Orsino, and seems genuinely fond of him. Since she is so secure in herself and in a benign inner world, we assume that she must know what she wants. Olivia makes us think that the Duke has many virtues (1.5.262–66). Still, he disconcerts us at the end of the play. He turns on Cesario, calls him a dissembling cub. With comic stubbornness, Orsino persists in idealizing Olivia; when at long last she enters, he exclaims: "now heaven walks on earth." But when he finds that she has wed Cesario he degrades her to a "marble-breasted tyrant." We may simply regard this as the death throes of his former ways. Still, his wish for revenge on Cesario has narcissistic overtones:

> But this your minion, whom I know you love,
> And whom, by heaven, I swear I tender dearly,
> Him will I tear out of that cruel eye
> Where he sits crowned in his master's spite.
> (5.1.123–26)

He will "sacrifice the lamb that I do love, / To spite a raven's heart within a dove." The situation—and rhymes—insure that we do not take this as much more than comic excess. And Viola's willingness to die is another—now preposterous—indication of her constancy. Still, we hardly need to have these traits emphasized once again. If we are at all attuned to Orsino's narcissistic mode, this outburst suggests that he has not entirely changed. We are left with the possibility that Viola idealizes Orsino, thinks him better than he is—and right up to the end.

The Essential Feste

Alan S. Downer

Quite often Shakespeare's fools are the wisest characters in his plays. Typically, it is up to the fool to
point out the follies of others, and in this Feste is no
different. However, as drama expert and Princeton
University scholar Alan S. Downer explains, Feste is
more deeply involved in the play than simply being
the commentator.

Twelfth Night is the fool's night and, as such, the
fool alone recognizes the foolish attitudes and language of the others—things aren't as they should be.
In order to set everything straight, Feste begins exposing the truths he sees disguised in language by
using language: he cleverly baits Olivia with a riddle,
he mocks Orsino with a song, and he teases and torments Malvolio to the point of groveling. Feste's commentary in these instances does nothing to advance
the action of the play, yet indirectly Feste's confound-
ing of these characters is responsible for driving Sebastian to Olivia. And this, according to Downer, is
the decisive action that "cuts the comic knot" of the
love triangle and reveals Feste's important connection
to the play's resolution.

The familiar convention of the Twins Confused is . . . employed by Shakespeare for purposes beyond the convention.
The unraveling of identities is not the end but the means to
the end of his comedy. And, in order that the confusion of
brother and sister may be convincing, he is forced to resort
to another convention of his stage, the "breeches role." Like
the conventional recognition scene, however, the conventional disguise becomes essential both to the plot and to the
basic idea of *Twelfth Night*.

Viola is most explicit as to the reasons for concealing her
identity in man's clothing. Both she and the audience un-

Excerpted from "Feste's Night," by Alan S. Downer, *College English*, 1952.

derstand clearly the motive of her act; there is no self-deception involved. Yet this disguise, innocently undertaken for the best of reasons, works a certain amount of havoc. Poor Olivia is so charmed by Viola's "outside" that she loses her heart to a dream. . . .

Feste, too, is disguised both in costume and in behavior. His suit is motley, the uniform of the Fool, and he carries the tabor and perhaps the bauble as his badge of office. When, however, Olivia calls him a fool—and we must return to this scene again—he points out that "cucullus non facit monachum" [a cowl does not make a monk, I, V, 54–55]. And as the man inside the monk's robe may be anything but a monk in spirit, so he, Feste, wears not motley in his brain. His disguise, like Viola's, is a kind of protection; he is an allowed fool and may speak frankly what other men, in other disguises, must say only to themselves. . . .

Disguise, of course, is not merely a matter of costume and pose. When Viola informs her master that she is all the daughters of her father's house and all the brothers too, she is masking her meaning in words, in a riddle. "A fustian riddle" betrays Malvolio, and in the second wooing scene between Olivia and Viola there occurs a passage of stichomythia, a device of dialogue that had its origin in riddling speech:

> OLIVIA: I prithee tell me what thou thinkst of me.
> VIOLA: That you do think you are not what you are.
> OLIVIA: If I think so, I think the same of you.
> VIOLA: Then think you right. I am not what I am.

It is by words alone that Sir Toby maintains his ascendancy over Sir Andrew, by pun and false logic and sheer volubility convincing him that he is not what he is, an asshead and a coxcomb and a knave. By words alone he brings about the duel between Andrew and Viola and so fills each fencer with false ideas of the other's skill that both are defeated before a sword has been crossed. His facility with words traps him at last, bringing him into open conflict with Antonio and with Sebastian and forcing the surrender of his freedom to Maria as recompense for her own cleverness in trapping Malvolio with a riddling letter.

Feste's whole art and function depend upon his talents as a "notable corrupter of words," and he has much wisdom to utter on what we should probably call the problem of semantics. He concludes one wit combat by declaring that "words are grown so false that I am loath to prove reason with them." In many ways he is the central figure of the play, the symbol of its meaning. The plot could get on without him, no doubt; his practical function as message-bearer could be taken over by Fabian, who has little enough to keep him busy. But he is no mere embellishment. Without Feste, *Twelfth Night* would not be the enduring comedy it is but another romantic farce like *The Comedy of Errors*. *Twelfth Night* is Feste's night. . . .

FESTE'S CONTRIBUTIONS TO ARRANGEMENT

The Fool is as conventional in Shakespearean comedy as the intriguing slave or parasite in [plays by] Plautus or Molière. But, while Feste shares some of the characteristics of [such characters] he does not, like them, dazzle our eyes by juggling the elements of the plot into a complex pattern which only he can sort out for the necessary fortunate conclusion. Until the last act of the play, he does little but jest or sing. But for all his failure to take a positive part in the intrigue—emphasized perhaps when he drops out of the baiting of Malvolio—for all that he is not, that is to say, a protagonist, he nonetheless propounds the theme which gives *Twelfth Night* its unity and makes a single work of art out of what might have been a gorgeous patchwork.

A brief examination of the matter of the comedy will suggest the basis for such a conclusion. *Twelfth Night* is compounded of two, perhaps three, "plots," more or less independent actions, each of which must be rounded off before the play is concluded. In the first, Duke Orsino's eyes must be opened to the true nature of love that he may marry Viola; in the second, Malvolio must be reduced from the deluded superman to fallible humanity; in the third, which is closely tied with the first, Sebastian must be substituted for Viola in the affections of Olivia.

The structure is skilfully contrived not only to keep all three plots going and maintain a reasonable connection among them but to emphasize the similarity of their themes. Like most panoramic drama, the play may be divided into three organic movements rather than the meaningless editorial division into five acts. The first of these movements, from the introduction of Orsino to Viola's discovery that she has charmed Olivia (I, I–II, 3), is concerned almost exclusively with establishing the triangular love affair. Toby, Andrew, and

Maria are brought on to whet our appetites for their plot, and, just before the movement ends, Sebastian appears that we may be reassured all will come right before the play is over. However, we should note a speech of Feste's made to Maria during his first appearance (I, 5), in which he refers obliquely to the common subject of the separate actions: "If Sir Toby would leave drinking, thou wert as witty a piece of Eve's flesh as any in Illyria." If all were as it should be and according to the order of nature, Toby would wed Maria. But Toby drinks, and the Duke loves Olivia, and Olivia (as we shall see in a moment) loves Viola. All most *un*natural.

In the second movement (II, 3–IV, I) the love triangle remains unchanged, and the trapping of Malvolio occupies

---

FESTE'S SONG PORTRAYS HIS DARK TRUTHS

In his book Love and Society in Shakespearean Comedy: A Study of Dramatic Form and Content, *Richard A. Levin believes Feste is linked to the "antiromantic," darker undercurrents running through the play. Here, Levin, an associate professor at UC Davis, examines the closing song, concluding that Feste patronizes the audience by acting as false counselor.*

Feste's role as a false counselor helps to clarify the meaning of his final song. Critics agree that the song closes *Twelfth Night* with arresting somberness, but they argue over the song's function. One view is that the song readmits into the play the "reality" that comic form has thus far held at a distance. Another interpretation emphasizes that the song narrates the unhappy experience of a rake or ne'er-do-well and thereby reminds the audience of the limits of festivity. Finally, a few critics regard the song as reliable commentary on the action of the play. I myself believe that the song does comment on the play, but not accurately, for we are now Feste's only audience and he offers us the false counsel he heretofore offered others.

I assume that by choosing a first-person narrative in the song, Feste intimates that the experiences of his persona are comparable to his own. He suggests, therefore, how his disillusionment developed. As a small boy, he made no demands and was therefore indulged. As an adult, however, he learned about the real nature of society:

But when I came to man's estate,
  With hey, ho, the wind and the rain,

most of the action. We observe the offense for which he is to be punished, the plotting of revenge, and the success of the scheme. Sebastian has again made only a token appearance, but in the final scene of the movement (III, 4) all three actions are brought together with the greatest of ease as the deluded Malvolio is handed over to Toby, and Andrew and Viola are inveigled into a duel from which both are rescued by the intervention and arrest of Sebastian's friend, Antonio.

The final movement, the last two acts of the play, is in a sense Sebastian's. Mistaken for Viola, he brings about a fortunate unknotting of the love tangle, rescues his friend Antonio from the clutches of the Duke, and forces a confession of their machinations from Toby and company. The point to notice here

---

> 'Gainst knaves and thieves men shut their gate,
>   For the rain it raineth every day.
>
>   (393–96)

The "great house," which may stand by synecdoche for society itself, has gates to protect the privileged life within. The "knaves and thieves," Feste perhaps implies, are simply those at a disadvantage—Sir Toby, after all, though as undeserving as any, enjoys a snug berth, and Antonio has been deemed a "thief" simply because it suited Orsino to do so (5.1.69). Whether this interpretation is correct in detail or not, Feste certainly likens the "wind and the rain" to the buffeting by fortune that unprotected people experience.

After portraying further stages of his disillusionment, Feste makes another claim: that the whole world has grown old, not merely himself:

> A great while ago the world begun,
>   With hey, ho, the wind and the rain,
> But that's all one, our play is done,
>   And we'll strive to please you every day.

The implication of the first line is that the world is now long past innocence; the Golden Age is a vanished dream. When Feste breaks off with "But that's all one," he is patronizing the audience as he patronized Orsino and Olivia and the others; he implies that we—his privileged audience—do not want to hear his darker truths. One should answer that these truths are his, not ours.

Richard A. Levin, *Love and Society in Shakespearean Comedy: A Study of Dramatic Form and Content.* Newark: University of Delaware Press, 1985, pp. 162–63.

is that Feste is the character who, innocently enough, drives Sebastian into Olivia's arms. It is Feste's only direct contribution to the action of the play; it is also the single decisive action which cuts the comic knot; and it is a visual dramatic symbol of his relationship to the whole play. It is the action of a man whose professional function is to perceive and declare the true state of affairs in the face of scorn, threats, and discouragement from the self-deluded. Shakespeare has in fact prepared us for this action at several important points earlier in the play.

KEEN INSIGHTS LEAD TO EXPOSURE

On his first appearance, with Maria, Feste demonstrates not only that he is able to more than hold his own in a wit combat but that he is shrewd enough to see the true state of affairs in the household. A moment later, with the license of an allowed fool, he is demonstrating to Olivia the folly of her resolution to withdraw from the world for seven years in mourning for her brother.

> FESTE: Good madonna, why mournest thou?
> OLIVIA: Good fool, for my brother's death.
> FESTE: I think his soul is in hell, madonna.
> OLIVIA: I know his soul is in heaven, fool.
> FESTE: The more fool, madonna, to mourn for your brother's soul, being in heaven. Take away the fool, gentlemen [I, 5, 72–78].

The little passage is in the most artificial of dialogue forms, stichomythia, and it is perhaps only a bit of logic-chopping, but it presents the common-sense view of a sentimental and un-Christian attitude.

The exposure of Olivia takes place in the first movement of the play. In the second movement Feste undertakes to tell the Duke a few plain truths, but, since the undeceiving of the mighty is ticklish business, he goes about it in an oblique manner. . . .

It is as early in the morning as the love-smitten Duke would arise from bed. He enters, calling at once for music, and requests Cesario (that is, Viola) for that "old and antique song" they heard last night. While his servant Curio goes in search of Feste to sing it, Orsino proceeds to analyze it for us. The description is famous and explicit:

> It is old and plain,
> The spinsters and the knitters in the sun,
> And the free maids that weave their thread with bones,
> Do use to chant it. It is silly sooth,

And dallies with the innocence of love
Like the old age [II, 4, 44–49]. . . .

It is a love song, but not impassioned, not from the point of view of fervent youth. It dallies with the harmless pleasure of love as if the experience were but the memory of the old, a memory recollected in tranquillity. Whereupon Feste sings:

Come away, come away, death,
  And in sad cypress let me be laid.
Fly away, fly away, breath;
  I'm slain by a fair cruel maid.
My shroud of white, stuck all with yew,
  O prepare it!
My part of death, no one so true
  Did share it.

In the second stanza the love imagery becomes more extravagant.

Not a flower, not a flower sweet,
  On my black coffin let there be strown;
Not a friend, not a friend greet
  My poor corpse, where my bones shall be thrown.
A thousand, thousand sighs to save,
  Lay me, O where
Sad, true lover ne'er find my grave,
  To weep there. . . .

Feste seems to have been mocking, indirectly, the Duke's passion. "Come away, death" is indeed a love song, but it can hardly be said to dally with the innocence of love. This would explain the Duke's abrupt, "There's for thy pains," and his immediate dismissal, not only of the singer, but of his entire court. . . .

And Feste, going off, dares a parting thrust. "Now the melancholy god protect thee," he says, and bids him put to sea to make a good voyage of nothing. In this scene, I suggest, Feste "exposes" the Duke as he has earlier exposed Olivia. By mocking them both, he points out that their loves are sentimental and foolish. . . .

THE FOOL SPEAKS PLAINLY

The parallel exposing of Malvolio, which is capped by Feste in the third movement, is the clearest statement of the theme in action, since it is unencumbered by romantic love, an element which can blind an audience to the true state of affairs as effectively as it can blind the romantic lovers. Malvolio, in this play, is plain text. . . . Malvolio would not only be virtuous, he would have others so, and he would define the term. It is a cause of delight to discover that the elegant creature with snow-broth in his veins, so superior to the drunken carousing of Toby, the witty trifling of Feste, the dalliance of Olivia—that this man of virtue is only human, like ourselves. And in this exposure, that the whirligig of time may bring his revenges, Feste is permitted to play the visually dominant part.

The action is so arranged that, of all the conspirators, only Feste has a scene alone with Malvolio, in which, for nobody's pleasure but his own, he teases and torments the benighted steward and reduces the proud man to a state of wretched groveling: "I tell thee," cries Malvolio at last, "I am as well in my wits as any man in Illyria," and Feste replies, "Well-a-day that you were, sir.". . .

Thus it is Feste's function in both parts of the action to make plain to the audience the artificial, foolish attitudes of the principal figures. Malvolio loves himself, Orsino loves love, and Olivia loves a ghost. This, says Feste, is unnatural, against common sense. In this similarity of situation and Feste's single-minded attitude in each case lies the unity of *Twelfth Night*, its theme.

Feste states it clearly. Since he is primarily a singing fool, he states it in song:

> What is love? 'Tis not hereafter;
> Present mirth hath present laughter. . . .
>   Youth's a stuff will not endure.

Feste's philosophy is as old as the hills, as old as the comic attitude, the acceptance of the facts of life. His philosophy, however, goes somewhat deeper than a mere sentimental optimism.

> Journeys end in lovers' meeting
>   Every wise man's son doth know.

As a wise man's son, or as an understanding fool, he sees to it that there shall be a meeting of true lovers at the end of the journey of Viola and Sebastian. In his scene with Malvolio he even discards his priestly disguise and appears in his own motley to restore the vision of the self-blinded man. And, by his introduction of Sebastian to Olivia, he makes possible the shedding of all disguises both physical and spiritual at the dénouement.

THE LONELY FOOL MAKES A WISE MAN

Critical opinion has been somewhat divided about Feste. There is general agreement about his remarkable cleanspokenness; he has been called the merriest of Shakespeare's fools, and the loneliest. He has been taken to be the symbol of misrule that governs the Twelfth Night activities. Yet, when the recognition scene is over, all the characters romantically paired off, Malvolio reduced to a very human bellow—"I'll be revenged on the whole pack of you!"—and Feste prepares to sing his foolish little epilogue, does he not seem to be something more than merry, or lonely, or the spirit of misrule?

Observe him, alone on the great stage which is the emptier for the departure of the grandly dressed ladies and gentlemen who have crowded it during the last scene, and the quieter after the vigorous excitement that attended the dénouement: the twins united, the marriage and betrothal, the explosion of Malvolio, the brawling of Andrew and Toby. Feste is perhaps older than the other characters, "a fool that the Lady Olivia's father took much delight in." But he has been, for a fool, a rather quiet character; no loud, bawdy jokes and very little slapstick. His brain is not parti-colored: *cucullus non facit monachum.* As Viola observes:

> This fellow's wise enough to play the fool,
> And to do that well craves a kind of wit.
> He must observe their mood on whom he jests,
> The quality of persons and the time;
> Not, like the haggard, check at every feather
> That comes before his eye. This is a practice
> As full of labor as a wise man's art.

It is the function of this fool to speak the truth, however quizzically he must phrase it. It is his task to persuade his lord and lady *not* to be fools. It is the task of comedy, too.

And now he is alone. Now he sings his lonely, foolish song:

> When that I was and a little tiny boy
> With hey, ho, the wind and the rain, etc. . . .

> But that's all one, our play is done,
> And we'll strive to please you every day.

It is, after all, as he reminds us, just a play. But it has its purpose for being, just as the great tragedies have. *Twelfth Night* is Feste's night, and we may look to be well edified when the Fool delivers the Madmen.

Olivia: The Real Heroine?

John W. Draper

This excerpt from the late professor John W. Draper, author of several books on Shakespeare, exposes the Lady Olivia as the true heroine in the central role of *Twelfth Night*. Draper supports his argument with evidence found in the text such as repeated reference to Olivia by other characters, her drawn-out introduction, and the ending in which her choice of husband governs the others' destinies. Not only is Olivia the central figure but, according to Draper, she is possibly the best independent woman Shakespeare ever created.

The Lady Olivia is a realist in a romantic situation: her youth and charm and wealth make her the cynosure [center of attention] of neighboring sheep's eyes, and everyone has plans to marry her off or to be married to her. Thus, while the castaway Viola desperately seeks a husband and protector, the much-bereaved but hardheaded Olivia seeks to avoid wooers, and so gives time for more and more to cluster, buzzing and droning about the honeypot of her attractions until at last she finds a suitable candidate; and then she swiftly follows the ancient maxim of *fortiter in re* [fortiter in re, suaviter in modo: strongly in deed, gently in manner]. Until she has hit upon her choice, she cannot drive off the others, and so must conceal her plans; she adopts an impenetrable veil of mourning, matches her woman's wit to her instant need, and . . . confuses and evades her suitors. Indeed, she is a realist in a romantic situation; and, as she prolongs this situation, she becomes more and more the axis on which the others' lives and expectations turn: to her own household, her marriage is the all-absorbing question; so also to Orsino and his household, and also to sundry satel-

Excerpted from *The "Twelfth Night" of Shakespeare's Audience*, by John W. Draper. Published by Octagon Books, a division of Hippocrene Books, Inc. Reprinted with permission from Hippocrene Books, Inc.

lites and hangers-on, who sigh and protest devotion in their several ways, disharmonious with one another, and (did they but know it) most disharmonious with the secret aspirations of their mistress.

UNVEILING OLIVIA

Although Olivia appears in only six scenes and speaks fewer lines than Viola or Sir Toby, she is truly the crux of *Twelfth Night*. Her role of melancholy mourning—seclusion, veil, and fertile tears—keeps her behind the scenes. Indeed, she appears but once in the first act and not at all in the second; but repeated reference to her makes her a pervading presence, and she is the center of the plots, which, as in contemporary Italian comedy, chiefly concern her lovers. . . .

According to Elizabethan stage convention, the introduction of a character generally gave a clue as to his personality, his place, and his importance in the play; and there is probably no one in Shakespeare who has a more lengthy and elaborate introduction than Olivia. Her appearance is a sort of climax to Act I, most amply and ingeniously prepared for. . . .

Indeed, though the Countess takes up but part of a single scene, she dominates the act; and her meeting with Viola not only gives it a brilliant climax of color and grouping upon the stage but also starts the major complication, which in the end defeats the well-laid plans of steward and knights and duke. Surely, the playwright Shakespeare, having given Olivia such an introduction, must have considered her crucially important.

Modern critics, allured by the romantic Viola, are inclined to disagree; and disagreeing with Shakespeare is a critical impasse. To a few, she seems more or less significant; to none, very attractive. Dr. [Samuel] Johnson [noted writer and critic] complained that her marriage "wants credibility." [Shakespeare scholar and translator, August Wilhelm von] Schlegel speaks of "the proud Olivia . . . . entangled by the modest and insinuating messenger of the Duke," as if she were entirely a pawn in the game. . . . More recently, the Arden [a collection of Shakespeare's work] editors declare her "an admirable foil" to Viola, whom they take to be the heroine: despite her "habit of dignity," she has "something of the spoiled child about her," and she lacks Viola's "readiness to repartee and quick resourcefulness"—this shrewd young lady who manages to dominate her unruly household and her persistent lovers, and finally confounds them all by a marriage of her own choice that leaves her (as she intended) the permanent mistress of the situation! The Tudor editors realize that she is "the central figure" of the play, "endowed with an engaging dignity and humanity"; but they do not seem to understand her shrewd designs. The new Cambridge editors declare her "plainly a self-deceiver," a shallow amateur in melancholy. These opinions are certainly diverse. Olivia seems indeed to have confounded not only Orsino and Sir Toby but also modern commentators—good evidence that she and her schemes are truly feminine in Shakespeare's subtlest manner.

OLIVIA: AN INDEPENDENT WOMAN

Olivia's mind and education, and something of her character, appear in the very style of her discourse. Her high place and the proprieties of mourning require of her plain speech rather than the skipping repartee of comedy; and this plain speech implies an incisive, direct mind, a will that knows what it wants, and at least the appearance of candor. . . . Indeed, her short, sharp speeches have the incisive quality of command rather than the submissive tone of female dependence.

The wide gamut of her allusions, especially in her first scene to give the keynote of her role, show a mind that was widely schooled in serious and practical concerns. . . . Her education, if not deep, is at least well rounded; and, had she shown some knowledge of the Classics, one might fairly term her a bluestocking [female intellectual] like Queen Elizabeth and the Countess of Pembroke. Many Elizabethans, however, especially the Puritans, objected to too much learning in girls; and, since only men might enter the universities, daughters could be educated only by costly private tutors. The preponderance of practical and the absence of Classical allusion in Olivia's discourse suggests that her education had come from her own eyes and ears, from casual reading and from conversation—a fine art in that age —rather than from the assiduity of a learned tutor.

Indeed, Olivia gives evidence of a clear head and a quick mind. She enjoys the combat of wit between Malvolio and Feste; and, though she is too dignified in her mourning to make one in it, she eggs on the contestants. She is competent at worldly-wise epigram: "O world, how apt the poore are to be proud?"; and ". . . . youth is bought more oft then begg'd, or borrow'd." She is quick-witted, and instantly invents the stratagem of the ring to oblige Viola to visit her again. She can endure plain speaking, and is not angry when Viola suggests that her fine complexion may be false and that she is "too proud." She can be patient with Feste, and can bide her time with Sir Toby. Indeed, she has poise and self-control. She has also a sense of diplomacy. She knows that bad news requires a lengthy introduction. She is suspicious of eulogy. She can ignore Sir Andrew, checkmate Sir Toby, restrain the Duke, and even get him to countenance her marriage with Sebastian by means of the double wedding—a final master stroke of policy that at once silences his suit forever and makes him give public recognition to Sebastian as her husband. No wonder she runs her household with "smooth, discreet, and stable bearing"! Truly, she had some right to think herself capable of ruling her father's lands—and, by the way, a husband. . . .

THE PLAYWRIGHT CREATES AN ELIZABETHAN FEMINIST

In drama, the family must be done away with if the daughter were to shine; and, in *Twelfth Night*, the traditional situation from Italian comedy of the girl and her many lovers receives a new and typically English turn: the girl, like a true Elizabethan feminist, marries herself off without benefit of kith or kin. . . . Sir Toby is clearly not her legal guardian. Her father, moreover, according to a common custom, had appointed her brother guardian in his will; but the brother's death had brought these plans to naught. Even if Sir Toby, moreover, had been Olivia's guardian, he could not have forced a husband of his choosing on her; for, in this regard, he had only the negative power of a veto. Thus Shakespeare, for the necessary purposes of the plot, has made the maiden Olivia her own mistress: her natural guardian was dead; the guardian appointed in her father's will was also dead—we must suppose too suddenly to name his own successor—and thus Olivia was left a petty counterpart of Queen Elizabeth, a young and affluent Countess; and the audience would easily understand her in this light.

Not without reason did the law provide guardians for unmarried girls; and Olivia's situation was beset with uncertainties and dangers. She must somehow shield herself from the unwelcome attentions of fortune hunters and of fools like Sir Andrew; and she ran a serious risk even of abduction and forced marriage to some miscreant who wished only to squander her patrimony as soon as wedlock gave him control of it. . . . Olivia in her position as self-guardian had a most exacting role. She adopts a screen of modest retirement that to the Elizabethans would doubtless seem a proof at once of her proper maidenly reserve and of her shrewd sagacity: if she accept the Duke, she has a master; if she refuse him face to face, she insults him; but, if she will not see him for a reason that all commend, she holds him checkmate. Thus she maintains the sacred atmosphere of conventual seclusion, but without the restrictions of an actual convent; and so she gets herself the maximum protection, with the minimum of restraint. . . . Who shall say that Olivia was not astute? . . .

Shakespeare, by giving Olivia the independence of Elizabethan ladies, motivates the old story, which required that she refuse the very eligible Duke, and choose instead a wandering youth of here and everywhere. The Countess is determined to dominate her husband; and so she will not wed a husband who both can and will dominate her. Some of Orsino's very virtues—his high position, age, and lusty manhood—are to Olivia the best reasons for refusing him. . . .

COMIC RESOLUTION THROUGH OLIVIA'S RESOLVE

The quadripartite triangle comprising the love affair of Orsino and Olivia with Viola and Sebastian is the least realistic episode in the play. . . . Olivia's strategy in this case is quite different from that with her other lovers: Orsino, she politely evades; Sir Andrew, she brusquely ignores; Malvolio as a lover never occurs to her; but Viola, and then by accident Sebastian, she woos and weds with no minced words and little restraint of action. The twins obviously surpass her in neither estate nor age, and she is so much in love that she takes a chance on their wit. She declares her passion to Viola apparently at their second meeting, is refused, but, like Orsino, will not so be answered. Again she urges, and once more is repulsed. Yet again, with a priest all ready, she comes upon her love—this time, not Viola but her twin brother—and the two are legally betrothed posthaste dispatch. One judges that Sebastian was as smitten with her at first sight as she had been with Viola—at least, one hopes so. Of course, at her next meeting with Viola who knows nothing of the wedding, she is again repulsed, and for a moment thinks that her husband has played her false. Then luckily, the complication of the twins is disentangled; Sebastian declares himself the lucky bridegroom, and all is well. Indeed, the Countess' love affairs were growing too complicated for her to manage; a summary wedlock with Sebastian was the obvious way to cut the Gordian knot, and she cleverly persuades the Duke to join with her in a double wedding that will commit him to a public acceptance of her marriage and so ward off all future complications. She handsomely offers to defray the cost of the wedding; and the cost will not be light; but politically it is worth the price. Each of Olivia's lovers pays a forfeit for paying her attentions: Orsino suffers from love-melancholy, and has to endure the ignominy of public refusal; Sir Andrew is bilked roundly by Sir Toby; Malvolio suffers gulling and imprisonment; but Viola, who does not pursue the lady of her own free will, suffers perhaps the most, for she must woo another for the man she loves; and she deserves the reward of the happy ending. Olivia no less so. . . .

OLIVIA, THE EPITOME OF SHAKESPEARE'S INDEPENDENT WOMEN

Olivia is perhaps the climax of the playwright's studies in the independent woman. . . . She proposes even after marriage to be her own master, and with a cleverness for which critics have given her little credit, without help of friends or relatives—in fact, in spite of them—she marries whom she will. . . .

Her decision to marry Sebastian governs the fate not only of [her four suitors] but also of Sir Toby, for he is thus obliged to safeguard his future through Maria rather than through Sir Andrew, and also of Viola, for she has no chance to marry Orsino as long as he pursues Olivia. The Countess, as more or less intentional arbiter of the main action, must be shrewd and determined and quick-witted; and Shakespeare found prototypes for just such a feminine figure in many contemporary noblewomen. He must, moreover, keep the audience's sympathy for this self-willed lady; and so, instead of putting her in the dubious position of rebelling against her male relations, he erases all of them from the scene, except the unprepossessing Sir Toby. He also makes two of her lovers, Sir Andrew and Malvolio, quite impossible; and, finally, he makes Olivia herself beautiful, young, and charming, so that, as in the case of Viola, we forgive all, not because we know all, but because forgiving a pretty woman is so much pleasanter than carping at her frailties —or rather, in Olivia's case, her woeful lack of frailties. Indeed, she rules the plot as Shakespeare revised it; and any effort to dethrone her throws the whole comedy out of joint. How can Viola be the heroine, and Sir Toby or Malvolio the comic hero, as most critics would suggest, when this hero and this heroine have little or no relation with each other in the plot? The identity of the hero is possibly open to question; but undoubtedly the heroine, as the early actresses who chose the role well knew, is clearly the Countess Olivia.

Malvolio's Ill Will as Cause for Revenge

Linda Anderson

Malvolio is a character that stirs up much contro-
versy among critics and audiences in general. He
creates an imbalance within the play which leads to
an ending that makes many uneasy. Few feel sympa-
thy for his character as the audience witnesses nu-
merous instances of his ill will, but at the same time
most do not feel that Malvolio's false imprisonment
is just. Furthermore, those critics who believe the re-
venge is justified cannot agree about the effect of the
revenge on the audience and on Malvolio's character.
In the following excerpt taken from Linda Ander-
son's book, A Kind of Wild Justice: Revenge in Shakespeare's Comedies, *the variety of ideas and reactions*
to Malvolio and the revenge carried out against him
are explored. Anderson perceives Shakespeare as di-
recting the audience in its reactions to Malvolio and
its acceptance of the revenge. By Illyrian standards,
says Anderson, Malvolio, who refuses forgiveness, is
truly mad, and the treatment he receives is nothing
more than poetic justice.

Although revenge is central to *Twelfth Night,* it is to the sub-
plot that we must turn to find it. At the center of the subplot
stands another of those Shakespearean characters so power-
fully imagined that for some readers they unbalance the
plays they inhabit. The alien Malvolio, both in himself and in
his effect on criticism, makes one think of the alien Shylock
[from *The Merchant of Venice*]; and, like Shylock, Malvolio
has his defenders. Nevertheless, despite [Muriel C.] Brad-
brook's contention that "a great deal of sympathy has been
wasted on Malvolio," most critics do not find him a sympathetic character. This is not to say, however, that there is

general agreement about him. There is disagreement over whether he may be a satire on a particular person or type of person, or whether he may be Shakespeare's satiric portrait of a Puritan.

Whether or not Malvolio is to be seen as a Puritan, critics generally agree that he is representative of a new order of values to which Shakespeare in this play shows himself unsympathetic. But there is less agreement about the plot against Malvolio: one theory holds that the steward is the victim of a sadistic plot that has no redeeming social value; on the other hand, some commentators maintain that the revenge taken on him is justifiable. Even among critics who agree that Malvolio deserves the revenge taken on him, however, there is disagreement about the effect of that revenge, both on our feelings toward Malvolio and on the character himself.

ILL WILL DRAWS NO ABSOLUTION

Like Shylock, Malvolio has become the focus for criticism of the play he inhabits, especially among his defenders; but sympathy for both characters seems to stem primarily from a modern distaste for the forms of revenge taken on them. A modern audience or reader cannot justify enforced conversion or false imprisonment of a sane person as insane; but our inability to justify such punishments does not absolve the characters who suffer them. Although Malvolio is a far less serious threat to Illyria than Shylock is to Venice and Belmont, he also has less reason for his objectionable actions. No one spits upon Malvolio; no one insults him until he has established himself as an obnoxious intruder. And while Shylock shows what may be interpreted as flashes of feeling for his daughter and late wife, Malvolio never shows the slightest charitable impulse toward anyone but himself.

Malvolio's very name alerts us to the ill will that is his hallmark, and his first lines set the tone from which he never deviates. The clown has been attempting, with both wit and wisdom, to persuade Olivia to give over her excessive mourning for her brother, and Olivia seeks Malvolio's opinion:

OLIVIA: What think you of this fool, Malvolio? doth he not mend?

MALVOLIO: Yes, and shall do till the pangs of death shake him. Infirmity, that decays the wise, doth ever make the better fool.

(1.5.73–77)

Malvolio is, in fact, perfectly content that the house should stay in a state of mourning, however excessive. He associates fun and laughter with weakness. Although this attitude is unattractive, especially in a comedy, we might view Malvolio as merely the obverse of the irrepressible Feste, if he did not immediately condemn himself:

CLOWN: God send you, sir, a speedy infirmity, for the
            better increasing your folly! Sir Toby will be
            sworn that I am no fox, but he will not pass
            his word twopence that you are no fool.

OLIVIA: How say you to that, Malvolio?

MALVOLIO: I marvel your ladyship takes delight in such a
            barren rascal. I saw him put down the other
            day with an ordinary fool that has no more
            brain than a stone. . . . I protest I take these
            wise men that crow so at these set kind of
            fools no better than the fools' zanies.

                                            (1.5.78–89)

By his attack on Feste, who has won our sympathy with his humor and good sense regarding Olivia, Malvolio offends us. Not only has he criticized Feste, but—if his opinion were taken seriously—he would endanger the clown's livelihood. Luckily, there is no chance that Malvolio's feelings in this matter will be respected, for Olivia, whose taste Malvolio has thoughtlessly disparaged, passes judgment on him for all of us:

O, you are sick of self-love, Malvolio, and taste with a distemper'd appetite. To be generous, guiltless, and of free disposition, is to take those things for bird-bolts that you deem cannon-bullets. . . .

                                            (1.5.90–96)

Prior to the revenge taken on him, Malvolio hardly speaks of another character but to malign, or to one but to threaten. He describes the disguised Viola as "of very ill manner" (1.5.153) and speaking "very shrewishly" (1.5.160). When we see him actually dealing with her, his behavior is contemptuous, certainly exceeding the bounds of his commission to return the ring (1.5.300–306):

Come, sir, you peevishly threw it to her; and her will is, it should be so return'd. If it be worth stooping for, there it lies, in your eye; if not, be it his that finds it. (2.2.13–16)

Typically, after an appearance by Malvolio, one or more of the sympathetic characters comments on his behavior; in this instance, Viola describes Malvolio as a "churlish messenger"

(2.2.23). Clearly, Shakespeare is taking some pains not only to show us Malvolio, but to direct our response to him.

Significantly, we have seen Malvolio's insolence toward Olivia, Viola, and Feste before seeing his more justifiable behavior toward Sir Toby's merry band. We are therefore more ready to side with the roisterers against Malvolio, especially since the injured and charming Feste is among them. Some critics have argued that, as Olivia's steward, Malvolio is merely performing his duty in attempting to quell what even Maria describes as "caterwauling" (2.3.72). There may be a degree of truth in this contention, although we do not in fact know what Olivia told Malvolio to tell Sir Toby and the others. True, he delivers a message as coming from her, but we know from his scene with Viola that he is capable of infusing his lady's messages with his own mean spirit. Even if he is delivering Olivia's sentiments, he does so in as offensive a manner as possible:

> My masters, are you mad? Or what are you? Have you no wit, manners, nor honesty, but to gabble like tinkers at this time of night? Do ye make an alehouse of my lady's house, that ye squeak out your coziers' catches without any mitigation or remorse of voice? . . . If you can separate yourself and your misdemeanors, you are welcome to the house; if not, and it would please you to take leave of her, she is very willing to bid you farewell. (2.3.86–92, 95–101)

When all of this has no effect on the "three merry men," Malvolio rounds on Maria, who seems rather an innocent bystander at this point, having attempted to calm the rioting and, after all, having no authority to control her lady's cousin:

> Mistress Mary, if you priz'd my lady's favor at any thing more than contempt, you would not give means for this uncivil rule. She shall know of it, by this hand. (2.3.121–24)

PLOTTING AGAINST MALVOLIO COMMENCES

Although we cannot entirely approve of Sir Toby—a sort of bush-league Falstaff—we can hardly keep from applauding his most coherent reply to Malvolio:

> Art any more than a steward? Dost thou think because thou art virtuous there shall be no more cakes and ale?
>
> (2.3.114–16)

Not only must the cakes-and-ale party prevail in Illyria, but Sir Toby's first question reminds us that Malvolio is the type of the biblical statement that "For thre things the earth is moved: yea, for foure it can not susteine it self," the first of which is "a servant when he reigneth" (Prov. 30:21, 22; although it is hardly likely that Sir Toby has this in mind). Malvolio in his pretensions *is* unbearable, and, aptly, these pretensions are the key to the revenge taken on him.

Maria, by far the clearest-headed of the lot, provides the most complete description of Malvolio even while plotting how to use his pretensions against him:

> The dev'l a puritan that he is, or anything constantly but a time-pleaser, an affection'd ass, that cons state without book, and utters it by great swarths; the best persuaded of himself, so cramm'd (as he thinks) with excellencies, that it is his grounds of faith that all that look on him love him; and on that vice in him will my revenge find notable cause to work.
> (2.3.147–53)

Maria's plot is a notable comic revenge just because it does play off of the self-love that is Malvolio's principal comic flaw. Some of his other flaws, however, abet and extend the revenge. Fabian joins the plotters because Malvolio has gotten him into trouble with Olivia over a bear-baiting (2.5.7–8). As the plot is being put into action, Maria provides another of her vivid descriptions of Malvolio:

> Get ye all three into the box-tree; Malvolio's coming down this walk. He has been yonder i' the sun practicing behavior to his own shadow this half hour. Observe him, for the love of mockery; for I know this letter will make a contemplative idiot of him. Close, in the name of jesting! [*The men hide themselves.*] Lie thou there [*throws down a letter*]; for here comes the trout that must be caught with tickling. (2.5.15–22)

The remainder of this scene beggars all description. It need only be said that Malvolio in soliloquy, as he thinks, reveals an insolent, over-weening, and self-deluding character. If he had not previously revealed himself as such an unpleasant person, we might be moved to pity such total self-delusion; as it is, the fact that he aids in his own entrapment, by making sense of "M.O.A.I." and resolving to follow the insane advice given in the letter, only adds to the fun. . . .

In his next appearance, spurred on by Maria's advice, Malvolio gives his unattractive character free rein. He makes indecent suggestions to Olivia, sneers at Maria and Sir Toby, and interprets Olivia's use of the word "fellow" in a manner complimentary toward himself (3.4.29–31, 34–36, 88–90, 75–78). Finally, he reveals his contempt for all of them:

> Go hang yourselves all! You are idle shallow things, I am not

of your element. You shall know more hereafter. (3.4.123–25)

But Malvolio in adversity is quite a different character; then the "barren rascal" Feste becomes "good fool" repeatedly and is begged for favors (4.2.84–119). Although this is understandable behavior, it does not suit with Malvolio's previous pride, and it reinforces our image of him as a "time-pleaser."

A Controversial Plot Conceived by a Motley Crew

The nature and intent of the plot against Malvolio have been the subject of considerable controversy. . . . Maria develops and directs the scheme, although she eventually relinquishes control of it. But because the original idea is hers, her character is important to understanding the meaning of the revenge taken on Malvolio. There seems to be, however, little agreement as to what her character is.

Part of the difficulty of analyzing Maria is that, while a major plotter, she is only a minor character. She does not tell us her feelings; she speaks only to characters such as Olivia and Sir Toby, from whom she may be concealing her true intentions. But what she says and what she does are of a piece. She says that she will "gull [Malvolio] into a nayword, and make him a common recreation," make him an ass (she has previously told him "Go shake your ears"), and "turn him into a notable contempt" (2.3.134–35, 168–70, 125; 2.5.203–4); all of this she does. In addition, she provides hilarity for her fellow conspirators (3.2.68–69). When Olivia calls for Malvolio, Maria prepares her to assume that he is mad (3.4.8–13). Whether or not Maria is sincere in her unconcern for Malvolio's sanity, it is Sir Toby who extends the jest to the dark room; in the same speech, however, he reassures us that they will eventually "have mercy on him" (3.4.135–41, a reassurance repeated, this time out of fear of Olivia's anger, at 4.2.66–71).

Certainly . . . the device of the letter, in which he finds himself "most feelingly personated" (2.3.159) by one who hates but understands him, is simply brilliant, and the appeal to him of the supposed love letter perfectly accords with Maria's description of his vanity. Whether she has any intent to reform him must remain an open question, although her reference to "my physic" may indicate some such aim, however secondary to the "sport royal" that is the main object of the plot (2.3.172–73). That her revenge, whatever its purpose, is approved within the world of the play is proved by the fact that Maria is rewarded for it; true, her reward—marriage to Sir Toby—may not be an unmixed blessing, but presumably it is to Maria's taste.

Feste, who has perhaps the best reason to hate Malvolio, takes little part in the revenge until Malvolio is imprisoned. Then the "fool" mocks the "madman," nonsensically as Sir Topas and rationally as himself. Ultimately, however, the revenge taken on Malvolio is simply to force him to see himself as others see him. However cruel this revenge may seem to us, and regardless of its effectiveness in altering Malvolio's behavior, it is a just revenge. For, by the standards of Illyria, Malvolio, with his self-love and self-delusions, and his lack of a generous, guiltless, and free disposition, *is* mad. And it is a measure of the disregard in which Shakespeare holds him that the revenge plot against him is conceived and carried out, not by a significant character of the stature, for example, of Portia [from *The Merchant of Venice*], but by a comic cabal of a gentlewoman, a servant, a fool, a clown, and a drunkard. . . .

MALVOLIO'S UNKIND WORDS AND THE UNFORGIVEN

Malvolio's letter is both ill-bred and foolish. In it he falsely accuses and threatens a lady who is not only his social superior and employer, but who has always treated him graciously and now has him entirely in her power (as he thinks):

> By the Lord, madam, you wrong me, and the world shall know it. Though you have put me into darkness, and given your drunken cousin rule over me, yet have I the benefit of my senses as well as your ladyship. I have your own letter, that induc'd me to the semblance I put on; with the which I doubt not but to do myself much right, or you much shame. Think of me as you please. I leave my duty a little unthought of, and speak out of my injury.
>
> The madly-us'd Malvolio.
> (5.1.302–11)

Although, as Orsino remarks, "this savors not much of distraction" (5.1.314) as far as the sense of the message, it is surely a mad letter as coming from a servant to his mistress, a commoner to a great lady, or a prospective suitor to his beloved. That Malvolio can take such a tone toward Olivia, no matter what his injuries, can only increase our distaste for him, as do his accusations when he finally confronts her:

MALVOLIO: Madam, you have done me wrong,
             Notorious wrong.

OLIVIA: Have I, Malvolio? No.

> MALVOLIO: Lady, you have. Pray you, peruse that letter.
> You must not now deny it is your hand;
> Write from it if you can, in hand or phrase,
> Or say 'tis not your seal, not your invention.
> You can say none of this. Well, grant it then,
> And tell me . . .
> Why have you suffer'd me to be imprison'd,
> Kept in a dark house, visited by the priest,
> And made the most notorious geck and gull
> That e'er invention play'd on? Tell me why!

(5.1.328–44)

In giving Olivia the lie, Malvolio is wrong in courtesy, in deference, and in fact. But Olivia nevertheless responds to him with her customary graciousness

> Alas, Malvolio, this is not my writing,
> Though I confess much like the character;
> But out of question 'tis Maria's hand.
> And now I do bethink me, it was she
> First told me thou wast mad. Then cam'st in smiling,
> And in such forms which here were presuppos'd
> Upon thee in the letter. Prithee, be content.
> This practice hath most shrewdly pass'd upon thee;
> But when we know the grounds and authors of it,
> Thou shalt be both the plaintiff and the judge
> Of thine own cause.

(5.1.345–55)

This generous response, however, draws no answering generosity—nor even an apology—from Malvolio. Instead, generosity is shown by one of the revengers, who takes the burden of blame on himself, defends the justice of the plot, and expresses hope for reconciliation:

> FABIAN: Good madam, hear me speak,
> And let no quarrel nor no brawl to come
> Taint the condition of this present hour,
> Which I have wond'red at. In hope it shall not,
> Most freely I confess, myself and Toby
> Set this device against Malvolio here,
> Upon some stubborn and uncourteous parts
> We had conceiv'd against him. Maria writ
> The letter at Sir Toby's great importance,
> In recompense whereof he hath married her.
> How with a sportful malice it was follow'd
> May rather pluck on laughter than revenge,
> If that the injuries be justly weigh'd
> That have on both sides pass'd.

(5.1.355–68)

Lest this speech fail to justify the revenge taken on Malvolio, he is made to condemn himself in his final response to Olivia's sympathy and Feste's explicit moralizing:

OLIVIA: Alas, poor fool, how have they baffled thee!

FESTE: Why, "some are born great, some achieve greatness, and some have greatness thrown upon them." I was one, sir, in this enterlude— one Sir Topas, sir, but that's all one. "By the Lord, fool, I am not mad." But do you remember? "Madam, why laugh you at such a barren rascal? And you smile not, he's gagg'd." And thus the whirligig of time brings in his revenges.

MALVOLIO: I'll be reveng'd on the whole pack of you. [*Exit*]
(5.1.369–77)

Feste, who has been repeatedly praised throughout the play (2.4.11–12; 3.1.60–68; 5.1.24), has proved that this revenge, at least from his standpoint, was no more than justice; as Malvolio has denigrated his fooling, so he has helped to undermine Malvolio's reputation for rationality. . . . What has been done to Malvolio is relatively harmless and altogether deserved, and it is this kind of revenge that Feste is describing.

Feste's idea of revenge, however, is not Malvolio's, and many critics have found Malvolio's exit line a disturbing element, often on the assumption that the (self-)expulsion of Malvolio is somehow a judgment on Illyria and its inhabitants. But it seems a bit harsh to condemn Illyrian society on the basis of Malvolio's dissatisfaction with it. Although Shakespeare weaves his plots together with great skill, the happiness of the lovers has in fact nothing to do with the revenge taken on Malvolio. Nor is it correct to call this revenge mere "practical jesting": each of the major plotters has a score to settle with Malvolio, and that is what they do. But their revenge has a limit; in the end [as Eleanor Prosser contends] "Illyria seeks only Malvolio's goodwill, and with such charming people it may win him over. . . ." Whether or not Malvolio can be "converted" is a moot point; but if it is assumed that he cannot be, the assumption condemns him, rather than Illyria, whose inhabitants go much farther than those of any other comedy to make peace with the outsider in their midst.

The contrast between the behavior of Malvolio and that of Olivia and Orsino could hardly be more pronounced, and it is this contrast that damns Malvolio and finally prevents him from being a sympathetic character. Malvolio rejects the offered reconciliation and threatens the innocent as well as the guilty, whereas Olivia and Orsino, who have in no way wronged Malvolio, continue even after his vow of vengeance to placate him. Such charity speaks well for Olivia and Orsino, but by this point it is difficult to care what happens to Malvolio. Even if it can be argued that Malvolio did not, because of his injuries to Feste, Fabian, and the others, deserve what was done to him, certainly he earns his punishment retroactively in the last scene. He is freely offered forgiveness and refuses it, and for this he cannot be forgiven: [Porter Williams Jr. concludes] "No one in *Twelfth Night* entirely escapes the darkness of ignorance, but at least those who come to know generous love and friendship escape time's harshest revenges. Those who escape make it clear why the others suffered, for comedy thrives on poetic justice.". . . And poetic justice, in *Twelfth Night,* is accomplished through comic revenge.

CHAPTER 3

Themes and Concepts

READINGS ON
TWELFTH NIGHT

Twelfth Night Displays Multiple Moral Themes

Barbara Hardy

In this section from her supplement to *Twelfth Night*, literary scholar and critic Barbara Hardy cautions readers against making the common error of viewing self-deception as the only theme in the play. Although she hesitates to discount the theme of self-deception, she does ultimately demonstrate its weakness and, instead, comes to acknowledge the greater strength of other moral-based themes such as pride and folly. Hardy discusses these other themes in direct relation to the characters, concluding that theme and character are inseparable in Shakespeare's work.

There seems to be some direction and consistency in the moral criticism made in this comedy. Sir Andrew, Malvolio and Olivia have something in common. But this does not mean that we can boil down all the moral implications to a single theme. . . .

NO SINGLE THEME

Most scholars agree that the Elizabethans had a pronounced love of variety. Many Elizabethan comedies, with their multiple action, their song, dance, spectacle, plays-within-the-play, have much in common with the later Variety of music-hall, revue, radio and television. The tidy-minded scholar, even while accepting this, has a habit of preferring one answer to two or three, and in much of the discussion of *Twelfth Night* there seems to be a marked tendency to pick on a single formula for the theme. *Twelfth Night* is like most of Shakespeare's comedies, with the possible exception of the narrower didactic comedy of *Love's Labours Lost*, in being very rich in moral implications. Its pattern has the shifting variety of Feste's taffeta or opal, and is composed of many shades of human weakness and—I want to stress this—of human virtue.

A popular label in many commentaries is Self-Deception. I was taught at school that this was The Theme of the play, and many of my students take this so much for granted that they sometimes go to great lengths to apply it to all the characters and situations. I do not want to deny that Self-Deception is *a* theme. [Sir Arthur Thomas] Quiller-Couch, in his introduction to the New Cambridge edition of the play, tries hard to reduce several characters to this moral interpretation. We can certainly agree that Orsino deceives himself about the nature of love, that Olivia deceives herself about the need to mourn her brother in seclusion from the world, and that Malvolio deceives himself about Olivia's love for him. There is Self-Deception in these three characters, but the dramatic emphasis and the actual consequences are not all that similar. The critic can extract a theme here, but only by ignoring the flow of the play.

Orsino, for instance, is not entirely responsible for his fantasy: he persists partly because he is encouraged by Olivia's romantic mourning. She does not give the real sensible reason for refusing him—he has many fine qualities, she admits, but she cannot love him—until she speaks to Cesario; and even after that, for reasons of her own, she admits Orsino's embassy. What the audience first hears is Valentine's report that he has been turned away because of her vow. We need to say all this in order to recognise the emphasis placed on Orsino's illusion. We need also to compare it with Olivia's. Whereas Orsino persists until the end, Olivia's Self-Deception is brief. She drops it indeed during the very first scene in which the audience sees her, and for the rest of the play what is emphasised seems to be less Self-Deception than the deceitful male disguise of Viola. In Malvolio's case there is both Self-Deception and a very elaborate plot to deceive him, and the comic exposure and punishment of Malvolio places rather more emphasis on the evils of killjoy hypocrisy than on Self-Deception. I am not suggesting that this is all there is to it, but merely pointing out that it will not do to consider this play as a specialised dramatic discussion of a theme which is not only common to most comedy, but is moreover only one amongst several other moral themes in this play.

We need not do any forced interpretation, ignoring the dramatic emphasis, if we assume that there will probably be several themes. I would not argue that all comedies have Shakespeare's moral variety, but one of Shakespeare's great virtues is his refusal to simplify even in comedy. I suggest that we could make a list of several other themes as prominent as Self-Deception.

We could call it a play about Pride, which is present in Orsino, Olivia, Malvolio, and the other characters. Even Viola is accused of Pride by Olivia, and Feste's motive for baiting Malvolio is the injury to his professional Pride. It is in many cases Pride which causes the fall.

Or we could call it a play about Folly. This is *Twelfth Night*, the Feast of Misrule, when law and order are turned upside down and Folly given its head. A Count is rejected for

---

APPEARANCE REFLECTS THE TRUE SELF

Adding to the many thematic interpretations of Twelfth Night, *Brown University's Karen Newman—Professor of Comparative Literature, English, and Women's Studies—considers a Renaissance theme: appearance as a reflection of the true self. The confusion caused by Viola's disguise exemplifies the popular neo-Platonic idea that love and appearance are connected, and Viola's purpose, then, is to lead Olivia and Orsino to discovery of the loves they seek.*

Olivia does not fall in love with Cesario's soul . . . but with his "perfections" which crept in through her eyes. The quality of her love is not undermined by the winning appearance of the man she loves, for his identity all along is subsumed in what Viola/Cesario calls her "outside" (II, ii, 17). Through that outside Olivia has "insight" into Sebastian's nature and identity. The epicene [both male and female] figure of Cesario can be compared to a *trompe l'oeil* perspectivist painting [a painting style that fools the viewer]. When Olivia sees him from her point of view, she "sees" Sebastian; when Orsino looks at Cesario, he "sees" Viola. The figure of Cesario illustrates the ambiguous Renaissance attitude toward the verbal-visual problem which fascinated poets and theorists alike. Cesario's "outside" is both an accurate and a mistaken reflection of reality; his sexual ambiguity embodies both twins and neither.

One of the recurring themes of the play is whether or not appearance reflects the true self. In her first scene Viola speculates on the captain's inner nature:

a page, and a woman at that. Olivia drops her foolish vow in a foolish susceptibility to outside appearance. The grave steward apes madness and is handed over to Sir Toby, drunken Lord of Misrule. The Fool plays Sir Topas. Everyone, except the Fool, is made a fool of in these reversals, and Folly is given almost a ritual celebration in the baiting of Malvolio.

Folly is given its head, but criticised too. The Fool, as in other plays, is given the task of calling wise men fools. Olivia, Malvolio, Sir Toby, and Orsino are all accused of being mad or foolish. Viola and Sir Andrew are the only characters to call themselves fools.

We could go on, but I hope the point has been made. Shakespeare does not make one criticism of one failing. Nor indeed does he content himself with attack. His dramatic

> And though that nature with a beauteous wall
> Doth oft close in pollution, yet of thee
> I will believe thou hast a mind that suits
> With this thy fair and outward character.

(I, ii, 48–51)

Later in III, iv, Antonio mistakes Cesario for Sebastian and is rebuffed. He laments that "to his image, which methought did promise/Most venerable worth . . . Thou hast, Sebastian, done good feature shame." Though "a beauteous wall/Doth oft close in pollution," the action of the play argues that outward appearance finally reflects inward truth, even in the complex case of Cesario. To fault Shakespeare's conception of identity in human relations by saying that they are reduced to physical appearance alone is to ignore the importance in the Renaissance of appearance as a speaking picture of the inner self. Such an attitude was no doubt influenced by widely diffused neo-Platonic doctrines which taught that visible beauty bespoke hidden reality. Throughout the sixteenth century and certainly in Shakespeare there is an uneasy trust in the relationship between the visual sign and its inner meanings, if one is initiated, like Viola, into the rites of "seeing." Viola's role is to lead both Olivia and Orsino to recognize in Cesario what they seek in love.

Karen Newman, "Magic Versus Time: *As You Like It* and *Twelfth Night*," *Shakespeare's Rhetoric of Comic Character: Dramatic Convention in Classical and Renaissance Comedy.* New York and London: Methuen, 1985, pp. 104–105.

rendering of positive moral strength is an important feature of his comic spirit.

CHARACTER AND THEME ARE INSEPARABLE IN SHAKESPEARE'S MORAL BALANCE

Even characters who are presented critically are endowed on occasion with admirable qualities. Orsino can admit, at the cost of contradicting himself, that men exaggerate and may be less constant than women. When we first meet Olivia she rebukes Feste and Malvolio with sense and gravity, and does not impress us as being a romantic self-deceiver. It is true that we must not fall into the old trap of treating every detail as a psychological clue. Orsino's comments are there partly in the interests of the dramatic irony and Olivia's rebukes are important guides to the character of Feste and Malvolio and start off their quarrel. But although such details contribute to good theatrical situations I do not think we can ignore the way in which they affect our impression of the speakers. They do something to modify our first view of Orsino and our first account of Olivia, and they fit with difficulty into a view of Self-Deception as the only theme.

In Olivia's case there are many examples of sense and unromantic honesty which are plainly part of dramatic portraiture. When she talks about her love for Viola she is self-critical and matter-of-fact. She knows that her eye is too great a flatterer for her mind, she knows she is being headstrong and unreasonable. In the dialogues with Viola she has dignity, sense, and a wry humour, which make her a person too complex to be fitted into the usual themes. We might indeed argue that the romantic mournful Olivia is one we are *told* about but never shown. She is not present in these lines:

Why then methinks 'tis time to smile again (3.1)

and

Be not afraid, good youth, I will not have you (3.1.)

There are many comedies which criticise harshly and some which present no normal moral standard within the play. [Shakespeare's colleague and rival Ben] Jonson and [English Restoration playwright William] Wycherley, though very different from each other, are two examples of pejorative satirists of this kind. Shakespeare combines satire and sympathy, praise and blame, and this is one reason for calling this play good-tempered. We can draw up a list of virtues which correspond to the weaknesses. If there is Self-Deception, there is Candour and Insight. If there is Pride, it is true and false, with humility thrown in for good measure. If it is about killjoy criticism it is also about Enjoyment and Gusto. And opposite qualities often appear in the same character. But Shakespeare does not merely temper his criticism within weak characters, he also shows strength. Viola is the main source of all these qualities I have just mentioned and although she is involved, by accident, in Deception, Folly, and Misunderstanding, she reacts with honesty, sense, and insight. The problem of theme, as I hope you realise, cannot be separated from character.

The Game of Romantic Love

Robin Headlam Wells

Through close analysis of *Twelfth Night*, Professor Robin Headlam Wells of the University of Hull in England reveals that the characters are players in a game of romantic love. Wells, an expert on popular Elizabethan concepts and viewpoints, considers the classical and medieval origins of the game and its rules, well known to the Elizabethans. He examines the ability of the characters as players as well as the necessary trappings of the game: wealth, leisure time, and unrequited love. However, as Wells notes, there is a dark tone which prevails in the comedy so that romantic love in Illyria is fleeting along with the youth of the players. He concludes that the songs about love which permeate the play become symbolic of this ephemeral quality of romantic love.

Like Shakespeare's other romantic comedies, *Twelfth Night* portrays a world apparently dominated by fortune. In a play about anything as capricious as romantic love this is natural enough. As Orsino says in his opening speech, "so full of shapes is fancie / That it alone, is high fantasticall" (I.i.14–15). It is because, as Bottom says, "reason and loue keepe little company together" (*A Midsummer Night's Dream*, III.i.132) that lovers are so vulnerable to fortune. . . .

It is the folly and at the same time the irresistibility of romantic love that is Shakespeare's great comic theme.

ROMANTIC LOVE: ITS GAME RULES AND REQUIREMENTS

Twelfth Night differs from the other romantic comedies in two respects; first, because it conspicuously lacks the kind of moralizing judgments that are normally found in the comedies and love tragedies; and second, because of its emphasis on the brevity of youth, and therefore of romantic love. But if love is sad in *Twelfth Night* it is not because "Warre, death, or sicknesse, did lay siege to it" (*MND*, I.i.142), or even because of parental interference. In fact there are no parents in the play. Unlike most of the other comedies, which divide their time between two worlds—a holiday world of romance and laughter, and a contrasting world of harsh domestic, political or commercial realities—*Twelfth Night* has only one location. . . . Illyria contains no natural obstacles to impede the course of love. The romantic confusions in this land of Cockaigne [imaginary land of luxury and ease] are all self-generated. Moreover, despite the widely held view that they are self-deceivers, the major characters know exactly what they are doing. They are playing a game. That game is called romantic Love.

It might be thought that the most essential characteristic of romantic love is its spontaneity. When played as a game, however, it is the reverse. Romantic love has two features that are common to all successful games; it is of compelling interest to the players; and its rules are both complex and very precise. Those rules had been codified by many writers including, most notably, Ovid in the ancient world, and Andreas Capellanus and Guillaume de Lorris in the Middle Ages. The Elizabethans knew them by heart. . . .

The fact that rules are essential to games of every kind does not mean that powerful emotions may not be involved: as any poker-player knows, in many games the ability to conceal strong feelings is one of the marks of a skilful player. Like the successful gambler, the player in the game of love must adopt an "aquentable" social manner. But inwardly he will be tormented by the vicissitudes of his passion. . . . In short, the lover is a type and example of mutability; like fortune itself. . . .

The vicissitudes of love catalogued at such length by Guillaume are the result of unrequited passion. The anguish, the torment, the bitter-sweet joy experienced by the lover are all the consequence of unfulfilled desire. When the thirst for passion is slaked, all these emotions disappear and are replaced by different ones. Love may blossom or it may wither; but once the conditions essential for its existence have been removed, it will no longer be romantic love. That can only flourish when desire is met by impossible obstacles. . . .

Though not so essential, certain other conditions are also necessary if the game of love is to approximate to the level of

the high art described by Guillaume. Medieval representa-
tions of the court of Venus describe the romantic setting of her
temple with flowers, music and sweet odours augmenting the
aphrodisiac effects of food and wine. Among her courtiers are
not only Youth, Grace, Nobility and Charm, but also Elegance,
Affability, Courtesy and Patience. But the most illustrious of
them is Wealth, for only a monied society can afford the
leisure that can free the mind from other distractions and allow it to devote itself exclusively to the business of passion. . . .

Romantic love is above all a social art, relying partly on
gesture and performance, but also on the written, spoken
and sung word. Although, as the beautifully constructed
wooing scenes in *Sir Gawain and the Green Knight* show so
well, the game of love can be played perfectly satisfactorily
by two players in private, it is obvious that far greater scope
is offered to skilful performers if there is a knowledgeable
audience to appreciate their art. Finally, it is money alone
that can provide the costumes, the professionally produced
music and the food that create a sympathetic environment
in which to act out the rituals of love.

ORSINO AS DEDICATED PLAYER TO LOVE GAMES

The opening scene of *Twelfth Night* immediately establishes
Orsino's court as a neo-medieval temple of Venus waiting for
its goddess to emerge, like Viola, from the sea. With its music, its ease, its luxury, its canopies of flowers and its poetic
grace, Illyria's ducal palace is dedicated to one purpose
alone: homage to the goddess of love. As the master of so
much wealth Orsino can take his pick from among the
fairest ladies in Illyria. However, he must choose carefully,
for the game of love cannot progress beyond the first move if
the lady is not unattainable. But Orsino is an experienced
player. He chooses someone who fits his purpose beautifully, a lady who has vowed to immure herself for seven
years in memory of her brother's death. . . . A hedonist
Orsino may be, but he cannot be accused of self-deception
when he shows so clearly that he knows exactly what he is
doing. Declaring his passion for Olivia "with fertill teares, /
With groanes, that thunder loue, with sighes of fire"
(I.v.256–7), he is every inch the correct lover described by
Guillaume. When his servant informs him that Olivia is un-
available, he does not collapse in hysterics, like Romeo [of
Romeo and Juliet]. But then why should he? It is, after all,

only a game. Instead, he asks Valentine to lead him away "to sweet beds of Flowres" to plan his next move, for "Loue-thoughts lye rich, when canopy'd with bowres" (I.i.41-2). His is a polished and knowing performance.

With the arrival of Viola at Illyria's court of Venus a new dimension is added to the game of love: Orsino now has a go-between to "act his woes" (I.iv.26) to Olivia. But, more important, he also has a willing and sympathetic audience at the spectacle of his passion. The nature of that passion is epitomized in the song he arranges to be performed for Viola in act II scene iv:

> Come away, come away, death;
> And in sad cypresse let me be laide;
>   Fye away, fie away, breath,
> I am slaine by a faire cruell maide:
> My shrowde of white, stuck all with Ew,
>   O, prepare it.
> My part of death no one so true
>   Did share it.
>
>   Not a flower, not a flower sweete,
> On my blacke coffin, let there be strewne;
>   Not a friend, not a friend greet
> My poor corpes, where my bones shall be throwne;
> A thousand thousand sighes to saue,
>   Lay me o where
> Sad true louer neuer find my graue,
>   To weepe there.

Though no contemporary setting of Shakespeare's lyrics has been identified, there are numberless analogues in the contemporary lute song repertory testifying to the irresistible appeal for the Elizabethans of this kind of melancholy song. As it lingers self-indulgently over the funeral arrangements for a death we know to be feigned, Feste's romantic dirge serves both a mimetic and an affective function: it is intended not only to mirror in music the feelings that are its subject, but also to evoke in Viola a sympathetic response to Orsino's chosen plight. When it is over she is silent. But this should not be read as the disillusioned reaction of one who perceives that the man she loves is no more than an idle voluptuary. Viola, no less than Orsino, is addicted to the "sweet pangs" of unrequited love. It is her song as much as his. If Viola's disguise prevents Orsino from seeing in her a possible opponent for him in the game of love, he does recognize her skill as a player. . . . He tries to draw her out and persuade her to reveal something of her true self. But Viola is only too aware of the dangers of unguarded self-revelation and counters his moves with such skill that he is moved to compliment her on her game: "Thou dost speake masterly," he tells her (II.iv.21).

EVEN EXPERT PLAYERS VIOLATE THE RULES

Viola's successful performance is testimony both to her talent as a player and also to her knowledge of the rules of the game of love. That knowledge is perhaps best revealed in her exchanges with Olivia, where it is she who now has the upper hand. Her reply to Olivia's question at I.v.251 regarding the correct presentation of love is a model catechist's [one who participates in oral questioning as a test, usually religious] response. . . .

> VIO: If I did loue you in my masters flame,
> With such a suffring, such a deadly life,
> In your deniall I would finde no sence,
> I would not understand it.
> OLI: Why, what would you?
> VIO: Make me a willow Cabine at your gate,
> And call upon my soule within the house,
> Write loyall Cantons of contemned loue
> And sing them lowd euen in the dead of night:
> Hallow your name to the reuerberate hilles,
> And make the babling Gossip of the aire
> Cry out *Olivia:* O you should not rest
> Betweene the elements of ayre, and earth
> But you should pittie me. (I.v.248–60)

Viola's words are, of course, full of irony. Not only is she inviting Olivia to make a fool of herself by adopting a masculine role in the game of love, and thereby violating one of its most fundamental rules, but she is herself acting a part. Moreover, she relishes that part, taking conscious pleasure in her talent, and sufficiently confident of her own performance to be able to laugh at its absurdity.

The ability to laugh at your own performance is a valuable asset to the player of a game as essentially absurd as romantic love. Another important quality that Viola possesses is patience. . . . Viola's little allegory in act II scene iv shows that she is well versed in love's lore. But despite her archly histrionic representation of herself as Patience on a monument wanly smiling at grief (II.iv.109–14), she never relaxes her guard in her verbal sparring with Orsino. She may drop hints of her feelings towards the duke, but she does not lose her self-possession. The dangers of doing so are made clear in the second of her three private interviews with Olivia.

Like Orsino and Viola, Olivia is an experienced player who recognizes the importance of concealing one's true feelings. For all its romantic accoutrements, the game of love can be a harshly competitive affair. Beneath the surface talk of "Roses of the Spring" (III.i.146) there may be lurking "scorne," "contempt" and "anger" (142–3). Perceiving that she is in danger of falling "prey" to her "enemy" (125; 122), Olivia knows that "'tis time to smile agen" (123). But having wisely decided to save face by allowing Viola to leave, she then commits an unforgivable error: she asks Viola what her real feelings towards her are: "I prethee tell me what thou thinkst of me?" (135). Blushing with embarrassment at such a *faux pas* [blunder] (143–4), Viola tries to restore a sense of decorum to their game by shifting the exchange back to its proper level of equivocation. But the damage has been done and Olivia later regrets that

> There's something in me that reproues my fault:
> But such a head-strong potent fault it is,
> That it but mockes reproofe.   (III.iv.193–5)

But if she lacks the self-possession that is the mark of the truly accomplished player, Olivia does at least know how to lose gracefully. Acknowledging her defeat, she turns loss into gain by making a joke of the whole affair:

> Well, come again to morrow: far-thee-well,
> A Fiend like thee might beare my soule to hell.   (III.iv.206–7)

GAME RULES ARE TOO SOPHISTICATED FOR MALVOLIO

Twelfth Night portrays a sophisticated, elegant social world in which the major characters are all adept and skilful players in the game of love. Whether they lose or win they are alike in the pleasure they take in the verbal sparring that is really the essence of their game. But there is one character who does not enjoy the game of love. Malvolio's humiliation is due not to want of skill, but to ignorance of the game's most basic rules. Indeed, with his puritan sensibility he is antipathetic to the very idea of play. Little wonder that he is detested in Illyria.

Malvolio has presumably read his text-books and is aware that the way to a lady's heart may well begin with haberdashery [a man's clothing accessories]. . . . His error is to mistake game for earnest and to attribute to fortune ("'Tis but Fortune, all is fortune" (II.v.21)) what is in fact the work of comic design. The gulf that divides the puritan from his adversaries is epitomized by the way each responds to music. Act II scene iii shows Sir Toby and Sir Andrew at their most convivial, cracking puerile jokes and singing drunken catches "without any mitigation or remorse of voice." Their merriment is interrupted by Malvolio. Reproving them for their irresponsibility, he demands of them with dour self-righteousness "Is there no respect of place, persons, nor time in you?" (88). Feste and Sir Toby respond, not with a simple riposte, but by weaving a magic net of sound in which the helpless Malvolio can only flounder and gasp. In a buffoonish antiphony they sing alternate lines from a recently published popular song. The song is from Robert Jones' *First Booke of Songes and Ayres* (1600) and tells of a foolishly vacillating lover who cannot bring himself to leave his cruel-hearted mistress:

> Farewel dear love since thou wilt needs be gon,
> Mine eies do shew my life is almost done,
>> Nay I will never die,
>> So long as I can spie,
>> Ther by many mo
>> Though that she do go
> There be many mo I feare not,
> Why then let her goe I care not.
>
> Farewell, farewell, since this I finde is true,
> I will not spend more time in wooing you:
>> But I will seeke elswhere,
>> If I may find her there,
>> Shall I bid her goe,
>> What and if I doe?
> Shall I bid her go and spare not,
> Oh no no no no I dare not.
>
> Ten thousand times farewell, yet stay a while,
> Sweet kisse me once, sweet kisses time beguile:
>> I have no power to move,
>> How now, am I in love
>> Wilt thou needs be gone?
>> Go then, all is one,
> Wilt thou needs be gone? oh hie thee,
> Nay, stay and doe no more denie mee.
>
> Once more farewell, I see loth to depart,
> Bids oft adew to her that holdes my hart:
>> But seeing I must loose,
>> Thy love which I did chuse:

> Go thy waies for me,
> Since it may not be,
> Go thy waies for me, but whither?
> Go, oh but where I may come thither.

> What shall I doe? my love is now departed,
> Shee is as faire as shee is cruell harted:
> Shee would not be intreated,
> With praiers oft repeated:
> If shee come no more,
> Shall I die therefore,
> If she come no more, what care I?
> Faith, let her go, or come, or tarry.

Olivia's arrogant admirer has probably never heard of Jones' song, and in any case, the script has not yet been written for the play in which he himself is to perform the role of foolish lover. But it is clear enough to Malvolio that Feste's and Sir Toby's innuendos refer to him in some way that is not favourable. With his natural suspicion of music and its powers of exciting the passions, the puritan is here symbolically trapped and caught by what he most deprecates. When he has gone Maria diagnoses his problem. "Marrie sir," she tells Sir Toby, "sometimes he is a kinde of Puritane" (131).

A distaste for puritan sanctimony is something that Maria shares with her mistress. Olivia's censure of Malvolio's dyspeptic puritanism is in effect a defence of social games-playing:

> OLI: O, you are sicke of selfe-loue, *Maluolio,* and taste with
> a distemper'd appetite. To be generous, guiltlesse, and
> of free disposition, is to take those things for Birdbolts,
> that you deeme Cannon bullets: There is no slander in
> an allow'd foole, though he do nothing but rayle.
> (I.v.85–90)

But if we are expected to endorse Olivia's plea for a generous and free disposition that can laugh at raillery, there is more than a little truth in Malvolio's counter-attack on his tormenters. There is a real sense in which not only Maria, Sir Toby and Sir Andrew, but also Orsino, Olivia and Viola are "ydle shallowe things" (III.iv.118). . . . It is precisely because they do not need to work for a living that they are able to commit themselves so exclusively to the service of their goddess. Theirs is a life dedicated, no less than Sir Toby's, to play. Where he and his companions are content with a buffoonery that requires few rules, their play is of a different order. They have raised the game of love to a sophisticated art.

Their lives are a performance. But, like any performance, it is an essentially transitory one. Critics of *Twelfth Night* often remind us that this is a play whose title hints not only at the festive origins of its mood, but also at the fact that holidays presuppose a workaday world to which we must all sooner or later return. But there is a larger sense in which the aristocratic world of Illyria is overshadowed by change.

AN EPHEMERAL EXPERIENCE: SONGS REFLECT ROMANTIC LOVE

The theme of mutability pervades *Twelfth Night*. But it is expressed most poignantly in Feste's beautiful song in act II scene iii:

> O Mistris mine where are you roming?
> O stay and heare, your true loues coming,
>   That can sing both high and low.
> Trip no further prettie sweeting.
> Journeys end in louers meeting,
>   Euery wise mans sonne doth knowe.
>
> What is loue, tis not heerafter,
> Present mirth, hath present laughter:
>   What's to come, is still vnsure.
> In delay there lies no plentie,
> Then come kisse me, sweet and twentie:
>   Youths a stuffe will not endure.

In Thomas Morley's eloquently simple setting *O Mistress Mine* evokes the sweetness and the delight of courtship and anticipates the happy conclusion of loves journey, suggesting idealistically that such unions always receive the blessing of age and wisdom. But the facile optimism of the first stanza is qualified by the radically different tone of the second. Despite the assertion that "Journeys end in louers meeting," it insists on the impermanence of "present laughter" and concludes with the commonplace reminder that "Youths a stuffe will not endure. . . ."

The themes implicit in *O Mistress Mine* are rehearsed for the last time in Feste's valedictory song. The world evoked in this balladeer's version of the ancient *topos* [a standard rhetorical theme or topic] of the four ages of man is a bleak and loveless world in which human beings do not gain wisdom with age and in which the only principle of constancy is the rain that raineth every day. . . .

Twelfth Night reminds us of how "the whirlegigge of time, brings in its reuenges" we are brought back from the world of self-indulgent games to the reality not of work, but of mutability. When Orsino tells Viola that "women are as Roses, whose faire flowre, / Being once displaid, doth fall that verie howre," she caps his maxim with an equally sententious couplet:

And so they are: alas, that they are so:
To die, euen when they to perfection grow.   (II.iv.37–40)

Although she is talking, like him, simply of youth and love, there lies behind her words that sense of the transitoriness of civilization which the Elizabethans inherited from the late Middle Ages. It is a commonplace embodied in some of the age's greatest literature that not only flowers and women, but also civilizations, begin "to die, even when they to perfection grow." The idea is never explicitly articulated in the play. The most you can say is that, with its sense of sadness and dereliction, this play seems to reflect that sense of national decline that is such a characteristic feature of the period.

For the Cavalier lyricists writing on the eve of revolution romantic love was a uniquely appropriate theme because it embodied so vividly their sense of mutability. Like the societies that created it, romantic love is fragile, artificial and above all impermanent. For, paradoxically, no sooner are the lover's wishes fulfilled than romantic love must die. . . . This is why the happiness of *Twelfth Night*'s conclusion is tinged (as almost every critic of the play points out) with sadness. The multiple marriage, which in Elizabethan comedy conventionally symbolizes the restoration of social and personal harmony, here spells the death of romantic love. In the happiness of the marriage partners lies their sorrow. It is this paradox that *Twelfth Night*'s songs embody.

In a general sense it is obvious that *Twelfth Night*'s music reflects its mood of self-indulgent melancholy: as Viola says, "It giues a verie eccho to the seate / Where loue is thron'd" (II.iv.20–1). But there is a more important sense in which the play's music enacts its theme. Feste's art songs not only express but actually embody the paradoxical truth about romantic love that is the play's subject. Beautiful, brief and sad, they are like concrete symbols of the love they describe. . . . they are poems, that is, which enact aesthetically not the visual but the abstract nature of their subject.

As lyrics on the printed page these songs are not much more than pretty clichés, stereotyped variations on the conventional commonplaces of a literary tradition. But when set to music and performed on the stage they take on a different meaning. Unlike the reader, who can return to the words on the page as many times as he or she wishes, the audience in the theatre hears the songs only once. A fixed and permanent artefact is for the audience a transitory experience. The brevity of these songs is part of their meaning: like the love they describe, they are not only beautiful and sad, but also ephemeral.

Madness in Paradise: Restoring Peace to Illyria

Barbara K. Lewalski

Illyria is one of Shakespeare's many places of retreat, but, unlike the other places, the characters who retreat to Illyria do not leave it and are not altered by it. Rather, these characters—Viola and Sebastian—enter Illyria and they restore the peace to this "refuge." According to Harvard English professor Barbara K. Lewalski, although there is the presence of good will and celebration, there is also madness, disorder, and self-delusion which requires rectification. Feste and Maria are able to assist with partial restoration of the order through their insight and wit, but it is up to the outsiders to restore the peace. Lewalski perceives the twins as the fulfillment of the Christian promise of Divine Love that is celebrated on Twelfth Night as the Epiphany—the revelation of the Christ-child to the Magi. As such, only the twins who represent perfect order and perfect love—the body and the spirit represented in Christ—can restore Illyria from the disorder and madness.

Illyria is one of several idealized locales in Shakespeare's romantic comedies and romances, a "second world" markedly different from and in most respects better than the real world by reason of its pervasive atmosphere of song and poetry. Its dominant concern with love and the "good life" (that is, the life of revelry), and its freedom from any malicious villany. Other idealized locales such as the Forest of Arden [in *As You Like It*], the forest of *A Midsummer Night's Dream,* Prospero's island [in *The Tempest*], and Perdita's pastoral refuge [in *The Winter's Tale*], present what . . . [critic] John Vyvyan

Excerpted from "Thematic Patterns in *Twelfth Night*," by Barbara K. Lewalski in *Shakespeare Studies: An Annual Gathering of Research, Criticism, and Reviews,* edited by J. Leeds Barroll. Reprinted with permission from Barbara K. Lewalski.

labels "retreats in the wilderness" into which characters move from the world outside, within which they establish new comic relationships and clarifications, and from which they then return to the real world. But the case with Illyria is different: the characters who enter it from outside, Viola and Sebastian, do not leave it again; moreover they are not formed or altered by it, or in it, or under its influence, but they are themselves the chief agents in reordering and perfecting Illyrian life.

ILLYRIA EMBODIES GOOD WILL, NEEDS RESTORATION FROM MADNESS

Something of the special quality of Illyria is indicated by the first use of the name in the dialogue, as Viola specifically contrasts Illyria with Elysium:

VIOLA: What country, friends, is this?
CAPTAIN: This is Illyria, lady.
VIOLA: And what should I do in Illyria?
            My brother he is in Elysium.   (I.ii.1–4)

At the same time, however, Illyria is related to Elysium through the melodic, romantic sound of the two words and their identical syntactical positions. Indeed the dominant Illyrian concern with song, music, poetry, good cheer, and love gives the place an idyllic, Elysium-like atmosphere. This idyllic aspect may be more precisely defined when one considers that the avowed antagonist of Illyria's accustomed life and activities is Malvolio—Bad Will—whose name is justified and interpreted by Olivia's comment, "O, you are sick of self-love, Malvolio, and taste with a distempered appetite. To be generous, guiltless, and of free disposition, is to take those things for birdbolts that you deem cannon bullets" (I.v.85–88). If Malvolio's "Bad Will" (self-love) constitutes the antagonistic force to the life of Illyria we may be directed by this fact to the recognition that the Elysium-like quality of this place emanates from a festival atmosphere of *Good Will* which has banished active malice and radical selfishness and has created a genuine community. These terms invite recall of the Christmas message proclaimed by the angels, rendered in the Geneva bible [London, 1599] as "peace on earth, and towards men good will. . . ." Illyria would seem to be a realm ready for, open to, and perhaps already experiencing in some measure the restoration and "peace" promised in the angelic message: the charity of the play's spirit is such that Malvolio himself is invited at the conclusion to share in this special condition. This context gives significance to the full title of the play, *Twelfth Night: Or, What You Will.* Instead of being merely an invitation to whimsical response and interpretation the subtitle would seem to point to the thematic opposition of Good and Bad Will in the play, and to the fact that the promises of the Christmas season attend upon or include the spirit of Good Will.

But if Illyria is in some respects related to Elysium as a place of Good Will exhibiting the spirit of the season, it is also a place much in need of the restoration and peace of the Christmastide promises. The name Illyria may be intended to suggest illusion in the sense of distortion, disorder, and faulty perception of self and others; at any rate, as [the critic John Russell] J.R. Brown has pointed out, these are all dominant features of Illyrian life. [The critic C.L.] Barber notes that "madness" is a key word in this play: almost every character exclaims about the madness and disorder afflicting other people and sometimes himself as well. Malvolio coming to stop the midnight revels of Sir Toby and Sir Andrew asks, "My masters, are you mad?" (II.iii.80). Sir Toby in his cups is said by Olivia to speak "nothing but madman" (I.v.101–102). Malvolio's ridiculous behavior after he is gulled by Maria's letter is termed a "very midsummer madness" (III.iv.51). Olivia identifies her love-madness with what she thinks to be Malvolio's real lunacy, "I am as mad as he, / If sad and merry madness equal be" (III.iv.13–14). Orsino describes his fancy as "high fantastical" (I.i.15). Sebastian subjected to the apparently gratuitous attack of Andrew Aguecheek asks, "Are all the people mad?" (IV.i.25). Feste asks the supposed lunatic Malvolio, "Tell me true, are you not mad indeed? or do you but counterfeit?" (IV.ii. 110–111). This pervasive "madness," while it is not malicious or vicious and may even be in some respects restorative, nevertheless leads each person whom it afflicts towards a culpable self-centeredness and a potentially dangerous indulgence of emotional excess. Illyria is badly in need of restoration to order and peace, but such a restoration as will also preserve the merriment, sponteneity, and sense of human community displayed in the "mad" state.

CHARACTERS OF MADNESS AND "DISORDERED PASSIONS"

Malvolio, by repudiating any share in the Illyrian "madness," shows himself more lunatic than any, for he repudiates thereby the greatest goods of human life and the common bonds of human kind, love and merrymaking. His fundamental "bad will" is shown both in his attempted repression of merrymaking which calls forth Sir Toby's immortal comment, "Dost thou think, because thou art virtuous, there shall be no more cakes and ale?" (II.iii.105–106), and in his loveless, wholly ambition-motivated aspiration to wed his mistress Olivia. . . . One whose self-regard, self-delusion, and absurd ambition cause him to exclude himself deliberately from human merriment and human love is obviously a greater madman than the most abandoned reveller or the most fantastic lover in Illyria, and Maria's trick, which causes Malvolio to be taken for a lunatic, points symbolically to the real lunacy of his values. . . .

Sir Toby Belch, Sir Andrew Aguecheek, and Fabian represent the life dedicated to good cheer and merriment, song and revelry, which is constantly escaping from "the modest limits of order" (I.iii.7–8). But though usually engaging and harmless this love of disorder and revelry also shows a less attractive side: Toby reveals his capacity for selfish manipulation in defrauding his boon companion Andrew Aguecheek out of his fortune on the pretext that Andrew has a chance for Olivia's hand, and Andrew demonstrates the same trait by aspiring to Olivia chiefly as a means to recoup the fortunes wasted on revelry. Also, Toby's jests sometimes have a potential for unconscious cruelty: witness the pain caused to Viola disguised as Cesario when Toby engineers a dual between Cesario and Andrew.

Olivia displays two varieties of disordered passion. Her melancholy takes the form of excessive grief and ostentatious mourning rituals for her dead brother, appropriately described in Valentine's exaggerated language: "The element itself, till seven years' heat, / Shall not behold her face at ample view: / But like a cloistress she will veilèd walk, / And water once a day her chamber round / With eye-offending brine" (I.i.27–31). This melancholic grief gives her some common bond with that scorner of pleasure and love, Malvolio: she herself declares that his "sad and civil" demeanor is appropriate to her state (III.iv.4–5), and he suggests the same point when he denies her any community of feeling with Sir Toby, "she's nothing allied to your disorders" (II.iii.89). But Toby knows well that he is "consanguineous," that he is "of her blood" (II.iii.71). That Toby has the right of it is clear when Olivia falls madly in love with Viola-Cesario, developing hereby a new madness which acts in some ways as a restorative in that it draws her away from the bad will, the self-love that Malvolio represents and fixes her devotion upon a worthy object. . . .

The Duke Orsino, indulging his unrequited passion for Olivia, is in the throes of another kind of madness—love-melancholy—characterized by giddy appetite, unregulated fancy, self-indulgence. . . . He gives way to, and indeed takes pride in, the "unstaid and skittish" behavior which he thinks proclaims him a lover, and seems oblivious to the self-contradiction in his logic when he first proclaims to Cesario that men's fancies in love are "more giddy and unfirm, / More longing, wavering, sooner lost and worn, / Than women's are," and a few moments later observes that women's love lacks "retention. / Alas, their love may be called appetite, / No motion of the liver but the palate, / That suffers surfeit, cloyment, and revolt" (II.iv.17, 32–34, 95–98). Orsino's disorder also has its darker side: it is based upon self-delusion, for the viewer sees that Orsino is in love with *love* rather than with Olivia; it leads to disregard of the lady's feelings in being unable to love him, manifested especially when he urges Cesario to "leap all civil bounds" in pressing his suit; and it leads finally to a frenzy of jealousy and hurt pride wherein he offers violence to his beloved page Cesario: "I'll sacrifice the lamb that I do love / To spite a raven's heart within a dove" (V.i.124–125).

MARIA AND FESTE: ILLYRIAN NATIVES WITH RESTORATIVE QUALITIES

Opposition to the forces of self-love and disorder in Illyria is offered by certain characters who embrace wholeheartedly the human activities of love and merrymaking but who are preserved from "madness" by positive ordering principles within themselves and who project these principles as forces to restore and reorder the community.

Maria embodies one such restorative force within Illyria: sheer wit. Early in the play Feste points to her special quality, terming her "as witty a piece of Eve's flesh as any in Illyria" (I.v.25–26). Maria employs her wit as contriver and executor of the masterful plot against Malvolio: her faked letter is cleverly framed so as to confirm Malvolio's self-delusions about Olivia's regard for him, and the letter's recommendations that Malvolio affect yellow stockings, cross-garters, constant smiles, and surly behavior are brilliantly calculated to insure his self-exposure. The power of Maria's wit is thus addressed to the revelation and punishment of the "madness" involved in self-delusion, self-love, and hypo-critic affectation of virtue. Maria's wit becomes an instru-ment for further reformation when Sir Toby Belch out of sheer delight in her witty plot offers to marry her: there can be little doubt from her success in managing Sir Toby and his associates throughout the play that she will succeed henceforward through wit in controlling Toby's excesses without in the least repressing his gaiety.

The clown Feste is the second force working from within to reorder and perfect Illyria. In many respects he is Malvolio's opposite, incarnating the spirit of festival Good Will. He fre-quents Orsino's court as well as Olivia's house, takes part in the midnight revels of Sir Toby, and masquerades as Sir Topas the clergyman coming to exorcise "Malvolio the lunatic," ex-plaining this ubiquity in the following terms, "Foolery, sir, does walk about the orb like the sun; it shines everywhere" (III.i.37–38). His foolery is a consciously adopted and con-trolled foolery which is a far cry from the madness and disor-der rampant in Illyria; it is compacted of wit and song and is firmly aligned with the forces of love and merrymaking, but is conscious also of other perspectives and harsh realities.

One aspect of Feste's restorative role is his function as "li-censed Fool" exercising his wit to stalk wise men's folly: as Viola declares, "This fellow is wise enough to play the fool, / And to do that well craves a kind of wit. / . . . For folly that he wisely shows, is fit; / But wise men, folly-fall'n, quite taint their wit" (III. i.58–66). Feste's jest displaying Olivia as a fool in mourning for a brother whom she believes to be in heaven, achieves considerable success: its curative effect upon Olivia is immediately evident in her compliment to his wit, her defense of the fool's role against Malvolio's diatribe, and her keen insight into Malvolio's "self-love." But Orsino is less responsive to the fool's jest upon his giddy love melancholy—"Now the melancholy god protect thee, and the tailor make thy doublet of changeable taffeta, for thy mind is a very opal" (II.iv.72–74)—although his discordant passions are often soothed by that other important aspect of the fool's role, his song. Feste also undertakes the care of the reeling Sir Toby when his drunkenness has progressed to the stage of "madness," declaring, "the fool shall look to the madman" (I.v.131–132). . . .

VIOLA AND SEBASTIAN ENTER, RESTORING PEACE

The forces of wit and festival—of Good Will—can do much to reorder and restore Illyria but they cannot do everything. They can in large part reclaim Olivia from melancholic surrender to excessive grief, they can control and care for Sir Toby, they can expose the real "lunacy" of Malvolio and cast him forth as comic Satan into the bondage and darkness which was supposedly the fate of Satan himself at the nativity of Christ. But they cannot reform Malvolio, they cannot deal effectively with the love disorders of Orsino and Olivia, and they cannot restore the community as a whole to the "peace" that is the special promise of the season. For this a force must come from outside, presenting a pattern of perfect love and perfect order, and having power to produce these qualities in the community. Such a force enters the Illyrian world in the persons of the twins, Viola and Sebastian.

Though the two are dramatically separate, Viola and Sebastian represent thematically two aspects of the same restorative process. This fact is suggested partly by an identity in their physical appearances so absolute that they themselves recognize no differences: Viola declares, "I my brother know / Yet living in my glass. Even such and so / In favor was my brother, and he went / Still in this fashion, color, ornament" (III.iv.359–362), and Sebastian seeing Viola in her disguise as Cesario asks, "Do I stand there?" (V.i.218). More important, there is a remarkable identity in the events of their lives: both endure a sea tempest, both are saved and aided by good sea captains, both are wooed by and in a manner of speaking woo Olivia, both are forced to a duel with Andrew Aguecheek, both give money to Feste, both are in the end betrothed to their proper lovers. By these parallels the twin motif is made to do much more than to provide occasion for comic misapprehension and misunderstanding, though it does that also in good measure.

Viola, disguised throughout the play as the page Cesario, is the embodiment of selfless love (as Maria is the embodiment of wit and Feste of festival foolery); as such she provides a direct contrast to the self-centered passions of Orsino and Olivia and at length inspires both to a purified love. . . . Because her love is selfless, Viola is able to embrace love fully, freely, and at once, to share in the common human turbulence of feeling attending upon love without ever giving way to the madness and disorder that accompany the selfish passions of Orsino and Olivia; she is thus a pattern of the ordered self as well as of selfless love. In this respect Viola is specifically contrasted with Olivia: both have lost (as they suppose) dearly beloved brothers, but Olivia has disordered herself and disrupted her household by giving way to excessive grief whereas Viola steels herself to act in accordance with the needs and necessities of her situation. Viola is also directly contrasted with Orsino: both are victims of unrequited love, but whereas Orsino gives way to love-sick posturing and giddy behavior, Viola can endure with patience. . . . But in thus waiting upon time she never forces any issue: after her encounter with Antonio who mistakes her for Sebastian (III.iv) she is reasonably sure that her brother is alive—"O, if it prove, / Tempests are kind, and salt waves fresh in love" (III.iv.363–364). But despite the steadily mounting pressure upon her resulting from the mistaken identities—Antonio's rage, Olivia's chiding, Orsino's offer to kill her—she gives no hint that she has a twin brother who may hold the key to the confusions. The epiphany must be allowed to come when it will, and she endures in patience until the revelation is given.

Sebastian's role is to bring to determination the issues which Viola begins, and to resolve the difficult situations which she must endure until his manifestation. Whereas Viola must constantly give selfless love and service to others, Sebastian is able at once to inspire selfless, devoted love for himself: his friend Antonio risks danger and imprisonment to minister to Sebastian's needs in the strange town, and later risks life itself for him in undertaking a duel in his supposed defence. The pattern is repeated when Olivia (thinking him Cesario) proclaims her love for him at first sight and proposes a betrothal. His immediate decision to accept that betrothal despite his perception that it is grounded in some error, and his forthright response to the attack of Andrew and Toby in which he gives each a "bloody coxcomb," show a power of firm determination which make possible the restoration of order to the land.

TWIN MOTIF REPRESENTS CHRIST
EPIPHANY OF TWELFTH NIGHT

The complementary roles of Viola and Sebastian in Illyria may on the basis of what has been said be seen to reflect the dual nature and role of the incarnate Divine Love, Christ, in accordance with the Christmastide theme implied in the play's title [*Twelfth Night*]. . . . Viola's role alludes to the human dimension, Christ's role as patient servant, willing sufferer, model of selfless love. Her offer to Orsino, "And I, most jocund, apt, and willingly, / To do you rest a thousand deaths would die" (V.i.126–127) is perhaps the most direct verbal reference to this role. Sebastian reflects the divine dimension, pointed up especially in Antonio's language to and about Sebastian: "I do *adore* thee so / That danger shall seem sport" (II.i.42–43) and again, "to his image, which methought did promise / Most venerable worth, did I *devotion*" (III.iv.342–343), and then in disillusionment, "But, O, how vile an *idol* proves this *god*" (III.iv.345) [Italics are author's emphasis]. The bloody pates dealt out to Toby and Andrew present Sebastian in the role of judge and punisher, and the final betrothal to Olivia suggests Christ's role as destined "husband" of the perfected soul and of the reordered society, the Church.

In the "epiphany" in the final scene when Sebastian is at length manifested and the double identity is revealed, some of the language points directly to the theological dimension here noted, but at the same time resists simplistic allegorical equations. When the twins are first seen together by the company the Duke's comment suggests and reverses the usual formula for defining Christ as incorporating two natures in one person, observing that here is "One face, one voice, one habit, and two persons" (V.i.208). Antonio makes a similar observation, "How have you made division of yourself? / An apple cleft in two is not more twin / Than these two creatures" (V.i.214–216). But the other formulation, a mysterious duality in unity, is suggested throughout the play in Viola's dual masculine-feminine nature, and is restated in the last scene in Sebastian's words to Olivia, "You are betrothed both to a maid and man" (V.i.255). Elsewhere in the final scene Sebastian denies any claim to "divinity" in terms that at the same time relate him to such a role: "I never had a brother; / Nor can there be that deity in my nature / Of here and everywhere" (V.i.218–220). And again, "A spirit I am indeed, / But am in that dimension grossly clad / Which from the womb I did participate" (V.i.228–230).

Sebastian and Viola do indeed bring the "peace" of the season to Illyria through a reordering of its life and its loves. . . . The right betrothals are made though Viola may not yet put off her disguise: that must wait upon finding the sea-captain who has her "maid's garments" and who "upon some action / Is now in durance, at Malvolio's suit" (V.i.267–268). When we remember that Malvolio has been identified as comic devil the line seems to point to the condition of mankind held in durance by the devil's "suit" as a result of the Fall [from Grace], and reminds us that only after the atonement for that Fall has been made may Christ's passive, suffering servant's role be put aside. Sir Toby and Sir Andrew have endured the token punishment for their disorders meted out by Sebastian, Toby will wed Maria and reform, and even Malvolio is freed and invited to participate in the general "peace" if he will, "Pursue him and entreat him to a peace" (V.i.369). The Duke's concluding statement shows him taking firm hold of affairs in his kingdom for the first time since the play began, auguring well for the preservation of the land in order and peace. And the Duke's declaration that the weddings will take place when "golden time convents" suggests that the reordering made possible by this fictional embodiment of the significance and themes of Christmastide looks forward to the reëstablishment of the golden age, or in Christian terms, to the millennium. . . .

Bringing the Twelfth Night celebration to a close, Feste reminds us that the world we live in is a very great distance from the land of good will that is Illyria, that the restorative forces which had a comparatively easy time there have much more resistant materials to work upon in the real world, and that the golden age foreseen as imminent at the end of the play is in the real world only a far-off apocalyptic vision.

The Theme of Give and Take

Richard Henze

According to Colorado State English professor Richard Henze, critics of *Twelfth Night* have reached completely contradictory conclusions regarding themes in the play. Agreeing that *Twelfth Night* is a play of opposites, he asserts that there is one particular dualism that unpins the whole comedy. To him, *Twelfth Night* is about generosity and desire —give and take—and a search for balance between the two. He64 holds up Viola as a model of generosity, freely giving of herself to make others happy, and depicts Feste as the embodiment of taking. Feste's taking is not the selfish, covetous desire of Malvolio; rather Henze idealizes Feste as a generous taker, one who is gracious in accepting what is offered by others. Given these extremes, Henze argues that the other characters exhibit traits that fall somewhere along the range of generosity and desire. Furthermore, in order to participate in the festivity of the play's conclusion, the characters have to make some effort to harmonize the extremes and become free and generous givers and takers.

Critical interpretations of *Twelfth Night* are notable for the variety of contradictory meanings that their makers attach to the play. The play has been called, among other things, a vindication of romance, a depreciation of romance, a realistic comment on economic security and practical marriage, an account of saturnalian festivity, a "subtle portrayal of the psychology of love," a play about "unrequital in love" because of self-deception, an account of love's wealth, a dramatic account of Epiphany and the gift of Divine Love, a moral comedy about the surfeiting of the appetite so that it

Excerpted from *"Twelfth Night:* Free Disposition on the Sea of Love," by Richard Henze. First published in *The Sewanee Review*, vol. 83, no. 2, Spring 1975. Copyright © 1975 by the University of the South. Reprinted with permission from the editor and the author.

"may sicken and so die" and allow "the rebirth of the unencumbered self." Various critics have variously described the
chief character in the play to be Malvolio, Viola, Olivia, or
even Feste. The complexity of the play is such that each of
these opinions is supported by considerable textual evidence. The play is about the vindication of romance and the
depreciation of romance, but the romance that is vindicated
is that of Viola and Sebastian reunited and chosen by love
and not that of Orsino and his selfish, conventional, melancholic seclusion in a bower of flowers. The play does deal
with both practicality and prudence—Viola tells us her very
practical reasons for joining the duke' s household, for example; but the play also shows saturnalian festivity in full
sway under Sir Toby Belch, master of the holiday. The play
shows Viola's epiphany of love and Toby's surfeit of the appetite—Viola's love fulfilled and Malvolio's love unrequited.

PRIMARY OPPOSITION: GIVE AND TAKE

I should like to propose a solution to this puzzle of interpretations: that *Twelfth Night* is a play about opposites and that
each of the interpretations above tends to treat just one of a
pair of opposites in the play. The primary opposition in the
play is the one implicit in the title, *Twelfth Night; or, What
You Will:* epiphany and the divine gift of love or earthly appetite, desire, and choice. But as the play's action proceeds,
oppositions become much more complicated and subtle
than the single one in the title as they grow to include oppositions between characters, between actions, between images, and finally between the present mirth of the play and
the continual indiscriminate rain of Feste's concluding song.

The most obvious opposition in the play is that between
giving and taking: whether it is better to give or to receive is
a question that the play continually poses and answers ambiguously. Viola gives freely, Sebastian takes unhesitantly.
Maria gives, Toby takes. Orsino gives, Feste takes. Critics
have described very well the giving side of the play, but not
very fully at all its opposite—the constant taking of the play.
The generosity is obvious: Viola gives freely of her money
and herself; she even offers to give her life finally if Orsino
will take it. Antonio, until he is captured, gives his money
and himself for Sebastian; then he asks for his money back
and regrets his generosity. Orsino gives money somewhat
generously to the fool, himself very insistently to Olivia;

Olivia matches Orsino by taking care to preserve Malvolio even while she forces herself upon Viola. Maria gives sport that delights Toby and deludes Malvolio. Sebastian gives himself to Olivia; Orsino finally gives himself to Viola. Gifts in the play are multiple even though giving is not always generous.

But taking is just as important in the play, and most evident in Feste's constant begging for tips and bribes, although Feste only begs so long as someone is bountiful toward him; he is never very insistent but is often even hesitant in his pleas: as he says, "I would not have you to think that my desire of having is the sin of covetousness" [V.i.44–46]. Just as free from greed—and no beggar at all—is Sebastian in his acceptance of Olivia. Olivia and Orsino, on the other hand, lack full freedom from covetousness, although they covet persons rather than money. Less hesitant and more covetous still are Toby in his attempts to get Andrew's money and horse, Andrew in his attempt to get Olivia, and Malvolio in his conceited assurance that Olivia loves him and that he will soon have power over Toby.

FESTE AND VIOLA ESTABLISH THE NORMS OF GIVE AND TAKE

Feste describes in the play a norm for getting what he wills without taking what others would not have him take. He differs from Sebastian in that he does not repay what he gets with a like gift; he differs from the other takers in his lack of covetousness, even though his profession is to beg. He is the generous taker.

The other norm, that of generous giving, is defined by Viola as she gives herself and her services to Orsino, money to the fool, and half her purse to Antonio. The others in the play, with the exception of Sebastian, violate one or both of the norms established by Feste and Viola. Orsino gives himself to Olivia, but he also tries to claim her as Antonio did his ship. Olivia seems to be generous: "What shall you ask of me that I'll deny,/ That honour, sav'd, may upon asking give?" Yet she tries to buy Viola-Cesario with a show of wealth. Antonio is extravagant in his generosity toward Sebastian, but he is also a "salt water pirate" and very concerned about his own safety in spite of his hazard of himself. Malvolio's offer of himself is gross conceit; Andrew's is gross foolishness. Maria gives Toby sport but seeks to end Malvolio's freedom. Only Viola consistently gives freely and graciously with no expectation of profit or power; only Feste consistently takes freely and graciously without disturbing another's bounty and without giving himself in return.

The range in the action of the play is suggested by the characterization of Viola and Feste. Viola becomes the embodiment of gracious, nearly divine Twelfth Night giving, Feste of festive Twelfth Night taking. Yet, though they seem to contradict each other, Viola and Feste are more alike than they are unlike, for they share the essential qualities of graciousness, civility, and free disposition; they are both careful not to intrude on someone else's free disposition.

Free disposition in the play involves two things: that one be generous with one's money and one's self where the money and self are freely desired—and that one graciously accept what one is freely offered if to accept the gift does not intrude on the free disposition of giver or recipient. To be simply generous is not enough, for generosity can become terribly selfish if it is imposed on one who does not desire it. Simply to take is likewise not enough, for graciousness requires that one take only what one is freely offered. Viola and Feste demonstrate the right kind of generosity and the right kind of graciousness; Malvolio, on the other hand, neither generous nor gracious, opposes both Feste and Viola. As the characters become more like Viola and Feste and less like Malvolio, they acquire generosity, graciousness, and true civility.

THE FESTIVE FINALE FINDS BALANCE

The freedom that Orsino and Olivia finally acquire, freedom to give where the gift is desired, is the true festivity that Feste himself tends to symbolize in the play. Here the distinction is between Feste's true festivity and the belching, oversatisfied, what-shall-we-do-else sport of Toby. There will be cakes and ale to be sure, but cakes and ale are not all that life is. Feste's sport inspires generosity without intruding on free disposition; he begs only as long as one is freely generous, then he allows bounty to sleep a while. Toby on the other hand has no concern whatever for others' freedom. His sport is terribly ungenerous, endangering even Viola—free disposition itself—as well as Andrew and Malvolio. His sport is too indiscriminate, too little inclined to take into account person, time, and circumstances. . . .

A proper attitude toward festivity, the play implies, is one that recommends Feste and his freedom even while it rejects the excess of Toby Belch. But one's choice is not always that simple. Maria, for example, has to choose between Malvolio and Toby: in that case Maria, the embodiment of wit, properly prefers Toby's freedom to Malvolio's self-love; but she recognizes, at the same time, that Toby is out of order. So does the fool: he too prefers Toby's attitude to Malvolio's, but he sees Toby for the drunk that he is.

The names of the characters indicate their symbolic qualities. Viola is both musical and free in volition; her counter-image, Malvolio, is the embodiment of ill will who intrudes on free disposition. Feste is festive; his counterimage, Belch, is surfeited. Toby Belch, until his marriage to Maria, threatens to replace Twelfth Night's generous festivity with uncivil sport. For what you will to be fully satisfactory, it must be Viola's what you will and not Malvolio's. For the festivity of Twelfth Night to be fully satisfactory, it must be Feste's graciousness, not Toby's rambunctiousness.

The movement of the play is from ill will to true festivity, generosity, and the harmonic feast of marriage and friendship. Sebastian's arrival signifies the approaching success of the characters in arriving at that point, for Sebastian is a compound of Feste and Viola, one who freely gives and just as freely takes. He furnishes the single embodiment of the Twelfth Night spirit that Viola and Feste together define, and the final opposition of the play is the thorough opposition between Sebastian and Malvolio rather than the superficial one between Feste and Viola. Twelfth Night becomes what you will; desire and generosity operate in accord.

Variations on Metamorphoses and Doubling

William C. Carroll

From his book *The Metamorphoses of Shakespearean Comedy*, Professor William C. Carroll of Boston University explores the variety of forms metamorphosis takes in *Twelfth Night* as revealed through water imagery, language, character disguise, imitation, and doubling. Carroll keenly reveals the patterns of metamorphosis within the play which manifest in the transforming of characters such as Viola, who is reasonably in control of her transformation, and Malvolio, who resists change. To further the complexity, these metamorphoses are reflected in the characters' speech, especially Feste's commentaries, which manifest as appropriate "double talk." The idea of doubling is also found in the Viola/Sebastian pairing as well as in Malvolio's descent into madness which produces the second "mad" Malvolio. As Carroll points out, the qualities of the play that allow for the exponential metamorphoses—the doublings, false identities, and quick-changing language—can further extend beyond the characters and the play to the actors and the audience and their connection with the text.

The multiple powers of metamorphosis govern the action throughout *Twelfth Night:* mysterious energies which turn two into one and one into two, and mimetic impulses which lead people to become actors, donning disguises and willingly turning themselves into what they are not. Shakespeare again adopts the Plautine mode in this play [as he did in *The Comedy of Errors*], but broadens and complicates his borrowings until he has produced something quite new and strange. . . .

LIQUIDS AND LANGUAGE DEMONSTRATE THE PLAY'S "OSCILLATING RHYTHM"

Water—the central element of transformation—from tears and from the sea, engulfs most of the characters in *Twelfth Night.* Olivia "water(s) once a day her chamber round / With eye-offending brine" (I.i.30-1), and Sebastian in turn will mourn his lost Viola: "She is drowned already, sir, with salt water, though I seem to drown her remembrance again with more" (II.i.30-1). Viola has been washed ashore by the sea, believing her brother drowned. But the Captain offers a kind of hope: after the shipwreck, he saw Sebastian tie himself

> To a strong mast that lived upon the sea;
> Where, like Arion on the dolphin's back,
> I saw him hold acquaintance with the waves
> So long as I could see.
>   (I.ii.14–17)

The Captain's glimpse of Sebastian overcoming flux and peril in the metaphoric guise of Arion . . . offers an emblem of how one can surrender to and still triumph over the mere elements.

Throughout the opening scenes of *Twelfth Night,* questions of constancy and order, and images of the sea, receive special emphasis. Toby Belch . . . is ordered by Maria to "confine yourself within modest limits of order" (I.iii.9), as if that were possible. But Toby is only the most extreme of those characters in the play who defy conventions, resist limits, and spill over boundaries. Feste links together all in the play who are done in by liquids:

OLIVIA.   What's a drunken man like, fool?

CLOWN.   Like a drowned man, a fool, and a madman.
           One draught above heat makes him a fool, the
           second mads him, and a third drowns him.
                   (I.v.129–32)

Even his language partakes of the play's typical oscillating rhythm, as he works a triple transformation on a single idea, each version of the drunken man revealing yet another kind of transformation, which "makes . . . mads . . . [and] drowns him."

Feste's most common rhetorical tool—the figure of anti-metabole (or *commutatio*), in which sentence elements are glibly reversed—reflects a verbal metamorphic capability which matches the other changes in the play. Here, for example, he quotes a non-existent authority:

For what says Quinapalus? "Better a witty fool than a foolish wit." . . . For give the dry fool drink, then is the fool not dry. Bid the dishonest man mend himself: if he mend, he is no longer dishonest; if he cannot, let the botcher mend him. Anything that's mended is but patched; virtue that transgresses is but patched with sin, and sin that amends is but patched with virtue. (I.v.36–7, 44–50)

If this "simple syllogism" won't do, he goes on, "what remedy?" Certainly Viola puts up more resistance to these verbal gymnastics:

VIOLA.	Dost thou live by thy tabor?
CLOWN.	No, sir, I live by the church.
VIOLA.	Art thou a churchman?
CLOWN.	No such matter, sir. I do live by the church; for I do live at my house, and my house doth stand by the church.
VIOLA.	So thou mayst say, the king lies by a beggar, if a beggar dwell near him; or, the church stands by thy tabor, if thy tabor stand by the church. (III.i.1–10)

Resisting such glib reversals of language or of love is one of Viola's chief functions (though she experiences her own radical changes), and this pattern of change versus constancy is seen repeatedly. Feste ironically agrees with Viola in this case: "You have said, sir. To see this age! A sentence is but a chev'ril glove to a good wit. How quickly the wrong side may be turned outward!" (II.11–13). He goes on to lament that "words are grown so false I am loath to prove reason with them" (I. 25) and describe himself, not as Olivia's fool, "but her corrupter of words" (I. 37). One of Shakespeare's constant interests in the comedies is the instability of language, its power to change, and its own plasticity. To transform a sentence into its opposite meaning is, like all change, both wonderful and fearful. The deep connection between metamorphosis and unstable language is everywhere stressed, and emphasized in Viola's ability to do anything with words, but to be wise about which changes in them are truly significant.

VIOLA'S WILLPOWER AND EXPONENTIAL TRANSFORMATIONS

Between Orsino's instability in love and Olivia's obstinacy in continuing to mourn her brother stands Viola. In her disguise as Cesario she represents a loving, clear-sighted constancy more sensible and endearing than Olivia's rigid devotion to— as the line so ambiguously reads—her "brother's dead love"

(I.i.32). In her disguise-taking and common sense about her own lost brother, Viola exhibits a capability for intelligent, willed change that the others would do well to imitate. . . .

Viola's ability to change when she will and yet also to be constant—to be and not to be—distinguishes her from all others in the play. Shakespeare suggests in her energies, as he does earlier with Julia in *The Two Gentlemen of Verona,* a distinction between active and passive metamorphosis, between a willed embrace of flexibility and the kind of rigidity which Olivia displays at the beginning of the play. But Viola's decision to disguise herself is, as in many of the comedies, vague in its reasoning; Shakespeare seems to bow to the convention without bothering to explain it, but we can also see something urgent and compulsive in the repeated urge to conceal one's self, to become someone else:

> Conceal me what I am, and be my aid
> For such disguise as haply shall become
> The form of my intent.
> I'll serve this duke.
> Thou shalt present me as an eunuch to him.
> (I.ii.53–6)

The form of her intent is never made clear—she wishes not to "be delivered to the world, / Till I had made mine own occasion mellow, / What my estate is" (II. 42–4)—but once the plot begins we turn toward the results of such change. Still, there is something appropriate to this vagueness; Viola shows herself to be adventurous and vital, entertaining the offered fallacy as Antipholus does [in *The Comedy of Errors*], and we are no doubt supposed to believe that playing a role has appealed to these qualities. . . .

Viola perceives (and she is the first of Shakespeare's comic heroines to do so) that disguise can be dangerous. Becoming someone else entails remaining in character at all times, or being judged "insane," as happened in *The Comedy of Errors.* When Olivia falls in love with Cesario, Viola marvels:

> I am the man. If it be so, as 'tis,
> Poor lady, she were better love a dream.
> Disguise, I see thou art a wickedness
> Wherein the pregnant enemy does much.
> How easy is it for the proper false
> In women's waxen hearts to set their forms!
> (II.ii.25–30)

This speech wittily registers transformation on several levels—as male actor to girl to "man" again, as love, as dream, as disguise, as wax set in a form; and, in its ironic self-consciousness, it reminds the audience once again of its own complicity in helping to create a mimetic transformation. Viola's assertion "I am the man" is true and false at once, a pointed rendering of the complex and paradoxical process of transformation at work here: of being (woman) and not-being (man). Her self-consciousness about all this marks a sharp difference between her and the helpless protagonists of *The Comedy of Errors,* moreover. In every comedy following *Errors,* Shakespeare makes at least one character, usually female, aware of the powers of change, even if she can't fully control or understand them. But even Viola is unaware that she herself is doubled by a living brother. Thus Shakespeare doubles the possibilities of transformation, by mirroring Viola's mimetic transformation with the situational transformation engendered by doubling. The complexities of *The Comedy of Errors* increase exponentially in *Twelfth Night.*

PERSONAE SERVE AS TEMPORARY IDENTITIES FOR THE CHARACTERS

The search for identity, a popular psychoanalytic theme of Twelfth Night, *is directly related to the idea of metamorphosis, specifically in connection with the characters whose identities fluctuate throughout the play. In this excerpt from James P. Driscoll's book* Identity in Shakespearean Drama, *identity is interpreted according to psychologist Carl Gustav (C.G.) Jung's concept of the "personae" as a mask that the characters wear.*

Without the stability that family bonds provide, social and real identity becomes uncertain; consequently, the identities of Viola, Olivia, Sebastian, and Orsino (along with those of the other major characters) are repeatedly questioned, asserted and explored:

> Conceal me what I am (I.ii. 54)
> What kind o' man is he? (I.v. 159)
> Of what personage and years is he? (I.v. 163)
> Are you a comedian? (I.v. 194);
> Are you the lady of this house? (I.v. 197)
> If I do not usurp myself, I am (I.v. 198)
> You do think you are not what you are; (III.i. 151)
> I am not what I am (III.i. 54)
> I am your fool (III.i. 157)
> For such as I am all true lovers are (II.iv. 17)

Viola calls herself a "poor monster," because as Cesario she is neither female nor male, neither Viola nor Sebastian, but a fusion of both. Like the Antipholi, too, Viola feels her own linguistic identity threatened by her situational transformation. She can no longer, in her role, make nominal assertions, but must describe herself as something Other, all potential forms of being, and yet also nothing:

> I am all the daughters of my father's house,
> And all the brothers too, and yet I know not.
> (II.iv.121–2)

As is appropriate for a fiction, she begins to speak of herself, in both her identities, in the conditional:

> My father had a daughter loved a man
> As it might be perhaps, were I a woman,
> I should your lordship.
> (II. 108–10)

When (or if) the audience begins to think about the still larger transformative fiction—boy to woman to man—it can

---

One face, one voice, one habit, and two persons, / A natural perspective, that is and is not! (V.i. 223–24)
What kin are you to me? What countryman? What name? What parentage? (V.i. 237–38)
I am not that I play (I.v. 196).

In Illyria, a land where nothing that is so is so, none (save Sebastian) are what they play. The wisest, Viola and Feste, have highly adaptable *personae* and are keenly alive to the crucial distinction between *personae* and real identities. Orsino and Olivia each have a hardened, inadaptive *persona*, which they conflate with conscious identity, and each has lost sight of real identity. Orsino the lover and Olivia the mourner are affected *personae*, which must be abandoned if they are to discover themselves and people the world. Viola, whose Cesario *persona* forms a deliberate disguise, knows herself and can penetrate the *personae* of Orsino and Olivia to perceive their real identities more clearly than they do. Sebastian adopts no disguise and his *persona* conceals nothing. Since, like Viola, he is self-aware, his conscious identity accords with his real identity. Yet the Illyrians make him other than what he is by attributing to him the social identity of Viola's Cesario *persona*. Consequently, much to Sebastian's bemusement, he accidentally becomes the beneficiary of Illyrian love madness.

James P. Driscoll, "Identity in Illyria," *Identity in Shakespearean Drama.* Lewisburg: Bucknell University Press, 1983, p. 92.

see the mimetic impulse as another form of metamorphosis, and wonder about its own role in all this. . . .

MALVOLIO'S RESISTANCE TO CHANGE IS FUTILE

One of Malvolio's least attractive traits is his maniacal resistance to transformation, his refusal to allow boundaries to give way (unless the ones between him and Olivia), especially the social boundaries which supposedly divide him from Toby Belch and set him apart from the rest of mankind. The more strongly he resists change, the more rigid his stance, the more certain it is to happen. . . . Malvolio will be forced into several transformations—first, an inner change wrought by desire and (self-) love; second, a physical change in his clothing and appearance; and third, a "possession" or "madness. . . ."

We should also remember that the plot against Malvolio involves language which is and is not Olivia's. Maria will forge "some obscure epistles of love" (II.iii.154), and the conspirators will "observe his construction of it" (I. 174). Olivia's true writing will be doubled by Maria ("on a forgotten matter we can hardly make distinction of our hands"—I. 160), eventually producing from Malvolio a second or doubled Malvolio—the "mad" one, the one made an ass. Malvolio shows himself all too susceptible to this doubling when it is reported that "he has been yonder i' the sun practicing behavior to his own shadow this half hour" (II.v.14–15), and he enters the scene quoting from his own imagined dialogue. So he is quite prepared to recognize or "read" false writing as true:

> By my life, this is my lady's hand. These be her very C's, her U's, and her T's; and thus makes she her great P's. It is, in contempt of question, her hand. (II. 84–7)

Malvolio's failure to make the letters and sounds cohere, much less to catch the double entendre, is quickly followed by another linguistic conundrum, which he does try to resolve. The letter's mysterious line, "M.O.A.I. doth sway my life, (I. 109) helps reveal Malvolio's motives in reading: "If I could make that resemble something in me!" (I. 117). Reading thus becomes an effort to double oneself, to find in letters something that "resemble[s]" oneself—a willed transformation that is, however, quite unlike Viola's, but more like Narcissus's. As if in mockery of the very attempt, Toby phonetically mirrors Malvolio: "O, ay, make up that." Eventually Malvolio will "read" the letter enough to transform it into his own reflection:

> M,O,A,I. This simulation is not as the former; and yet, to

crush this a little, it would bow to me, for every one of these
letters are in my name. (II. 135–7)

There must be a text behind the text, then, but the other text
is still just one's own reflection. Malvolio cannot escape this
"simulation" because he is so completely solipsistic. His
"love" turns out to be another manifestation of his self-love,
his surface transformations revealed as not essential ones.

The forged letter releases what meager powers of transformation lie within Malvolio and therefore makes possible his
adoption of the outward changes: "Be opposite with a kinsman,
surly with servants. Let thy tongue tang arguments of state; put
thyself into the trick of singularity" (II. 145–7). He is also to appear in yellow stockings, cross-gartered, and perpetually smiling. Like any metamorph, he must become the other that he already is: in this case, a fool. The "trick of singularity" is usually
glossed as something like the "affectation of eccentricity" but
the phrase also reminds us of Malvolio's problems with doubling. "Singularity" is a kind of role which one must "put thyself into." Thus "singularity" in the narrowest sense is impossible. He can't get out of himself. . . .

DOUBLING AND METAMORPHOSIS: FUSION AND FISSION

The final scene of *Twelfth Night* brings together all the questions about metamorphosis raised earlier in the play. Feste, for
example, explains to the puzzled Orsino how he can be "the
better for my foes, and the worse for my friends" (V.i.12–13);
this explanation is itself a figure of metamorphosis:

> Marry, sir, they [his friends] praise me and make an ass of me.
> Now my foes tell me plainly I am an ass; so that by my foes, sir,
> I profit in the knowledge of myself, and by my friends I am
> abused; so that, conclusions to be as kisses, if your four nega-
> tives make your two affirmatives, why then, the worse for my
> friends, and the better for my foes. (II. 17–23)

Turning "negatives" into "affirmatives," or men into asses is
all one. Orsino misses the point, even when Feste responds
to the gift of a gold coin, "But that it would be double-dealing,
sir, I would you could make it another" (II. 29–30). But when
he gives the other coin, Orsino can joke that he "will be so
much a sinner to be a double-dealer" (II. 34–5). This is a minor moment in a long scene, but these parables of transformation and doubling anticipate much of what is to come.

When the confusion mounts, Olivia must call in the Priest
to prove her marriage to Cesario, and his description of the

marriage suggests that a yet more profound kind of transformation has occurred:

> A contract of eternal bond of love,
> Confirmed by mutual joinder of your hands,
> Attested by the holy close of lips,
> Strength'ned by interchangement of your rings;
> And all the ceremony of this compact
> Sealed in my function, by my testimony.
>   (II. 155–60)

Already two have become one. The two lovers are never dis-
tinguished in this description—"your hands," "lips," and
"your rings" represent a single figure. A subtle alliteration
—contract, confirmed, compact—stresses the union of two
into one. The language of the passage, by turns legal and
formal—contract, bond, joinder, attested, interchangement,
testimony—witnesses the ritualistic joining together sym-
bolized by this ceremony. Such a reminder of the meaning of
marriage and its transfigurative power has an emblematic
status in this scene; so complete and so carefully crafted a
description is certainly unnecessary for the plot alone. The
final scene of *Twelfth Night* moves through this revelation of
two-in-one—marriage—to the discovery of still another two-
in-one—Cesario. Sir Andrew, for example, complains of the
double nature of "one Cesario," not realizing there are two
of him: "We took him for a coward, but he's the very devil incardinate" (II. 179–81). The pun accentuates the notion of
incarnation, of two-in-one which best describes Cesario
himself, and possibly even means incardinate—without
number. Perhaps we should remember here as well that
Twelfth Night marks the Eve of Epiphany, the announce-
ment of yet another incarnation.

At the greatest moment of confusion, threatened harm,
and accumulated paradox, Sebastian enters and the twins
confront each other and the rest of the troupe. Orsino's famous words gather up associations from this play and from
earlier works as well:

> One face, one voice, one habit, and two persons—
> A natural perspective that is and is not.
>   (11. 215–16)

In some plays contemporary with Shakespeare's, a simple discovery scene suffices to clarify confusion and reveal identity;
in others, such as [John] Lyly's *Gallathea*, a full metamorphosis will be required. In *Twelfth Night,* the discovery scene

must reveal the paradoxes of past transformations—and represent them linguistically as well as dramatically. . . .

Viola even for a moment wonders if Sebastian is a ghost, but he explains to Olivia the nature of the dual paradox:

> So comes it, lady, you have been mistook.
> But nature to her bias drew in that.
> You would have been contracted to a maid;
> Nor are you therein, by my life, deceived:
> You are betrothed both to a maid and man.
> (II. 258–62)

"Incardinate," "maid and man," "one habit, and two persons": the paradoxes all point to a mysterious transformation in which two become one and one becomes two. Marriage itself, as we have seen, is one paradigm of this process, and Cesario's fission another: a maid for Orsino, a man for Olivia, one for the master, one for the mistress. . . . The fission is also a translation of earlier and even contemporary magical resolutions in other plays. But the magic here is all Shakespeare's. What *Twelfth Night,* and especially its ending, offers us are successive moments of fusion and fission. . . .

LANGUAGE EXEMPLIFIES PARADOXES OF CHANGE AND PERCEPTION

Sebastian and Viola are and are not themselves; Cesario is and is not Cesario. . . . Throughout the play, moreover, similar paradoxes have been expressed. Viola/Cesario has twice given Olivia a similar veiled warning: "I am not that I play" (I.v.182); "I am not what I am" (III.i.143). And she has said of Olivia, "you do think you are not what you are" (III.i.141). Mistaking Sebastian for Cesario, Feste will parody the full extent of the confusion:

> No, I do not know you; nor I am not sent to you by my lady,
> to bid you come speak with her; nor your name is not Master
> Cesario; nor this is not my nose neither. Nothing that is so is
> so. (IV.i.5–9)

Feste's speech in one sense merely reflects the conventions of the usual appearance/reality theme, yet his speech has deeper resonances; his explanations and definitions proceed strictly by negation, as if to reflect our sense that metamorphosis is nothing. There is a logical difficulty, moreover, in the structure of the sentence "Nothing that is so is so" which seems curiously self-canceling and tautological [redundant] at the same time: that which is so is also not so. These cryptic references gain even more force from Feste's "old hermit of Prague" parody of them in the fourth act:

> "That that is is" . . . for what is "that" but that, and "is" but is?
> (IV.ii.15–17)

The reply comes in the fifth act: something "that is and is not." These enigmatic formulations all reflect the central mystery of metamorphosis we have been following, and suggest as well the role language plays in transformation. If antimetabole, one of the favorite figures of this play, reflected the possibilities of reversed transformation, these gnomic utterances [sayings] of negation seem the verbal form, perhaps even one cause, of transformation. Their duplicity is further doubled when the audience understands them even more ironically as the actors' allusions to their own counterfeiting.

Few characters in *Twelfth Night* have been merely themselves; they have also become not-themselves through transformation—through disguise, trickery, situation, and love. We find another confirmation of this duality when Malvolio's long-delayed letter defending his sanity is finally read. It doesn't matter when it is read, Feste says, because "a madman's epistles are no gospels" (V.i.286), as if only the Word need immediately find an audience. What follows is another demonstration of metamorphic powers as a species of mimesis:

OLIVIA.   Open't and read it.
CLOWN.   Look then to be well edified, when the fool
          delivers the madman. [*Reads in a loud voice.*]
          "By the Lord, madam"—
OLIVIA.   How now? Art thou mad?
CLOWN.   No, madam, I do but read madness. And your
          ladyship will have it as it ought to be, you
          must allow *vox*.
OLIVIA.   Prithee read i' thy right wits.
CLOWN.   So I do, madonna; but to read his right wits is
          to read thus.
          (II. 289–300)

To read a text is necessarily to *become* the author, then, as well as the reader. Thus Feste is and is not himself here, and, in a simpler version of this verbal mimesis, Malvolio has become the forgery he has read, cross-gartered and in yellow stockings. Viola too has become the fiction of counterfeit "Cesario"; and as she tells us earlier, she consciously "imitate[s]" her brother (III.iv.387). Still, beyond the characters there are the actors themselves, the technicians of the mimetic, who read a text in *vox* and take on another shape.

CHAPTER 4

The Play in Action

READINGS ON
TWELFTH NIGHT

Following a Disjointed Story Line

Jean E. Howard

Contrary to how a reader might interpret *Twelfth Night* through back-tracking and theme-based analysis of the text, the live audience does not have the luxury of rereading. Shakespearean theater expert Jean E. Howard examines the playwright's careful manipulation of the play which pulls together the disconnected scenes of the non-linear plot through contrasting aural (sounds, as in music and language), visual, and kinetic (the actors' movement and energy) devices. It is through Shakespeare's careful orchestration of these devices that he is able to maintain audience interest across a series of distinct episodes. Ultimately, Howard concludes, that tension builds throughout the play to a point at which the audience—knowing more than the characters on stage—becomes caught up in the frenzied stage action, fretting over the characters' self-deceptions and recognizing that Shakespeare is asking the viewers to apply the moral lessons exhibited onstage to their own lives.

That audiences do not respond to *Twelfth Night* as a fragmented and static work is largely due to Shakespeare's subtle orchestration of stage events. The progressive experience of the work has a meaningful dynamic of its own that underlies and gradually clarifies the rich thematic unity of the work. Retrospectively, of course, which is how most critics approach *Twelfth Night,* its thematic patterns are relatively clear. The play, above all, is about the dangerous egotism that makes the self the center of the universe, leading to illusions, disguises, and posturing. Characters who indulge their egocentric fantasies are led through a maze of mistakes

Excerpted from *Shakespeare's Art of Orchestration: Stage Technique and Audience Response,* by Jean E. Howard. Copyright © 1984 by the Board of Trustees of the University of Illinois. Reprinted with permission from the University of Illinois Press.

and embarrassing self-disclosures until, personal and social chaos at a peak, they are released into true and clarifying knowledge of the self. . . .

THE THEATRICAL EXPERIENCE

To say even this much about the thematic and psychological patterns in the play, of course, involves wandering back and forth, in retrospect, over its surface, imposing an abstract ordering paradigm upon events that, experienced sequentially, do not reveal a unifying meaning so readily. What this mode of criticism does, and it is a useful and necessary operation, is to spatialize a temporal phenomenon, to see it in one glance as a simultaneous whole. But in experiencing a play in the theater, the audience does not start here, with a summation of the play's overriding symbolic or psychological concerns, not even if we already know the play or know other romantic comedies of its type. In the theater we begin, not with abstract reflections on the sterility of egocentricity, but with the sound of a particular kind of music and a particular man's reaction to that music. What we subsequently experience is not a psychological treatise, but a particular succession of sights, sounds, and events that create a unique theatrical experience with its own tempo, rhythm, and pauses, its own moments of engagement and detachment, and its own natural points of emphasis. . . .

Orsino's Illyria is an emotional hothouse. Music and language are used to reveal an overwrought, self-indulgent psyche and a court devoted solely to the care and feeding of its count's emotional excesses. There is much here to interest an audience, but not much to engage its sympathies deeply. The brevity of the scene, the artificiality of its rhetoric, even the breaking off of its music are all devices for keeping an audience at some distance from what it is watching and hearing, even as the stasis and enervation of this court are indelibly impressed upon us.

What Shakespeare then does is present two scenes in which, again, relatively little happens. They are not linked together narratively, but they afford further tonal contrasts with the play's opening segment. The orchestration of the play's first three scenes, in fact, depends heavily upon the principle of contrast for its effectiveness. Successively the audience sees three groups of characters in three locales: Orsino and his followers in his court, Viola and the seamen on the coast, Toby and his friends at Olivia's house. Each succeeding scene is longer than the last (42 lines, 64 lines, 127 lines); and each is pitched in a different key, that is, each uses language in a strikingly different way to produce distinct tonal and kinetic effects. The differences are felt primarily because of the context the first segment establishes for the audience's perception of the next two. . . .

The energy and stringency of the [second] scene are primarily conveyed by the language employed as that language is heard against the aural ground provided by Orsino's lovesick mooning. The rhetoric of scene ii contains no conceits and hardly any metaphors, and it is swiftly propelled forward by Viola's logical questions. Language here is used as a means of finding out information and making decisions, not as a means of flaunting one's emotional sensitivity. After Orsino's speeches, it serves to heighten the audience's opinion of Viola. Vulnerable she may be, but she is not mired in an emotional bog.

When Toby, Maria, and then Andrew next come into view, the texture of what the audience hears undergoes another marked change. This is a scene of banter; in I.iii language is used for play, and the poetry of the two preceding scenes gives way to prose. The longest speech in this segment is Toby's nine-line exhortation to Andrew to demonstrate his talents in dancing; and for the most part the scene is devoted to quick-flying jests, though Maria's and Toby's fly somewhat faster, to be sure, than do Andrew's. Against the aural ground established by the businesslike dispatch of Viola's first appearance, the lighthearted expansiveness of this below-stairs world stands out sharply. Here, care is peremptorily banished as an enemy to life; and if a fat man is cast as Toby, as often occurs, his considerable girth becomes . . . a visual emblem of a life lived outside "the modest limits of order" (7–8). The scene itself sprawls; it is two or three times the length of the two that precede it, and what inner tension it has derives from wordplay and the exercise of nimble wits turning randomly to whatever topic lays to hand, not from Viola's purposeful march of questions.

What Shakespeare has done by stringing these three scenes together to form the opening movement of the play is to focus audience attention, not upon plot, but upon tonal and kinetic contrasts that illuminate some of the differing attitudes toward life and some of the different ways in which energy is expended in Illyria. . . .

PLOT THICKENS, PACE QUICKENS, AND AUDIENCE TENSION INCREASES

The second theatrical movement of *Twelfth Night* stretches from I.iv, Viola's first appearance in Orsino's court, to II.v, Malvolio's discovery and reading of Maria's letter; and it is orchestrated quite differently from the opening movement. What primarily unifies this movement theatrically is an increasingly insistent dialectic, felt in the language and pacing of successive segments, between languor and action, constraint and release. Of course, on the level of plot, more "happens" in this segment than in the first three scenes, so there is a quickening of audience desire to see what will next take place. For example, Viola, disguised as Orsino's page, attracts the amorous passion of Olivia and is attracted to Orsino; Sebastian emerges unscathed from the sea and sets out for Orsino's court; and Malvolio offends both Feste and Toby in ways that cry out for retribution. Clearly, with Viola, the audience now begins to look ahead with some impatience to see how time and the dramatist will untangle these knots. Simultaneously, however, the audience lives in the "now" of a carefully orchestrated succession of stage events, and the rhythm of the second movement of the play creates a second kind of tension, largely unrelated to tension generated by the quickening narrative, through the repeated frustration of theatrical energies of both a linguistic and kinetic type. . . .

In I.iv Viola appears in disguise. This is a crucial visual event, and good actresses usually are at pains to make it clear that a man's attire and a man's assertiveness are not entirely natural to Viola. The disguise, moreover, functions as the audience's first visual signal that Viola has done what she earlier promised she would do and that now a new phase of the action—Viola playing boy—is to begin. Further, the scene brings together what formerly had been separate: the melancholy count and the shipwrecked maiden. . . .

[In scene V] the constraints of Viola's disguise and her assigned role force her to adopt a cloying speech and a stance that she quite obviously—from her own interruptions of the script—does not find congenial. In turn, her clichéd text of love invites Olivia to sink into the sterile posture of the proud lady cynically repelling a tedious and unwanted assault. When Viola finally drops the script to tell how she would woo were she Orsino, the audience hears a marked aural shift. Viola's language surges with life, and Olivia's pose crumbles. She is released into love; and in the last thirty lines of the scene, her former hauteur gone, she asks questions and speaks with new energy and purpose.

But the audience is denied a love duet. . . . At the scene's end, Viola is still trapped in her disguise; Olivia has shed one false pose only to embrace another: no more a nun, she now

---

THE MAGIC OF PERFORMANCE

Known as The First Lady of the American Theatre, the ex-quisite Helen Hayes knew how to possess her role and her audience, even if only through the slightest gesture. As Viola in the 1940 New York production of Twelfth Night; or, What You Will, *she made her entrance shaking her foot, as if shaking the sand off it. A brilliant actress whose legacy lives on, Hayes was quite active in her career and even did tours overseas. Jill Johnson was helping out in postwar Korea when Helen Hayes visited the university in Pusan for a reading of selected scenes from Shakespeare.*

It was the spring of 1966 when we first heard the rumor through the post grapevine. But we didn't believe it. Helen Hayes? Coming here—to Korea? Impossible.

For the preceding six months, as program director of a U.S. service club at the base in Pusan, Korea, I had come to admire the indefatigable efforts of a people struggling to overcome postwar hardship and rebuild a nation. But cultural life at the base had been strictly starvation rations: an occasional showing of *Beach Blanket Bingo* or some Japanese science-fiction flick.

But the rumor was true, and gradually, in bits and pieces, we learned more. Miss Hayes was to give a reading of selected scenes from Shakespearean plays at a university in Pusan. Our Special Services officer arranged for our attendance, and on a cold and raw April evening five GIs and I, feverish with anticipation, set off for the program.

The performance hall was bare concrete—a narrow, unheated cave. We could see our breath as we took our seats. In the front, on a small podium, were a lectern and a table. In orderly rows of battered straight-backed chairs hundreds of male Korean university students waited, respectful and silent. The GIs and I were embarrassed when an insistent official led us to seats—obviously reserved for us—at the front. Then we

loves a woman whom she mistakes for a man. The audience once more sees—in Olivia's outstretched hand and Viola's recoil from the purse—and *hears*—in Olivia's questions and Viola's evasions—the pernicious consequences of disguise and false postures. Action is stymied; free and uncorrupted discourse is impossible; and it is the aural and visual orchestration of the encounter that directs the audience's attention to this impasse. . . .

waited—for ten, fifteen minutes. The silence and our prominent position made us increasingly uncomfortable. Finally, a quiet murmur rippled through the room and all eyes turned as a door near the podium opened.

There was no applause at her entrance, just respectful stares. Dressed in a wool plum-colored suit with no makeup and her gray hair tied up in a bun, she looked like someone's misplaced maiden aunt or a retired schoolteacher who had somehow gotten lost on an educational tour. Her nose was red, and, as she reached for her handkerchief, I remember thinking, What kind of people would force a sick old lady out on a night like this? She announced her program in a flat, croaking voice with several hesitations and repetitions. She was obviously ill at ease and that made me even more so. And then—she opened her script.

Suddenly her spine and shoulders straightened and her head went up. The voice took on a different timbre and a new strength; I could almost feel the power surging up through her body into her face and hands. I stared, fascinated, as a look of lovesick longing came into her eyes.

"Make me a willow cabin at your gate . . ."

As she launched into that famous speech of Viola's from *Twelfth Night,* her body swayed gently with yearning and, somehow, mine did too.

"Holla your name to the reverberate hills,
"And make the babbling gossip of the air
"Cry out, 'Olivia'! . . ."

As her hand reached out toward her beloved, so did mine. We were, both of us, transformed, transported to another place, another time, filled with passion and lyricism. As the speech ended, I wanted to jump up and shout, but, controlling myself, I remained seated and applauded politely with the others.

Jill Johnson, "Transformation: A Memory of Helen Hayes," *American Heritage,* October 1993, p. 28.

RESTRAINT AND RELEASE: THE FRENZY BUILDS

The dialectic between release and restraint that the whole second movement of the play embodies finds its final expression in the last three scenes of Act II: the midnight revels of Toby, the lovesick mooning of Orsino, and the boxtree scene. The orchestration of II.iii and II.iv is controlled by the various music that informs each. In II.iii, the below-stairs revelers jest, drink, and sing, in Malvolio's words, most uncivilly. They 'squeak out' their 'coziers' catches without any mitigation or remorse of voice" (83–84). Mitigation, in fact, is what the scene most wonderfully lacks. These are people in the mood for some excellent fooling, and so is the audience after observing Viola's becalmed and complicated situation. Sanctimonious Malvolio highlights, without really threatening, the exuberance of the revelers. They raid the wine cellar and sing carpe diem [Latin for seize the day] songs; he prates of manners and threatens to tattle to the lady of the house. When the scene ends with their plan to fool him with a false love letter, the audience is completely on their side and looks ahead with relish to the steward's mortification. But we are denied the immediate gratification of the plot's fulfillment, since the next scene plunks us down once again in the never changing, claustrophobic court of Orsino.

The Orsino scenes make clear that Shakespeare is effectively using both contrast and recurrence in the orchestration of this play. For the audience, the immediate impact of II.iv is felt in terms of its contrasts with II.iii. We move from a world of prose to a world of poetry, from jests to seriousness, from light airs to a melancholy dirge. . . . The tonal contrast between the two scenes is immense, highlighted by contrasts in music and language. The sense we get of blocked or frustrated energy is further heightened by the fact that II.iv deliberately uses aural cues to send the audience's mind back to the beginning of the play. There Orsino entered with the line "If music be the food of love, play on" (I.i.1); here he enters saying, "Give me some music" (II.iv.1). . . . When, in the specific theatrical context established by II.iii and the preceding scene, the audience is thrust once more into this world, frustration and uneasiness build up. We wait for release, and that need is partly satisfied and partly frustrated by II.v, the scene with Malvolio's reading of the letter that culminates the second movement of the play. . . .

Up to this point the audience has been experiencing, in successive scenes, a basic rhythm of restraint and release, has been hearing successive contrasts between affected and free-wheeling speech. Through the contrapuntal orchestration of II.v we simultaneously hear the constipated pomposity of Malvolio, imagining himself a count and unintentionally parodying the high-flown rhetoric of the real count, Orsino, and the scabrous jests and unrestrained oaths of Toby and his companions. The scene thus aurally highlights a central opposition in the play by exaggerating the affectations of the steward and the coarse energy of the observers.

As Malvolio preens, the audience takes satisfaction with the conspirators in seeing self-love so grotesquely display itself. At the same time, a certain amount of energy simply remains unreleased because the conspirators cannot leap out and laugh Malvolio into the ground without ruining their own joke. They are reduced to sputtering in the bushes, and some of the audience's laughter is directed at them in their fuming impotence. The scene helps to impart a sense of closure to this movement of the play. . . . But it also points attention ahead, not only to the completion of the letter trick, but to the final fulfilling eruption of pent-up energy. . . .

AUDIENCE SELF-AWARENESS INCREASES ALONG WITH TEMPO

The third movement of the play—acts III and IV—seems designed in part to engender in the audience various kinds of self-consciousness about its desires and stance as theatergoers. The third movement of the play contains more action and consequently is orchestrated somewhat differently than what has gone before. The movement begins slowly, but by scene iv of Act III, the pace quickens, reaching a crescendo of madness and confusion that is sustained right through Act IV, when temporary closure is achieved by the brief and stabilizing scene in which Sebastian follows Olivia to the altar to be wed and mistaken beginnings start to find their true conclusions. Increasingly, the pent-up energies of the play's beginning find chaotic and purgative release in physical violence, visual malapropisms [misdirected movements], and verbal excess. Twelfth Night madness overtakes the stage and catches up the audience in its confusion. . . .

Simultaneously the third movement of the play makes the audience self-regarding in yet another way. As critics of the play have shown [such as in *Shakespeare's Comedies* by

Bertrand Evans], it is unusual in the degree to which it puts the audience in a position of superior awareness vis-à-vis [face to face with] the characters. We typically know more than they do in situation after situation. One figure may know more than certain others; but we know more than any; and often a trickster in the midst of his trick unwittingly and unnervingly becomes the butt of someone else's joke. In the third movement of the play, the events are repeatedly structured to put us in this position of superior vision. Yet so insistently is this the case, that in the end we become self-conscious about our own actual omniscience. If the characters on the stage are so wrapped in blindness, are we really more all-knowing? If they live in a world of illusions, is not the theater itself just such a world? If they rely on time and chance for illumination, do not we rely on the dramatist? If they are malleable, so are we. Within the plot, the play repeatedly gives the lie to fantasies of omnipotence and one's control of the universe. The same humbling awareness, I would argue, becomes part of the theatergoer's experience. . . .

With III.iv a genuine sense of climax begins to build as action increasingly takes precedence over talk and as character after character begins to reap the fruit of his or her unnatural or affected posture. As each exposes his folly in its most extreme form, the audience is set free to laugh at a world gone utterly mad, until the laughter becomes strained by our growing awareness that things are spinning out of control. The arrival of Malvolio, yellow-stockinged and cross-gartered, sets the tone for much of the rest of the play's third movement and shows how visual malapropisms—i.e., the creation of appearances that miss their intended effect —are increasingly used to create laughter and focus attention on inappropriate behavior. . . . Shakespeare is also now quickening the pace of the action, and Malvolio no sooner struts out of sight than Andrew enters with his bizarre "challenge" for Cesario, and another joke unfolds.

In the subsequent action, Shakespeare creates a strong and complicated crescendo effect by presenting in rapid succession a series of stage actions notable for their escalating visual humor and for their increasingly strong overtones of violence. . . . Once again, visual humor is intense. At no point is the inappropriateness of Viola's male dress more comically and concretely brought home than when she is set the task of wielding a sword. Neither is the flaxen-haired Andrew much more valiant. . . .

But even at this point, when the madness on the stage would seem to have been played out fully and when our appetite for action has been well satisfied, we find out that this frenzied movement of the play has not reached its conclusion. One more fillip [snap of the fingers] remains, one more change to be rung on the theme of madness and disguise, and that is provided by the revelation of the imprisoned Malvolio and the sight of Feste capering about as Sir Topas. . . . But this scene is delicately handled. It is both the culmination of the farcical madness that has overtaken the stage for several scenes and the clearest signal of its impending collapse. . . . By now the audience is quite ready for less madness. Action we have had in abundance and also emotional release through laughter. But the mistakes and the misperceptions have almost ceased to be funny. We are reeling from the pace of events and sensitive—because of the repeated undermining of each character's fix on reality and because wished-for events have snowballed almost beyond the point at which we can take pleasure in them—to our dependence upon the dramatist for the security of our perceptions and the control of our pleasure and pain.

CLOSURE DOES NOT BRING HARMONY

What remains is the effecting of theatrical closure and the establishment of theatrical and moral equilibrium after the severe disturbance of both. The fourth movement of the play does just that. It brings illumination to the characters through release from disguises of every stripe, and it brings the theater event to a poised, if tenuous, conclusion, as linguistic and kinetic energy find expression in a scene that is both energetic and highly patterned. In fact, V.i is probably the most schematically orchestrated scene of the entire play. And it must be. A great deal happens in it, but the happenings do not spin out of control. Watching the scene, we feel what we so rarely feel in life, the perfect marriage of energy and restraint. The final movement of the play is four hundred lines long and falls into two distinct parts with the turn marked very precisely by Sebastian's final entry. Up to that point what is remarkable is the way in which Shakespeare orchestrates aural and visual events to create for a final time the sensation of impasse and frustration that results from mistakes of identity and the assumption of unnatural poses. One by one characters who have otherwise not shared a stage together assemble in one place, but their coming together at first does not result in the harmony one would expect.

The scene begins promisingly, however. The first striking event is the sight of Orsino walking the streets of Illyria and not holed up in his palace. We have come to expect that we will see him isolated from the world, listening to lugubrious music, and lamenting his unrequited love. It is a visual surprise, therefore, to observe him in the open air bantering with Feste and moving toward Olivia's. This visual cue signals that his claustrophobic self-imprisonment may be over. There is, furthermore, relief in seeing Feste once more in his characteristic role of fool, begging for money, and no longer disguised as a curate.

But as more characters enter—the visual crescendo underscoring a rising sense of anticipation—language once more becomes hopelessly entangled. Characters have so long pretended to be what they are not that, even when they genuinely try to communicate, they still speak at cross purposes. Each successive entrance merely compounds the confusion of identities, and questions fly thick and fast with few satisfying answers given. Antonio is clearly revealed as Orsino's old enemy, but he *seems* to be lying about his rescue of Viola. Olivia makes clear her love for Cesario, but either she or Viola *seems* to be lying about the wedding that is supposed to have occurred. Toby and Andrew clearly have taken a drubbing in a duel, but either they or Viola *seems* to be lying about who gave them that drubbing. Only when Sebastian enters can misunderstandings be resolved. . . .

REALISM IS NOT THE POINT

Students with a penchant for realism often object that it takes the twins an unconscionably long time to recognize one another. But, of course, realism is not the point. The point is that the tick-tock of question and answer, detail countered with confirming detail, is part of a ritual of recognition, a way of redeeming the self and language from the confusion into which both have fallen. And it is a theatrically necessary ritual, fulfilling a desire for direct, open, and reciprocated speech that has been frustrated for five acts. After the unanswered questions of the first half of the scene, the answered questions of Sebastian and Viola give special pleasure to characters and audience alike. Through them, characters find release from the prison of disguise and affectation in which they long have been locked. . . .

But the audience's experience is not over yet. It, too, must be released from the role of spectator and from the manipulations of the dramatist. For the spectator this release is effected by Feste's song. . . . By the way Shakespeare finally releases the audience from the play, he reminds us that, in the world beyond the theater, the forces which govern our experience are often less benign than the dramatist of *Twelfth Night* has been. Outside the theater, we are the pawns of time and chance, not the creatures of a generous playwright. And time and chance, while they sometimes bring ships safely to port, also bring pain, alienation, and frustration of desire. Feste's song, with its haunting refrain about the wind and the rain, is a chastening reminder of this truth and an important part of our experience of *Twelfth Night*. . . .

In short, Shakespeare finds in *Twelfth Night*, as in all his plays, a very specific theatrical vocabulary by which the enacted script communicates with its audience. This is a vocabulary, not just of words, but also of gestures, sounds, images, and movements that are woven together to create theatrical events of great complexity. In orchestrating these sensory elements of the implied performance, Shakespeare always keeps one eye on the audience. The full dramatic meaning of his works is realized only in our responses to them.

Interpretative Choices Reflect How the Play Is Perceived

Anthony B. Dawson

Anthony B. Dawson, professor of English and theater at the University of British Columbia as well as the author of several books on Shakespeare and an editor for The Internet Shakespeare Editions, examines different approaches taken by directors and actors in various productions of *Twelfth Night.* Dawson considers how decisions concerning the age of characters and how comically they are portrayed can affect the whole demeanor of the play. The characterizations of Maria, Feste, Malvolio, and Viola—who Dawson claims holds the reins to many moods—can affect the balance of comedy and pathos, thus altering how the play is ultimately received.

How old is Feste? The director's answer to that question will be one indication of his or her attitude toward *Twelfth Night* as a whole. In recent years it has become fashionable to give us an aging Feste, a precarious, vulnerable, melancholy fool whose wit is the brighter for the dark background. And, if Feste is old, the general emphasis is likely to be autumnal, with a sense of winter coming on and people buttoning up against the cold. At Stratford Ontario in 1980, William Hutt's quiet, dignified and haunting Feste even wore a wool scarf knotted around his neck. His age was matched by that of Maria, played by Kate Reid, who was a gentlewoman well past her prime, rather desperately seeking a match with a much younger Sir Toby Belch.

EXAMPLES OF CHARACTER RENDITIONS AND RELATIONSHIPS

"Autumnal" has, in fact, become something of a byword when applied to *Twelfth Night.* A play that in simpler days

was primarily a high-spirited romp has, on more careful examination, revealed the latent melancholy and complexity of
feeling that lie beneath the spirited surface. And this, I think,
has meant a real gain in our understanding. The essence of
Twelfth Night is the rich and delicate web of relationships
that it spins. If the previous age took its cue from the revelry
suggested by the festive associations of the title (the twelve
days of Christmas), the present age looks to the wintry landscape outside the brightly lit windows and to the quandaries
suggested by the ambiguous sub-title: "What You Will".

The play blends lyricism and mockery, sadness and wit,
melancholy and revelry. And, as with so much else in Shakespeare, no production can afford to neglect one side completely, though most directors will tend to weight their reading in one way or another. . . . Take, for example, the
character of Sir Andrew Aguecheek. Played usually as a
goofy, foolish knight, often tall, gangly and awkward, a butt
of the comic games of his intellectual superiors, an absurd
yes-man to Sir Toby, he nevertheless has his dignified and
slightly pathetic side. When Sir Toby says of the intrepid
Maria that "she's a beagle, true-bred, and one that adores
me", Andrew replies wistfully, "I was ador'd once too." This
line could be delivered as simply another of Andrew's many
attempts to keep up with Sir Toby, but how much richer it is
if we suddenly see a new side of the bumbling fool—a man
of some feeling who really was adored, once. . . .

To take [another] example, what is the relationship between Feste and Maria like? Each has a special place in the
household and both have been there for some time. Maria is
not a soubrette [a coquettish maid] nor a buxom serving-
girl; she is a gentlewoman of good family, a lady in waiting.
Most modern productions get this right, avoiding the old tradition of making her merely a wench. Giving her her right-
ful dignity will make a difference in her relationships with
the others in the house, including Feste. Theirs will not necessarily be a jocular, bouncy association based on clowning
and witty exchanges, but may easily be one in which their
mutual concern, based on a shared past, plays a central role.
. . . Their first dialogue together, at the beginning of I.v, will
set the tone. Maria scolds Feste in a familiar, teasing way:
"Nay, either tell me where thou hast been, or I will not open
my lips so wide as a bristle may enter in way of thy excuse.
My lady will hang thee for thy absence." Feste tries his

clown's method of witty avoidance, which she enjoys, but she comes back in a minute to the point: "Yet you will be hanged for being so long absent; or be turned away, is not that as good as a hanging to you?" The threat of losing his job, though he deftly brushes it aside, may indeed be a genuine one; economic reality edges in. In the 1985 Stratford Ontario production directed by David Giles, this whole dialogue was conducted as Maria helped Feste, who was distinctly old and frail, into his tattered motley. She held a pail up to him, he dunked his head in and came up white-faced. She was clearly his friend and knew his routines. Later, heeding her warning, he had to work hard to please Olivia and keep his job.

Both Maria and Feste are economically dependent, and each is aware of the other's position. Maria wants to marry Sir Toby—she "adores" him, but perhaps also she is looking for some kind of economic security (though Sir Toby too depends on the generosity of his niece or the gullibility of chumps like Andrew). At the end of their little dialogue, Feste, in his characteristically oblique way, alludes to her none-too-secret desire, which some recent Marias have shown to be rather desperate: "If Sir Toby would leave drinking, thou wert as pretty a piece of Eve's flesh as any in Illyria." Her response, "Peace, you rogue, no more o' that," shows again their familiar, teasing closeness and perhaps too a poorly concealed desperation (as Kate Reid played it), a quickly replaced dignity or an amused carefreeness.

As for Sir Toby, he is more than a comic drunkard, or a bumbling clown. As far back as [Harley] Granville-Barker's important production in 1914, he was treated properly as a gentleman, though one who is slightly down at heel. Nevertheless, subsequent directors and actors have often followed comic tradition and played the caricature. His age is uncertain, though it seems fitting that, as Feste and Maria are getting older, he seems to be getting younger. He carries the play's revelry on his shoulders, but he can also display a harsh and bitter side which cuts against the general festivity. . . .

Thus the interplay of feeling established early on, say in the little scene between Feste and Maria discussed above, can have interesting consequences in the finale. Such subtlety can be extended as well into what used to be called the "kitchen scene," the night of drunken revelry that Malvolio so rudely interrupts (II.iii). The traditional way of doing that scene was to load it down with exaggerated comic business, though at present we can hope for some signs of other feelings along with the madcap humour—a touch of sadness in Feste's song, an edge of belligerence in Sir Toby, or, again, a sense of solidarity between Feste and Maria. . . .

HOW MALVOLIO IS PORTRAYED WILL AFFECT THE MOOD

We have been neglecting Malvolio. What of him? More than any other character, he is subject to a variety of interpretations. Is he simply a pompous ass, and hence a fitting butt for the practical joke that undermines his hard-earned dignity? Is he a fool, a puritan, a man of some sensitivity, even if too earnest and self-concerned? Whatever he is, his is the star male part, and he has therefore been played by an array of brilliant actors. He has often evoked sympathy as well as laughter and contempt, especially at the end, where the treatment he undergoes at the hands of the comics seems to outweigh his crimes, and has thus reminded some critics of the treatment of Shylock [from *The Merchant of Venice*]. Overall, he has been played more for comedy than pathos, though usually comedy with an edge. [Sir John] Gielgud, in 1931, was [described in reviews as] "sere and yellow," a "Puritan to the core"; [Sir Laurence] Olivier, in 1955, was the lower-class fellow who had worked his way up, his affected speech sometimes slipping to reveal the broader vowels of his upbringing; Donald Sinden, in 1969, was "a Victorian cartoon Humpty Dumpty," pompous and absurd; Nicol Williamson in 1974 was, in the Gielgud vein, a "pinched Scottish elder," very tall and gangling with a ruff around his neck giving him a small detached-looking head on a grotesque body; Brian Bedford at Stratford Ontario in 1980 was broadly comic, complete with a teddy bear half-concealed under his nightshirt in II.iii, which inevitably led to a good deal of funny business. Back in the early part of this century, Beerbohm Tree played Malvolio with an earnest dignity that was both impressive and absurd; he was attended by "four smaller Malvolios, who aped the great chamberlain in dress, in manners and in deportment"; nevertheless, his ultimate loss of Olivia was emotionally telling. . . .

When Malvolio exits at the end, the subject of the Fool's ridicule and the others' laughter, his hopes to gain the fair Olivia (like those of the hapless Sir Andrew Aguecheek) for ever dashed, he shouts "I'll be reveng'd on the whole pack of

AN AUTUMNAL PLAY?

During the course of Trevor Nunn's eighteen years directing the Royal Shakespeare Company (Nunn began as an associate director while Sir Peter Hall was the managing director) he was interviewed by the prolific Shakespearean scholar Ralph Berry. Though he has yet to direct a stage version of Twelfth Night, *the director shares some of his impressions regarding the play that he was later able to apply to his 1998 cinematic production.*

Twelfth Night is capable of many different productions, in the sense that it is indestructible. It works even when people do appalling thing to it, like saying "wouldn't it be a good idea to make it about a country house society in the 1920s," or when Jonathan Miller writes a long programme note about the neo-Platonism of the play and does a production to prove it. . . . I saw Peter Hall's production of *Twelfth Night* and its autumnal setting and its melancholia seemed definitively right. He had touched a Chekhov-like [the Russian writer Anton Chekhov was known for his characterizations] centre in the play; it was unarguable. And when I saw John Barton's version of the play, it seemed to me that he had carried Peter Hall's perception further, and in a less nineteenth-century or operatic manner—John Barton's production was much more stark, more of the Elizabethan playhouse—and yet, in showing us that Belch, Aguecheek, Malvolio, Feste *and* Maria and Orsino were all of an age who would bitterly understand "Youth's a stuff will not endure" he'd unlocked fully the dark and melancholic half of the play, in contrast to which, while "golden time convents," Viola and Olivia and Sebastian play their games of disguise and romance. Recently it was suggested to me that we were quite wrong to think of *Twelfth Night* as an autumnal play: surely *Twelfth Night* is a winter play. Its relevance to the Twelfth Night festivities was not just that it was celebratory and joyous, but that Shakespeare clearly envisaged a bleak deep mid-winter situation, both climatically and emotionally—a much less funny play than tradition has made it. Immediately all kinds of images start to emerge from the text and yet, previously, every line of it seemed to be saying it's autumn and the leaves aren't quite dropping off the trees, and it's watery dawns and glorious sunsets.

Ralph Berry, "Trevor Nunn," *On Directing Shakespeare: Interviews with Contemporary Directors.* London: Croom Helm, 1977, pp. 60–61.

you." The festivity of the ending is at least temporarily disrupted, and a note of grievance and distaste enters in. Just how
much a director will allow this mood to intrude upon the dominant feeling of joy will affect profoundly the final taste of the
production. Some modulation of the mood is inevitable and
desirable. Even the most comic Malvolios are likely to bring to
this moment some feeling of pathos, as with Bedford's wince
at Olivia's friendly touch, which underlined his loneliness
and the shame he felt at his exposure. Nicholas Pennell's performance at Stratford Ontario in 1985, though it stressed
Malvolio's absurdity, elicited a sympathetic "oh" from the audience as he appeared dirty, downcast and bedraggled. His final line, with a significant pause after "reveng'd," was re-
strained and bitter. Pinched and puritanical Malvolios, such
as Gielgud's and Williamson's, are the least likely to excite
sympathy. Gielgud, for example, went out snarling and spite-
ful. With his patrician presence, Henry Irving in the last century made his exit frightening and vindictive—he clearly
meant mischief. No sympathy there, but a sense of danger undermining the final peace. . . . It is hard, then, to say how
Malvolio should, or predict how he will, be played. But any
performance will have to take account of both the comic absurdity—especially in the famous letter scene and its aftermath, when he appears smiling foolishly, in yellow stockings
and cross-gartered—and his earnest vulnerability, veiled as it
may be by pomposity or self-congratulation.

Malvolio and Feste are natural enemies, living in the
same household, each competing for place, and, presumably, taking any available opportunity to goad one another.
At the outset, Malvolio turns up his nose at Feste—"I marvel
your ladyship takes delight in such a barren rascal. I saw
him put down the other day with an ordinary fool that has
no more brain than a stone" (I.v.80–2). At the end Feste reminds Malvolio, rather cruelly, of his earlier words and the
price he has paid for them: "and thus the whirligig of time
brings in his revenges" (v.i.373–4). Perhaps we could say that
these two characters represent two poles of the play, and a
director's choices will lead him or her to weight one or the
other. The tendency over the last twenty years or so has been
to make Feste the spiritual centre. . . . ([The 1979 Royal
Shakespeare Company] even had him stationed on-stage
throughout). And Malvolio's role, though obviously important, has been correspondingly diminished. . . .

FABIAN'S NECESSITY, ORSINO'S TEMPERAMENT, AND OLIVIA'S AGE

The very minor but puzzling figure, Fabian, deserves a brief mention. He turns up at the end of Act II to take part in the plot against Malvolio, presumably because the latter has brought him "out o' favor with my lady about a bear-baiting here." Directors have not always known what to do with him, but he cannot be cut, since he is crucial to the trick played on Andrew and Viola (their "duel"). One of the most inventive answers to the question of who Fabian really is was Hugh Hunt's at the Old Vic in 1950. He made Fabian into a second fool, a younger rival to Feste, seeking the latter's spot in the household. This emphasized again the economics of Feste's position, and led to a nice moment in the last scene when Fabian is preferred over Feste in the reading of Malvolio's letter. The final song, poignant but unsentimental, thus seemed to suggest that Feste had been succeeded, and faced alone the "wind and the rain. . . ."

The interpretative question for both Orsino and Olivia concerns the degree of satire or comic mockery that may be directed at them. Orsino can easily be played as a luxuriating, slightly absurd, pampered aristocrat, with nothing more to do than lie around on this or that couch and have music feed his melancholy. The fact that he is the ruling duke of the principality seems to play almost no part in his life. One production that I saw had him constantly and elaborately mirrored, even directly above, so that when he lay down, as he often did, he could watch himself suffer. But he can also be given a degree of strength and presence, making Viola's love for him more credible, and turning his love-madness into, perhaps, a charming obsession, a brooding aberration, or even the inevitable result of a loving nature. Colm Feore, in David Giles's production, was strong, and used to command; his obsession with Olivia was clearly aberrant, stemming perhaps from the fact that he was unable to command *her*. His growing interest in Viola-Cesario thus suggested a truer relationship, blocked though it temporarily was by the confusion of sex. In general, though some "gentle satire" is certainly mingled with the "lyric strain," [according to Hunt] a winning, masculine Orsino is preferable to a swooning one.

As for Olivia, she has occasioned a wider range of interpretations. For many years, she was played as a dignified countess, somewhat older than the others, commanding her house with a sensible firmness and gaining from characters and audience a fair amount of respect. Peter Hall, in his "Chekhovian" [based on the style of Russian playwright Anton Chekhov] production at Stratford in 1958, revised all that, making her into [as one review noted] "a pouting doll, a gawky, giggling coquette," much younger than she had traditionally been. In [John] Barton's 1969 production, which developed some of Hall's ideas, she was also young and silly. Such an Olivia will necessarily affect our view of Orsino and his love, making him seem blinder and more foolishly obsessed than ever. She is now usually young, though at Stratford Ontario in 1980 she was considerably older and coolly dignified once again. This allowed for a distinctly agreeable Orsino, who lost little of our estimation despite his obsession. Nor was the silliness of either of them completely neglected. In Olivia especially, the sight of an older woman making a fool of herself in the face of such youngsters as Viola and Sebastian (though the former, unfortunately, was no spring chicken either) had both ironic and slightly distasteful consequences.

SUBTLETY, LIKE VIOLA, MODULATES THE PLAY

Both [Olivia and Orsino], and indeed the very life of the main plot of the play, revolve around Viola-Cesario. Her quickness, her lyricism, her good sense, her loyalty define the tone and dominate the action. She is one of Shakespeare's great comic heroines, but unlike the others she is remarkably helpless. . . . And she is the only one of these [comic heroines] to become the butt of a major joke—the mock duel in Act IV. . . . It is an unusual state of affairs to have the most attractive, most positive character in the play turn for a while into one of its dupes, but it is a measure of the kind of play we are dealing with. That mixture of lyricism and revelry, invocation and mockery, that I spoke of at the beginning is nowhere so richly embodied as in the person of Viola.

In II.iv, the many moods of the play gather softly around the heroine, and the trick will be for actress and production to hold and carry as many as possible: the gentle comedy of mistaken identity, the lyrical evocation of the shortness of youth and beauty, the deep sadness of Feste's song ("Come away, come away, death"), and especially Viola-Cesario's artfully ironic and melancholy story of his-her "sister" who "sat like

Patience on a monument, / Smiling at grief." This is one of those moments, infrequent but crucial, when the action stops and its opalescent tonalities are allowed to eddy freely:

ORSINO. For women are as roses, whose fair flow'r
    Being once display'd, doth fall that very hour.
VIOLA. And so they are. Alas, that they are so,
    To die, even when they to perfection grow!
                                            (II.iv.38–41)

Later, the lyrical voice is countered by the comic: "Say that some lady," says Viola, "Hath for your love as great a pang of heart / As you have for Olivia" (II. 89–91). But Orsino refuses to believe in such a possibility: "There is no woman's sides / Can bide the beating of so strong a passion / As love doth give my heart . . . they lack retention." The joke, of course, is on him. And Viola proceeds to tell her own story in a disguised way. Orsino is engaged by it; as Colm Feore and Seana McKenna played the scene at Stratford Ontario, he moved in towards her: "But died thy sister of her love, my boy?", to which she replied mysteriously, "I am all the daughters of my father's house, / And all the brothers too—and yet I know not." A pause; Orsino was standing *too* close to her. Deliciously confused feelings filled the moment. Then she broke away, returning to more comfortable ground: "Sir, shall I to this lady?"—"Ay, that's the theme." His constructed plot and artificially created emotions were easier for Orsino than these unfamiliar stirrings. [As noted by Stanley Wells] Judi Dench, speaking the above lines in Barton's 1969 production, gave "a tiny pause followed by a catch in the voice as she said 'brothers'"—a reminder, in the midst of her fiction, of the reality, to her though not to us, of her lost brother. Such subtle interplay between illusion and reality is both appropriate and necessary for a scene, indeed a play, in which the lyric and ironic voices are so finely modulated.

We get the same mixture in the final scene, where the recognition and unravelling are sandwiched between the climactic outbursts first of Sir Toby and then of Malvolio. Even within the recognition itself, there are ironic underlinings of the conventional features of such scenes. Can Viola really say to Sebastian with a straight face, "My father had a mole upon his brow?" She can and does, and the ironic reminiscence only adds to the sense of an exquisite stateliness, a measured formality which prolongs and encircles the act of recognition itself. J.C. Trewin describes how in the hands of an actress such as Peggy Ashcroft the moment can be magical indeed; after Sebastian's wondering question, "What countryman? What name? What parentage?" there was a long pause before Viola, "in almost a whisper (but one of infinite rapture and astonishment) answer[ed]: 'Of Messaline!'". . .

Viola, in keeping with the measured quality of the scene, forbears an embrace with her brother until "each circumstance / Of place, time, fortune, do cohere and jump / That I am Viola" (v.i.248–50). Orsino adopts the same manner as he moves to the faithless boy turned faithful woman: "Give me thy hand, / And let me see thee in thy woman's weeds" (II. 269–70). Again the embrace is postponed, the formality allowed. The scene, like many others in the play, manages to be both moving and funny, and calls for the kind of subtle playing that can evoke both reactions.

Feste and Fabian re-enter with the letter from Malvolio, and the mood again shifts. The latter's entrance and revengeful departure introduce a bitter note which echoes behind the processional exit of the happy couples, and we are left alone with the clown, who moves downstage, or stands in a spotlight as the other lights dim. Edward Atienza's poignant and versatile Feste, the spring of the 1985 Stratford Ontario revival, simply sat on a step, raindrops falling on his lute (his fingers tapped the wood as he looked quizzically to the sky). He sang, in a variety of appropriate voices, that last song, with its wonderfully ambiguous and evocative refrain: "With hey, ho, the wind and the rain . . . For the rain it raineth every day." Youth, marriage, revelry, the passing of time, all take their place under the sky and its unpredictable weather. But the play ends on an upbeat, with a reminder of the joy of playing, and of playgoing:

> But that's all one, our play is done,
> And we'll strive to please you every day.

Playing Viola

Zoë Wanamaker

Zoë Wanamaker, the award-winning British actress, describes her approach to taking on the role of Viola as well as all the problems of live performance including a perilous stage set and cumbersome clothes. With great consideration given to Viola's personality, Wanamaker perceives Viola as a catalyst in the play and acknowledges the responsibility of such a part. Wanamaker further discusses interpretations of ideas, themes, difficult scenes, and even the problematic ending.

I had played Viola some ten years before John Caird's Stratford production of *Twelfth Night,* in a version directed by Richard Cotterill for the Cambridge Theatre Company. The sense (the constant sense in doing Shakespeare) that that version had not come up to expectations left me, however, quite ready to accept a second invitation to attempt the part. . . .

OVERCOMING THE SENSE OF INSECURITY

To undertake a major role at Stratford is to be haunted by the past. As you go into the Royal Shakespeare Theatre you are faced with twelve-foot-high pictures of other actors who have done other performances of your part, and their history and their triumphs loom over you: "Follow that!" It's like coming to Mecca; the ghosts are all around and the fear of failure is very great. Having been brought up through the sixties when new work by new writers was the prime objective in my kind of theatre, the thought of speaking Shakespeare's verse on the Stratford stage was inevitably frightening.

This sense of insecurity remained when the production opened. Was I speaking the text as it should be spoken, was I being true to it, to the production, to the character? After a year in Stratford, a year of struggle to be relaxed in the role and yet to keep it fresh, we moved to London, to the Barbi-

Excerpted from "Viola in *Twelfth Night,*" by Zoë Wanamaker, in *Players of Shakespeare 2,* edited by Russell Jackson and Robert Smallwood. Copyright © 1988 by Cambridge University Press. Reprinted with permission from Cambridge University Press.

can, where, with some modifications to the set and alter-
ations to Viola's costume (and some cast changes too, including a new Olivia and a new Sir Toby), and some new
ideas that I had been mulling over during the break, I found
myself much more confident in the words and began to enjoy myself in the part. Confidence in the text as a springboard, an innate sense of not having to think about the
words or about saying them right, these things allowed the
play to become a conversation in which I was at home, to become organic. But a year to find that sense is a long time.

The basic aim of John Caird's production was to focus on
the pain of love. *Twelfth Night* deals with many kinds of love:
Viola's, the most pure, constant as the sea is constant, the sea
that gives her her life, and her brother his, and her brother
back to her; Malvolio's love, self-deluding, ultimately self-
centred; Olivia's love of mourning, for her father and, re-
flecting Viola, for her brother; Orsino's adoring love, which
puts woman on a pedestal; Antonio's faithful, painful love of
Sebastian; Maria's dogged love of Sir Toby; Sir Toby's love of
wasting time; each character disguising the truth about himself and from himself. The play is a fairly simple one, really,
a story about time, about growing up and growing old. It has
the concentrated quality of a chamber piece, and its form is
a complete circle, a point we tried to mark in our production,
which began with the sounds of storm and rain and ended
with Feste singing of them as these sounds returned. Illyria
seems to be a place that is frozen in time, where the social
order is locked, where self-delusion, disguise, and hierarchy
create an impasse for the people who live with them. And
then Viola arrives and her presence disturbs everyone and
moves the play through chaos and at last into seeming harmony but with that last strange coda of Feste's song, and
Malvolio still locked in self-delusion, disguised even to himself. The catalyst, the driving force of the play is Viola; and
the responsibility of that was on me.

To have played the part before was not helpful, not rele-
vant. I wanted to come to it as a blank sheet of paper, to let
it sit in my head while I was reading it, reading it once and
just trying to find where my instincts were on that first reading, what my first impressions of the play were, trying to
wipe out the old tunes of the way I had done it before. Much
of that early reading, too, was for the sounds, the rhythms,
the movement of the iambic line, which to me is not instinc-

tive but something I have to work at, a secret code to be penetrated, like music; but for this text, certainly, a wonderful route to the deeper flow of the play—and, indeed, to the simple process of learning the words, which for me (touched with dyslexia) is not an easy process at all. In these early stages I was looking for all the clues I could find about what kind of person Viola is, what other characters say about her, what would happen to the story of the play if she were taken away, but always concentrating on the actual structure of her text, the precise choice of words. . . . Rehearsals were, as ever, a tough and arduous search, a fumbling with the labyrinthine twists and turns of the script, a slow process of getting to know the other actors and their ideas, their interpretations of their roles; of argument and discussion and trying to fit it all in and to make the story of these people understandable and the play's ideas, wonderful and extraordinary, clear to an audience.

SETTING THE STAGE AND DRESSING THE PART

Eventually we got onto the set, designed by Robin Don and lit by David Hersey, a rocky landscape next to the sea, dominated by a tree, an autumnal-looking tree, its branches fanning out like a sea coral, above and beyond the proscenium arch. Costumes too were autumnal, in rusts and browns and olives, and traditionally Elizabethan. From the auditorium it was, I'm told, a very beautiful set, but for us, as we discovered at the technical rehearsals, there were huge problems, particularly with the terrain. The tree, and the rocky inclines, left an acting area only a few feet across, and though there was some levelling following the technical rehearsals, difficulties remained throughout the Stratford season. The set was partly supposed to represent a sort of nightmare, and the lighting was subdued to give an atmosphere of emotional turmoil, discovery of self, growing up, but the translation of these concepts into practical stage terms was not without difficulties for us. It was hard to find your light, and the unevenness of the floor was exacerbated by the eight-inch wide trough for the safety iron, in which many an ankle was in peril of being turned during the season; getting down from the top of the rocks at the back was hazardous; and the tree, which had looked so delicate on the model, the little veins of the coral like a lovely leaf-skeleton, had to be made much more substantial because of the need to dismantle it so often during the season for changes of play in the Stratford repertoire system. All these things were part of the disappointment (not unusual) of turning initial concepts and ideas into concrete, and sometimes cumbersome, reality. At the Barbican I think the set worked better, partly, no doubt, because we were more used to it, but also because the wider stage allowed more room on either side of it, and there was some more levelling out, and altered lighting. In London I was much happier, too, with my costume, which had been such a disappointment when I first wore it at the Stratford technical rehearsal. The thick corduroy trousers and waistcoat, which to me had always seemed lumpy, were changed to a light suede and I found myself much more relaxed and easy, able to use the pockets. I felt much more like a boy in it, and the sense of greater ease was increased by cutting my own hair very short and so discarding the wig which had always bothered me. Audiences, I think, enjoyed the literal quality of the set, the tree, the rocks, and the thunderstorm, and the music by Ilona Sekacz, beautiful and magical, and the sound of the sea which was ever present, the giver and taker of life, dark and threatening yet at the same time mysterious and romantic.

GETTING INTO THE PART

The young woman who enters this Illyrian world from the shipwreck I took to be about seventeen or eighteen years old, brought up with her twin brother Sebastian by their father (their mother is never mentioned in the play), a man, I felt, of great intelligence and warmth, since her relationship with her brother is so close and trusting. She has already learned (or inherited) that straightforward common sense, that unclouded attitude to life, that sense of being a person without prejudice—the qualities that are so wonderful about her. I suspect that the death of her father has been a great blow to her and that her relationship with her brother is all the stronger because of it. With him she is taking a summer cruise, we imagined, a tour in the royal yacht, and then the storm, and separation, and the rocky shore of Illyria, and the memory of her father's talk of Orsino and the decision to serve him as the sole link with the lost past.

Viola's disguise allows her to know Orsino in a way that would never have been possible otherwise. In three days he confides everything to this boy, this stranger, something he would never have done to a woman. The intimacy of confidence disturbs him—and this was something we tried hard to bring out in the production—the strange love for this boy is something that he cannot understand or explain. Viola is let into his mind, his confidence, his imagination, in such a way that inevitably she falls in love with him, with this extraordinary, erudite human being. The strange inevitability of Orsino's love for her was something we constantly tried to explore. . . .

MAKING A LASTING IMPRESSION

Into the locked-up stillness of Illyria [Viola] brings life, and chaos, and hope; she is the catalyst of the play, stirring up the place, forcing them all up into a spiral, to wake up, to discuss, to learn about themselves, turning their world upside down. She arrives in Illyria like a life-force: "What country, friends, is this?" (1.2.1).

The moment of Viola's entry changed significantly for me between Stratford and London. I tried to make the audience witness, as it were, to that terrible moment of loss, of parting from someone so close to her as her brother, by introducing a hopeless, helpless scream, almost of an animal, to bring focus immediately onto the pain of this person. In this short scene we see not only the initial pain, but also the positive qualities, her hope, her perception of others, her belief in the power of Time. In listening to the captain's story of Olivia, shutting the door, shunning life, I used to think that this could never happen to Viola, she would never do that, she does not think of men as a threat, emotionally or physically. Life for her is not to be lived behind locked doors. So from the idea of serving Olivia she turns to Orsino, to her memories of her father's talk of him, and then, instinctively, to the idea of disguise. She does not really know who she is—having lost her past she is in search of herself—she does not want to leave the place that provides the only hope of further news of her brother, and there in front of her is (or was in our production) Sebastian's trunk, which has been washed up with her. She opens it and finds his jacket, his doublet, and puts it on. And the smell of it, and the memory of him, means that in some way she keeps alive something of her brother, not just a piece of clothing but part of his soul, and by having that, through some sort of osmosis, the hope that he really is still alive is carried with her, always. "Conceal me what I am," and her hope begins to flow back and she decides to wait, to trust to Time, to use the confidence and hope that is in her to change the situation. And so from the despair of its opening this little scene moves to its wonderfully optimistic conclusion: "What else may hap, to time I will commit . . . Lead me on" (1.2.60, 64).

The meeting with Olivia, and the "willow cabin" speech, were always difficult for me, rather like a horse going up to a jump, I used to feel. The scene is a conversation between two women, very different women, though similar in age, Olivia perhaps a little younger than Viola. It is just two women talking and you see the different perceptions of both of them, especially of Viola, who associates very strongly with Olivia's emotions (she too has lost a father and, she fears, a brother) and understands them. The apparent finality of Olivia's "I cannot love him. / He might have took his answer long ago" (1.5.262–3) forces Viola into her big wooing speech; she has to make it, she has to do her appointed job, and she just happens to get carried away with it and so applies it to herself. And thus she admits to herself her love for Orsino by saying it out loud to another woman. The springboard for the willow cabin speech is her want, her need, to talk about her own love; it comes from the depth of her own imagination and she gets so carried away with it that she surprises herself. She has reached a new stage of self-awareness by the end of it.

DARK MOMENTS AND DEFENSIVENESS

On her way back from Olivia's house she is overtaken by Malvolio with the ring. She recognizes Olivia's motive, her self-delusion, immediately: "She loves me sure" (2.2.22). What to do with this ring was the source of some discussion during our rehearsals, for it is never given back or referred to again. Eventually it was decided that I should hang it on a twig of the stage tree where it was found again by Feste at the end of the play. (Some members of the audience saw this as further evidence of Feste's secret love for Olivia, which they also thought they discerned at other points in the production.) As far as Viola is concerned, the significance of hanging the ring on the tree was primarily to be rid of something which she cannot accept without compromising herself. She cannot accept the responsibility of that ring, for the love which it implies is not truly given to her, should not be

to her, and she does not want it to be to her. So she leaves it
there for Time (or whoever) to discover, and with its redis-
covery at the end we have the sense of the play coming full
circle again. "Time, thou must untangle this, not I" (2.2.40),
she says as she takes stock of her situation, not a reckless
surrender, but a declaration of trust and faith that Time, or
something, is going to make things change. When we reach
her next scene, however, her longest conversation with
Orsino, she is losing that faith and touching her lowest point
in the play.

The conversation between Orsino and Viola after the
singing of "Come away, death" I always felt a wonderfully
close scene and an absolutely heartbreaking one. For here
are two people in love who should love each other but cannot do so because one is incapable of seeing through disguises, not just hers but his own. Orsino deludes himself; he
is blind about women and how they should be treated; sup-
poses that they cannot be spoken to honestly or share the
thoughts and feelings of men. Viola in this scene is, I think,
in despair about her situation. All that Orsino says about
women is so terrible for her to hear, so mistaken:

> no woman's sides
> Can bide the beating of so strong a passion
> As love doth give my heart; no woman's heart
> So big, to hold so much; they lack retention.   (2.4.93–6)

Her reply, I felt, was defensive, and angry—"In faith, they
are as true of heart as we" (2.4.106)—and the argument that
follows catches her almost unawares. "Ay, but I know" . . .
"What dost thou know?", and there she is nearly found out;
through her unhappiness and frustration she has started
into something and she has to explain: "My father had a
daughter lov'd a man" . . . to explain in the best way that she
can . . . "as it might be". . . she's so close . . . "as it might be,
perhaps, were I a woman" . . . she is so close, so close to saying "I am a woman, and I love you," but she has to disguise
it, to disguise it in a way that tries to say to him that love is
not about dying and despair, as he seems to perceive it. "And
what's her history?", he then asks, and that's when she realizes her situation: "A blank, my lord; she never told her
love." That's something important, the difference between
him and her; this is what might happen to her—never to
speak, to remain silent and patient, for ever. "But died thy
sister of her love, my boy?" (line 119). He wants only to

know about the misery of it all and she is trying to educate him, to take him in another direction that he has never perceived. But he cannot see, and she has to go around: "I am all the daughters of my father's house, / And all the brothers too." She is here, I think, near to despair. "And yet I know not": the glimmer of hope is still there, but this always seemed to me her darkest moment. For Orsino, too, it is a strange moment, when he cannot decide, when he's nearly turned, and then habit, and confusion, and obsession take over again and he returns to his self-delusion: "To her in haste . . . my love can give no place" (lines 123–4). At the end of the scene we see Viola, for almost the only time in the play, really depressed.

CHANCE ENCOUNTERS AND THE PROBLEM ENDING

On the way to fulfil this gloomy mission, however, she meets Feste. The scene came after the interval in our production, at the top of the second act. Her relationship with Feste is another of the small joys of the play. He too is one of the play's outsiders: Malvolio, Feste, Antonio, Aguecheek, the Sea Captain, Viola—the play is full of loners. Feste, like all of Shakespeare's fools perhaps (but surely more so), has an extraordinary perception of life, an aptness of observation especially apparent in his scene with Orsino: "changeable taffeta . . . thy mind is a very opal" (2.4.74–5)—he is exactly right about Orsino. And here, interrupted on her way to Olivia's, Viola contemplates the skill of the man who is "wise enough to play the fool" (3.1.60), and finds the diversionary pleasure of playing with words. She is always discovering things about life, and taking time off during the play to talk to the audience about them . . . to share her sense of humour with them. Her relationship with Feste is an enjoyment of the mind—like her relationship with Orsino, if only they could break through to full understanding.

The chance of that comes by way of the recognition scene with Sebastian after her disguise has taken her through the comic absurdities of the mock duel with Aguecheek—comic and absurd for the audience, at least, though increasingly embarrassing and dangerous for Viola. The wonder of the recognition comes at an awful moment for her, as she is accused of having married Olivia, of beating Sir Andrew, wounding Sir Toby, denying the open-heartedness of Antonio's love, a crescendo of everything piling on top of her. And

then, there is her brother like something out of a fairy story
—just like a fairy story, indeed, that is what is so wonderful
about it, the sudden appearance of Sebastian, the apple cleft
in twain, the mirror of herself. It is a magical moment, the
resolution of confusion, the meeting of self, of each other;
the whirlpool and the tempest that brought them to Illyria
die down and suddenly there is wholeness again, the magical moment of seeing someone you thought was dead, the
other half of yourself. "Do not embrace me," she says
(5.1.251), unable quite to make that contact whole until she
knows again who she is by putting on her "maiden's weeds,"
rediscovering that other half of herself through the ritual of
dressing again as a woman.

After that comes Orsino's strangely hearty, and rather
awkward, declaration:

> Boy, thou hast said to me a thousand times
> Thou never shouldst love woman like to me.   (5.1.267–8)

Viola's reply is open and direct, honest and truthful as she
has been throughout the play. In front of all those people she
says:

> And all those sayings will I over swear,
> And all those swearings keep as true in soul
> As doth that orbed continent the fire
> That severs day from night.   (5.1.269–72)

They are almost her last words in the play. I always thought
it difficult for Orsino to make this sudden change from his
obsession with Olivia, however carefully we had tried to prepare for it in the "patience on a monument" dialogue. Viola
(unlike Rosalind in *As You Like It*) is denied her "woman's
weeds"; there is no marriage ceremony, not even a formal
offer from Orsino. "Let me see thee in thy woman's weeds"
he simply says, and a little later the bald statement that "a
solemn combination *shall* be made / Of our dear souls"
(lines 383–4). The scene is a difficult one to make work, a director's nightmare (like the last scene of *Measure for Measure*, perhaps), and I do not think that our production ever
really found it, though we worked hard at it and discussed
and argued about it for two years! Perhaps the problem was
just being a woman in 1983: putting out a hand to say I am
going to marry you seemed an anti-climax. Whatever it was,
our final scene never seemed to me thorough enough; it was
never fully clear to the actors so could not be to the audience. It is a very public scene, everyone gathered together, a

royal event with high and low characters all present and all their stories coming together, and I don't think we ever resolved its complexity or found the play's real ending. But then came the clap of thunder that marked the end of our production, and the returning darkness, and Feste finding the ring on the tree and singing of the wind and the rain. Things have come round full circle; they have reached a point of happiness—for some of the characters at least—but will they be happy ever after?

Chronology

CA. NOVEMBER 1556–SEPTEMBER 1558

Shakespeare's parents, John Shakespeare (the son of a farmer) and Mary Arden (daughter of a wealthy landowner), wed. Out of the eight children born to the Shakespeares, only five will live to adulthood.

1558

Elizabeth Tudor, age twenty-five, becomes the queen of England.

1559

The Elizabethan Settlement passes in Elizabeth's first Parliament, making her "supreme governor" of state and church; the Church of England is established, independent of the papacy.

1561

Francis Bacon, known for his scientific and philosophic investigations regarding systems of thought, is born. He dies in 1626 and is later a leading contender for authorship of Shakespeare's works.

1564

Stratford documents show the christening of William Shakespeare on April 26. His birthday is hazily established as April 23, coinciding with St. George's Day—the patron saint of England—and Shakespeare's own death date fifty-two years later; Christopher Marlowe, a rival dramatist to Shakespeare who is best known for *Doctor Faustus*, is born.

1569

Leading acting companies such as the Queen's Men and the Earl of Worcester's Men play the Guildhall in Stratford.

1572

The playwright Ben Jonson, Shakespeare's rival and friend, is born.

1574

The Common Council of London requires licenses for plays and their places of performance.

1576

The first public playhouse, the Theatre, is built by James Burbage, Richard Burbage's father, and John Brayne. It is located in Shoreditch, a northern suburb of London.

1577

A second public playhouse, the Curtain, opens near the Theatre.

1577–1580

Englishman Sir Francis Drake circumnavigates the world.

1582

Shakespeare, age eighteen, marries Anne Hathaway, age twenty-six, on November 28. Another record indicates a license issued on November 27 for the marriage between Anne Whateley and William Shakespeare; this is an odd coincidence or a mistake—nothing more is known about it.

1583

Susanna Shakespeare is born, christened on May 26, just six months after William and Anne Shakespeare married.

1585

Twins Hamnet and Judith Shakespeare are born, christened on February 2.

1588

Under Elizabeth's rule, the English defeat the Spanish Armada, thwarting Philip of Spain's efforts to invade England and giving England naval power.

CA. 1589–1594

Shakespeare writes his four earliest comedies, *Love's Labour's Lost, The Comedy of Errors, The Two Gentlemen of Verona,* and *The Taming of the Shrew,* in addition to *Henry VI,* Parts 1, 2, and 3, *Richard III,* and *Titus Andronicus;* he also publishes the poems "Venus and Adonis" and "The Rape of Lucrece," which are dedicated to his patron, Henry Wriothesley, third earl of Southampton.

1592

By summer, Shakespeare, age twenty-eight, is both an actor and a playwright; the outbreak of the plague closes down the theaters until the spring of 1594.

1593

The playwright Christopher Marlowe dies.

1593–1600

Shakespeare writes his *Sonnets,* which allude to a mysterious woman.

1594

After the theaters reopen from the plague epidemic, Shakespeare joins the Lord Chamberlain's Men; on December 28, *The Comedy of Errors* is performed at Gray's Inn on Holy Innocents' Day.

CA. 1594–1598

Shakespeare writes *Romeo and Juliet, Richard II, A Midsummer Night's Dream, King John, The Merchant of Venice,* and Parts 1 and 2 of *Henry IV.*

1596

Hamnet, Shakespeare's only son, dies at the age of eleven.

1597

Shakespeare buys New Place, the second largest house in Stratford. He also has a house in St. Helens Bishops Gate in London, where he maintains residence until he moves to a house on the Bankside in 1599.

1598

Shakespeare acts in Ben Jonson's *Every Man in His Humour;* in February, the Privy Council confirms licenses to the Lord Admiral's Men and the Lord Chamberlain's Men, allowing them to practice their plays (in playhouses) in preparation for playing before the queen; in December, as a result of a dispute with the landowner, Giles Alleyn, the Lord Chamberlain's Men (the company to which Shakespeare belongs) dismantle the Theatre building, carry the wood across the Thames, and reuse the timber to build the Globe.

CA. 1598–1601

Shakespeare writes the poem "The Phoenix and the Turtle" and the plays *The Merry Wives of Windsor, Much Ado About*

Nothing, Henry V, Julius Caesar, As You Like It, Hamlet, and *Twelfth Night.*

1599

The Globe Theater, of which Shakespeare owns a portion (about one-tenth), opens. Robert Armin, for whom Shakespeare most likely wrote the part of Feste in *Twelfth Night,* replaces Will Kemp, who had previously played the fools in the plays.

CA. 1601–1606

Shakespeare writes *Troilus and Cressida, All's Well That Ends Well, Othello, Measure for Measure, King Lear,* and *Macbeth.*

1602

On February 2, *Twelfth Night* is presented for Candlemas, the Christian celebration of the Assumption of the Virgin (as well as the pagan spring celebration), at Middle Temple Hall in London, as witnessed and reported in law student John Manningham's diary.

1603

James VI of Scotland becomes King James I of England, the successor Queen Elizabeth I finally names while on her death bed. (He rules until 1625.) The Lord Chamberlain's Men, Shakespeare's group, is honored by becoming the King's Men.

1606

A statute is issued against the use of profanity in the theater, thus prohibiting the use of the name of God, for which some believe Shakespeare substitutes "Jove."

1606–1608

Shakespeare writes *Antony and Cleopatra, Timon of Athens, Coriolanus,* and *Pericles.*

1607

Jamestown, Virginia, is founded, the first English settlement on the American mainland; on June 5, Susanna Shakespeare marries Dr. John Hall of Stratford.

1608

Shakespeare, Richard and Cuthbert Burbage, and the rest of the King's Men take over the second Blackfriars theater, which James Burbage had begun constructing in 1596; Shakespeare permanently retires to New Place; Susanna Shakespeare Hall gives birth to daughter Elizabeth, making Shakespeare a grandfather; Mary (Arden) Shakespeare dies in September.

1609

Shakespeare publishes the *Sonnets.*

1609–1613

Shakespeare writes his last plays: *Cymbeline, The Winter's Tale, The Tempest,* and most of *Henry VIII.* He collaborates with John Fletcher on *The Two Noble Kinsmen.*

1611

The first edition of the King James Bible is published.

1613

On June 29, during a performance of *Henry VIII* at the Globe, the theater catches fire and is destroyed.

1614

Until the discovery of law student John Manningham's dairy, *Twelfth Night* was considered Shakespeare's last play, originally dated 1614.

1616

In February, Shakespeare's youngest daughter, Judith, makes an unfortunate marriage to Thomas Quiney in Stratford. On April 23, Shakespeare dies.

1618

Twelfth Night is performed at court, possibly under the title of *Malvolio.*

1623

Seven years after his death, the first legitimate publication of Shakespeare's works, the First Folio, is published by his friends and colleagues John Heminge and Henry Condell, and entered in the Stationers' Register on November 8. This is the first known publication of *Twelfth Night.* Shakespeare's wife, Anne Hathaway, dies.

1625

Charles I succeeds James I as king of England.

1626

John Aubrey, author of *Brief Lives,* is born. He is one of the first Shakespeare biographers to add to the myth biographies of Shakespeare's multiple lives.

1632

Shakespeare's Second Folio is published.

1642

The English Civil War begins; theaters are officially closed.

1649

Charles I is beheaded; Parliament invites Charles II to return to England. He is crowned in 1661 as the new king.

1660

The theaters are reopened, this time with women in the female roles.

1661–1669

English diarist Samuel Pepys sees *Twelfth Night* no less than three times: once in 1661; once in 1663, which he records in his diary as "silly" and for which he finds no relation between the title and the play; and once again in 1668. It will be nearly seventy-five years before the play is once again performed as a whole.

1703

Charles Burnaby's *Love Betray'd; or, The Agreeable Disappointment,* an adaptation of *Twelfth Night* (which uses only about fifty lines of the folio text), is performed at Lincoln's Inn Fields under the management of Thomas Betterton. Published a month later, it does not seem to have done well at all and will be performed only once more, in 1705.

1741

The "modern history" of *Twelfth Night* begins when, after nearly seventy-five years of being off the stage, it is revived by Charles Macklin at Drury Lane, with Macklin playing Malvolio.

1770

David Garrick's Drury Lane revival of *Twelfth Night* gains prominence.

1794

Twelfth Night is performed in Boston, the first known U.S. performance.

EARLY 1800s

Scholars switch from considering *Twelfth Night* Shakespeare's last play, placing it instead in the middle period.

CA. 1804

Twelfth Night is performed in New York.

1810

John Philip Kemble publishes an acting edition of *Twelfth Night* with the first and second scenes switched.

1820

Frederic Reynold's operatic version of *Twelfth Night* is produced at Covent Garden; after seventeen performances it is revived again in 1825.

CA. 1900

Originating from the United States, Augustin Daly's production of *Twelfth Night* is embellished with music, appealing scenery, and moonlight, but the play is reduced to four acts, with Malvolio's scenes condensed and his dark room scene and final scene omitted.

1901

Sir Henry Beerbohm Tree's production (in three acts) with Maud Jefferies as Viola and Tree as Malvolio continues the tradition of elaborate spectacle and scenery and runs for more than three months to a steady audience totaling, by the end of the run, approximately 200,000 people.

1912

Harley Granville-Barker's famous production of *Twelfth Night* at the Savoy Theater is one of several productions around this time that returns to a simplified, less elaborate version of staging. (Gordon Craig and William Poel's productions are also simplified.)

1926-1933

While Terence Gray is director of the Festival Theatre at Cambridge, his production of *Twelfth Night* is simple but consists of a revolving stage and Sir Toby and Sir Andrew on roller skates.

1933

The teenage Orson Welles assists Roger Hill with designing and codirecting *Twelfth Night* for the Todd School production at the Chicago Drama Festival, using Welles's promptbook as the script. Welles's set consists of a twelve-foot-high book and pages that are turned as each new scene unfolds.

1937

In August, *Twelfth Night* is adapted for a CBS radio production with Orson Welles as Orsino.

1955

In Sir John Gielgud's Shakespeare Memorial Theatre production of *Twelfth Night*, Sir Laurence Olivier returns to a comical portrayal of Malvolio. Despite his director's wishes, Olivier insists on falling backward off a bench during the garden scene and, as noted by Gielgud, displays an extreme accent with a lisp calling to mind a "Jewish hairdresser."

1969–1971

John Barton's Royal Shakespeare Company production of *Twelfth Night; or, What You Will* is found to be quite harmonious. Judi Dench (who won Best Supporting Actress for *Shakespeare in Love* for her portrayal of Queen Elizabeth) is a strong Viola.

1974–1975

Peter Gill's production of *Twelfth Night* includes Elizabethan costumes but otherwise is quite contemporary, addressing both the psychological and sexual ambiguities of the characters. Bill Dudley's set design includes a huge picture of Narcissus gazing into a pool.

1980

The British Broadcasting Corporation (BBC) television version of *Twelfth Night* premiers.

1983

Zoë Wanamaker is a spirited and sensible Viola in John Caird's Stratford production.

1996

Former Royal Shakespeare Company director Trevor Nunn directs *Twelfth Night*, the first full-length film version in English.

FOR FURTHER RESEARCH

COMPILATIONS OF COMPLETE WORKS

G. Blakemore Evans and J.J. Tobin, eds., *The Riverside Shakespeare: The Complete Works.* 2nd ed. Boston: Houghton Mifflin, 1997.

Stephen Greenblatt et al., eds., *The Norton Shakespeare.* New York: W.W. Norton, 1997.

Richard Proudfoot, Ann Thompson, and David Scott Kastan, eds., *The Arden Shakespeare Complete Works.* Reading, MA: Addison Wesley Longman, 1998.

TWELFTH NIGHT; OR, WHAT YOU WILL:
INTERPRETATIONS AND EXPLANATIONS

Ralph Berry, "*Twelfth Night:* The Experience of the Audience," *Shakespeare Survey,* vol. 34, 1981.

Denise Bradshaw, "Directing the 'Dark Room' Scene (Act IV Scene 2)," November 1999. www.killay.demon.co.uk/essay1/htm.

Alan S. Downer, "Feste's Night," *College English.* Chicago: University of Chicago Press, 1952.

John W. Draper, *The* Twelfth Night *of Shakespeare's Audience.* Stanford, CA: Stanford University Press, 1950.

Terence Eagleton, "Language and Reality in *Twelfth Night,*" Critical Quarterly, vol. 9, 1967.

Barbara Everett, "Or What You Will." In R.S. White, ed., *New Casebooks:* Twelfth Night. New York: St. Martin's Press, 1996.

J.M. Gregson, *Shakespeare:* Twelfth Night. London: Edward Arnold, 1980.

Nancy K. Hales, "Sexual Disguise in *As You Like It* and *Twelfth Night,*" *Shakespeare Survey,* vol. 32, 1979.

Barbara Hardy, *Notes on English Literature:* Twelfth Night. Oxford, England: Basil Blackwell and Mott Ltd., 1962.

Richard Henze, "*Twelfth Night:* Free Disposition on the Sea of Love," *Sewanee Review,* April–June 1975.

Leslie Hotson, *The First Night of* Twelfth Night. London: Rupert Hart-Davis, 1954.

Maurice Hunt, "The Religion of *Twelfth Night*," *CLA Journal,* December 1993.

Harold Jenkins, "Shakespeare's *Twelfth Night.*" In Kenneth Muir, ed., *Shakespeare: The Comedies.* Englewood Cliffs, NJ: Prentice-Hall, 1965.

Walter N. King, ed., Introduction to *Twentieth Century Interpretations of* Twelfth Night. Englewood Cliffs, NJ: Prentice-Hall, 1968.

Clifford Leech, Twelfth Night *and Shakespearian Comedy.* Toronto: Dalhousie University Press, 1965.

Barbara K. Lewalski, "Thematic Patterns in *Twelfth Night*," *Shakespeare Studies: An Annual Gathering of Research, Criticism, and Reviews,* 1965.

J.M. Lothian and T.W. Craik, eds., *The Arden Edition of the Works of William Shakespeare:* Twelfth Night. London: Routledge, 1995.

Molly Maureen Mahood, ed., *Twelfth Night.* Harmondsworth, England: Penguin Books, 1968.

Lois Potter, Twelfth Night: *Text and Performance.* Houndmills, England: Macmillan, 1985.

Leo Salingar, "The Design of *Twelfth Night.*" In *Dramatic Form in Shakespeare and the Jacobeans.* Cambridge, England: Cambridge University Press, 1986.

Orson Welles and Roger Hill, eds., *The Mercury Shakespeare:* The Merchant of Venice, Twelfth Night, Julius Caesar. New York: Harper & Brothers, 1939.

Stanley Wells, ed., Twelfth Night: *Critical Essays.* New York: Garland, 1986.

R.S. White, ed., *New Casebooks:* Twelfth Night. New York: St. Martin's Press, 1996.

Porter Williams Jr., "Mistakes in *Twelfth Night* and Their Resolution: A Study in Some Relationships of Plot and Theme." In Walter N. King, ed., *Twentieth-Century Interpretations of Twelfth Night.* Englewood Cliffs, NJ: Prentice-Hall, 1968.

SHAKESPEARE'S COMEDIES

Linda Anderson, *A Kind of Wild Justice: Revenge in Shakespeare's Comedies.* Newark: University of Delaware Press, 1987.

C.L. Barber, *Shakespeare's Festive Comedy: A Study of Dramatic Form and Its Relation to Social Custom.* Princeton, NJ: Princeton University Press, 1959.

John Russell Brown, *Shakespeare and His Comedies.* London: Methuen, 1962.

Oscar James Campbell, *Shakespeare's Satire.* London: Oxford University Press, 1943.

William C. Carroll, *The Metamorphoses of Shakespearean Comedy.* Princeton, NJ: Princeton University Press, 1985.

Maurice Charney, ed., *Shakespearean Comedy.* New York: New York Literary Forum, 1980.

Bertrand Evans, *Shakespeare's Comedies.* New York: Oxford University Press, 1967.

R. Chris Hassel Jr., *Faith and Folly in Shakespeare's Romantic Comedies.* Athens: University of Georgia Press, 1980.

G.K. Hunter, *The Later Comedies*: A Midsummer Night's Dream, Much Ado About Nothing, As You Like It, Twelfth Night. Essex, England: Longmans, Green, 1962.

Ejner J. Jensen, *Shakespeare and the Ends of Comedy.* Bloomington and Indianapolis: Indiana University Press, 1991.

Alexander Leggatt, *Shakespeare's Comedy of Love.* London: Methuen, 1974.

Richard A. Levin, *Love and Society in Shakespearean Comedy: A Study of Dramatic Form and Content.* Newark: University of Delaware Press, 1985.

Karen Newman, *Shakespeare's Rhetoric of Comic Character: Dramatic Convention in Classical and Renaissance Comedy.* New York: Methuen, 1985.

Robert Ornstein, *Shakespeare's Comedies: From Roman Farce to Romantic Mystery.* Newark: University of Delaware Press, 1986.

Naseeb Shaheen, *Biblical References in Shakespeare's Comedies.* Newark: University of Delaware Press, 1993.

Patrick Swinden, *An Introduction to Shakespeare's Comedies.* New York: Barnes and Noble, 1973.

Jack A. Vaughn, *Shakespeare's Comedies.* New York: Frederick Ungar, 1980.

John Dover Wilson, *Shakespeare's Happy Comedies.* Evanston, IL: Northwestern University Press, 1962.

PRODUCTION AND PERFORMANCE OF SHAKESPEARE

Ralph Berry, *On Directing Shakespeare: Interviews with Contemporary Directors.* London: Croom Helm, 1977.

John Russell Brown, *Shakespeare's Plays in Performance.* London: Penguin Shakespeare Library, 1966.

Anthony B. Dawson, *Watching Shakespeare: A Playgoers' Guide.* New York: St. Martin's Press, 1988.

Jean Elizabeth Howard, *Shakespeare's Art of Orchestration: Stage Technique and Audience Response.* Urbana and Chicago: University of Illinois Press, 1984.

Hugh Hunt, *Old Vic Prefaces: Shakespeare and the Producer.* London: Routledge & Kegan Paul, 1954.

Russell Jackson and Robert Smallwood, eds., *Players of Shakespeare 2.* Cambridge, England: Cambridge University Press, 1988.

John H. Long, *Shakespeare's Use of Music: A Study of the Music and Its Performance in the Original Production of Seven Comedies.* New York: Da Capo Press, 1977.

Kenneth S. Rothwell and Annabelle Henkin Melzer, comps., *Shakespeare on Screen: An International Filmography and Videography.* New York: Neal-Schuman, 1990.

Arthur Colby Sprague, *Shakespeare and the Actors: The Stage Business in His Plays (1660–1905).* New York: Russell & Russell, 1963.

A.C. Sprague and J.C. Trewin, *Shakespeare's Plays Today: Some Customs and Conventions of the Stage.* London: Sidgwick and Jackson, 1970.

J.L. Styan, *The Shakespeare Revolution: Criticism and Performance in the 20th Century.* Cambridge, England: Cambridge University Press, 1977.

Peter Thomson, *Shakespeare's Theatre.* London: Routledge & Kegan Paul, 1983.

G. Wickham, *Early English Stages 1300–1660.* Vol. 2, pt. 1. London: Routledge & Kegan Paul, 1963.

SHAKESPEARE'S LIFE AND TIMES

Peter Alexander, *Shakespeare's Life and Art.* 2nd Amer. ed. New York: New York University Press, 1967.

Rebecca Brown, Shakespeare at School. July 1999. www.shakespeare.org.uk/schools.htm.

Anthony Burgess, *Shakespeare.* Chicago: Elephant-Ivan R. Dee, 1994.

Peter Hyland, *An Introduction to Shakespeare: The Dramatist in His Context.* New York: St. Martin's Press, 1996.

David Scott Kasten, ed., *A Companion to Shakespeare.* Oxford, England: Blackwell, 1999.

Dave Kathman, *The Spelling and Pronunciation of Shakespeare's Name.* April 2000. www.clark.net/pub/tross/ws/name1.html.

———, "The Stratford Grammar School," *Critically Examining Oxfordian Claims,* Part 2. April 2000. www.clark. net/pub/tross/ws/school.html.

Samuel Schoenbaum, *Shakespeare's Lives.* Oxford, England: Clarendon Press, 1970.

———, *William Shakespeare: A Compact Documentary Life.* New York: Oxford University Press, 1977.

Bruce R. Smith, *Roasting the Swan of Avon: Shakespeare's Redoubtable Enemies and Dubious Friends.* Washington, DC: Folger Shakespeare Library, 1994.

LITERARY CRITICISM OF SHAKESPEARE'S WORK

Isaac Asimov, *Asimov's Guide to Shakespeare.* New York: Avenel Books, 1978.

Linda Bamber, *Comic Women, Tragic Men: A Study of Gender and Genre in Shakespeare.* Stanford, CA: Stanford University Press, 1982.

Harold Bloom, *Shakespeare: The Invention of the Human.* New York: Riverhead Books, 1998.

John Russell Brown, *Shakespeare's Dramatic Style:* Romeo and Juliet, As You Like It, Julius Caesar, Twelfth Night, Macbeth. New York: Barnes and Noble, 1971.

Geoffrey Bullough, *Narrative and Dramatic Sources of Shakespeare.* 8 vols. New York: Columbia University Press, 1957–1975.

Irene G. Dash, *Women's Worlds in Shakespeare's Plays.* Newark: University of Delaware Press, 1997.

James P. Driscoll, *Identity in Shakespearean Drama.* Lewisburg, PA: Bucknell University Press, 1983.

Marilyn French, *Shakespeare's Division of Experience.* New York: Summit-Simon & Schuster, 1981.

Northrop Frye, *A Natural Perspective.* New York: Harcourt, Brace, and World, 1965.

Jean Elizabeth Howard, "Crossdressing, the Theatre, and Gender Struggle in Early Modern England," *Shakespeare Quarterly,* vol. 39, 1988.

William Ingpen, *The Secrets of Numbers.* London, 1624.

Mrs. Jameson, *Shakspeare's Heroines: Characteristics of Women Moral, Poetical, and Historical.* Philadelphia: Henry Altemus, ca. 1860.

Eleanor Prosser, *Hamlet and Revenge.* Stanford, CA: Stanford University Press, 1973.

John Vyvyan, *Shakespeare and Platonic Beauty.* London: Chatto, 1961.

Robin Headlam Wells, *Elizabethan Mythologies: Studies in Poetry, Drama, and Music.* Cambridge, England: Cambridge University Press, 1994.

Joseph Westlund, *Shakespeare's Reparative Comedies: A Psychoanalytic View of the Middle Plays.* Chicago: University of Chicago Press, 1984.

WORKS BY WILLIAM SHAKESPEARE

The Comedy of Errors (1588–1593)
Love's Labour's Lost (1588–1595)
Henry VI, Part 1 (1589–1591)
Henry VI, Part 2 (1590–1591)
Henry VI, Part 3 (1590–1591)
"Venus and Adonis" (1592–1593)
Richard III (1592–1593)
Titus Andronicus (1592–1594)
The Two Gentlemen of Verona (1592–1594)
"The Rape of Lucrece" (1593–1594)
The Taming of the Shrew (1593–1594)
Sonnets (1593–1600)
King John (1594–1596)
Richard II (1595)
Romeo and Juliet (1595–1596)
A Midsummer Night's Dream (1595–1596)
The Merchant of Venice (1596–1597)
Henry IV, Part 1 (1596–1597)
Henry IV, Part 2 (1597–1598)
The Merry Wives of Windsor (1597–1601)
Henry V (1598–1599)
Much Ado About Nothing (1598–1600)
Julius Caesar (1599)
As You Like It (1599–1600)
Twelfth Night; or, What You Will (1599–1602)
Hamlet (1600–1601)
"The Phoenix and the Turtle" (1600–1601)
Troilus and Cressida (1601–1602)
All's Well That Ends Well (1602–1603)
Othello (1603–1604)
Measure for Measure (1604)
King Lear (1605–1606)
Macbeth (1605–1606)
Antony and Cleopatra (1606–1607)

Timon of Athens (1607–1608)
Coriolanus (1607–1608)
Pericles (1607–1608)
Cymbeline (1609–1610)
The Winter's Tale (1610–1611)
The Tempest (1611)
Henry VIII (1612–1613)
The Two Noble Kinsmen (1612–1613)

INDEX

212